Sceptic

An Exposition of Spiritualism

Comprising two series of letters

Sceptic

An Exposition of Spiritualism
Comprising two series of letters

ISBN/EAN: 9783337424664

Printed in Europe, USA, Canada, Australia, Japan

Cover: Foto ©Lupo / pixelio.de

More available books at **www.hansebooks.com**

AN

EXPOSITION OF SPIRITUALISM;

COMPRISING

TWO SERIES OF LETTERS, AND A REVIEW OF
THE "SPIRITUAL MAGAZINE," No. 20.

AS PUBLISHED IN

THE "STAR AND DIAL."

With Introduction, Notes, and Appendix,

BY SCEPTIC.

LONDON:
GEORGE MANWARING, PUBLISHER,
8, KING WILLIAM STREET,
WEST STRAND.
1862.

TO

HENRY GEORGE ATKINSON, ESQ.,

F.G.S., &c., &c.

THIS
EXPOSITION OF SPIRITUALISM IS MOST RESPECTFULLY
DEDICATED, IN HUMBLE ACKNOWLEDGMENT
OF ADVANTAGES
DERIVED FROM THE STUDY OF HIS
ADMIRABLE "LETTERS ON THE LAWS OF MAN'S
NATURE AND DEVELOPMENT,"
AND OF HIS GREAT COURTESY IN IMPARTING IN-
FORMATION TO THE INQUIRING AND
PHILOSOPHICAL MIND,
BY HIS OBLIGED AND OBEDIENT SERVANT,

THE COMPILER.

PREFACE.

In issuing this volume it has been my sole object to place the phenomena of Spiritualism on their proper basis: whether I have succeeded or not, I leave to a discriminating and discerning public to decide. Without any pretensions to authorship, but by the kind permission of the Editor, I have collated the correspondence and other articles which appeared in the "Morning Star," in the Autumn of 1860 and 1861, which correspondence seemed to me to have been brought to an abrupt and somewhat unfortunate termination just when the question at issue had become of great practical importance, and was producing a corresponding interest in the minds of scientific and thinking men. With the view, then, not of exhausting a subject, which is in itself inexhaustible, nor of altogether setting the matter at rest, but of placing the whole question of Spiritualism on a rational and scientific PLANE, (to adopt the language of Mr. William Howitt, who has done me the distinguished honour to revise his own spirited and highly interesting letters), in furtherance of which, I have availed myself of the opinions of the talented Author of "The Philosophy of Necessity," together with numerous extracts from the well-known works of other distinguished writers, all duly acknowledged and bearing upon the subject, which, though too diffuse for the columns of a daily paper, I considered essential to the thorough investigation of the attested phenomena, and without which no inquiry could either profitably or satisfactorily terminate.

This, then, is my apology for again introducing the subject upon the public in the present form; and having given both the affirmative and negative opinions of the various correspondents, I opine I need not offer any further justification either of the book or its title; honestly believing it to be, as it announces itself, an EXPOSITION OF SPIRITUALISM. The notes appended to several of the letters are either explanatory of expressions in previous letters objected to by correspondents, or in continuation of the argument which was closed just when it jarred with religious views very generally maintained—and which, therefore, necessarily failed to find expression, though we look in vain for the Christianising and pacific influence of Spiritualism upon the millions in America, of whom Mr. Howitt, Mr. B. Coleman, and others speak or write. Nothing further remains to be said than that my sincere acknowledgments are due to others for the important assistance rendered in the interests of the work during its progress through the press.

January 17th, 1862.

CONTENTS.

	PAGE
Introduction	1
Notice of the Article "Seeing is Believing," in Blackwood's Magazine. "Star and Dial."	21

FIRST SERIES.

NO.		
1.	Howitt, William	22
2.	Buckland, James N.	31
3.	Faber	32
4.	Robins, William	36
5.	Lex	39
6.	Bird, John James	41
7.	Coleman, Benjamin	48
	Editor's Note	56
8.	A Barrister	57
9.	Senex	58
10.	A Lover of the whole Truth . . .	59
11.	A. S. L.	60

CONTENTS.

NO.		PAGE
12.	Braden, A. S.	62
13.	Sceptic	63
14.	W. S.	65
15.	A Lady	66
16.	M. D.	67
17.	Mitchell, Alfred M.	69
18.	Americanus	71
19.	B. A. Cantabrigiensis	73
20.	Bennett, J.	74
21.	Plummer, John	76
22.	Howitt, William (2nd)	81
23.	Collyer, Robert H., M.D.	90
	Editor's Note.	97
	Note by Sceptic	98
24.	One who has tried the Spirits	100
25.	Smith, William	103
26.	Gully, J. M., M.D.	110
27.	Harper, H. E. A.	116
28.	Leam	120
29.	Wyer, N. W.	121
30.	Wilkinson, W. M.	122
31.	Burroughs, Calman	125
32.	Bridges, Matthew	130
33.	Hoppey, James	132
34.	Williams, John, Catholic Priest	137
35.	Kidd, Charles, M.D.	140
36.	Harper, W. E. A. (2nd)	143
37.	Howitt, William (3rd)	146
38.	Collyer, Robert H., M.D. (2nd)	158
39.	Crosland, Newton.	165
40.	Snow, W. Parker.	166
41.	An Israelite	172

NO.		PAGE
42. Adams, W. Bridges	. . . .	174
Editor's Note (Conclusion of the discussion)	.	176
Letter by Chas. Bray, Esq.	. . .	177
Elucidation of Clairvoyance, extracted from J. W. Haddock's "*Somnolism and Psycheism*"		191

SECOND SERIES.

Review of the *Spiritual Magazine*, No. 20, "*Star and Dial*" 199

NO			
1. Coleman, W. T. .	. . . .	209
2. Bostwick, A. W. .	. . . .	214
3. Jones, John	. . . .	220
4. W. P. K. .	. . . .	222
5. Sceptic	. . . . .	226
6. Jones, John (2nd)	. . .	228
7. Adams, W. A.	. . . .	233
8. Barkas, T. P.	. . . .	236
9. Coleman, Benjamin	. . .	240
10. Wilks, T. .	. . . .	241
11. J. A. L.	. . . .	244
12. Sceptic (2nd)	. . . .	247
13. Buckland, James M.	. . .	252
14. Jones, John (3rd) .	. . .	253
Note by Sceptic.	. . .	256
15. Another Sceptic .	. . .	257
16. Dendy, Walter Cooper	. . .	257
17. A Critic .	. , . .	261
Note by Sceptic	. . .	265
18. Barkas, T. P. (2nd)	. . .	266
Note by Sceptic	. . .	269
19. A Spiritualist	. . . .	270
Notes by Sceptic	. . .	277

NO.		PAGE
20. Watchful		278
Notes by Sceptic		279
21. Sceptic (3rd)		280
22. Jones, John (4th)		287
Notes by Sceptic		289
Editor's Note		291
23. Barkas, T. P. (3rd)		292
24. S.		293
25. L.		294
Notes by Sceptic		298
26. Morrison, R. J.		298
Notes by Sceptic		303
Appendix and Notes		306

ERRATA.

Page 22, in motto from Sir Thomas Browne, *read* "confute their *in*credulity."

Page 25, speaking of Mr. Hume's visits to Lord Lyndhurst, *omit* " on one occasion for a whole fortnight."

Page 29, for "Euthyphon," *read* "Euthyphron."

Page 81, for "thunder of the Royal Society," *read* "blunder, &c."

Page 146, in motto from Sir Walter Scott, instead of "comprehension of the public," *read* "of the sceptic."

Page 148, for "act of puration," *read* "act of formation."

Page 151, for "attribute to a score, &c.," *read* "attribute them, &c."

AN EXPOSITION OF SPIRITUALISM.

INTRODUCTION.

Hitherto Spiritual life has been supposed not to be cognizable by the senses, but wholly a question of belief. Modern spiritualists, however, seem desirous to prove that supposition to be a fallacy, believing they have evidence to the contrary. On the other hand, those who hold life and mind, apart from organized matter, to be an utter impossibility, deny the correctness of their assumptions. In this article I shall combat the spiritualistic notions affirmed in the following correspondence, which, I much regret, was brought to a somewhat abrupt termination in the columns of the "Star and Dial," in August last, the reason for which was, it appears, the voluminous and discursive nature of the correspondence. *Vide* Editor's paragraph.

In man we behold a sentient being, inspiring the surrounding atmosphere, the no less vitalizing blood coursing through his system, while all the functions of life, both voluntary and involuntary, are duly performed. Again, we behold him motionless, void of intelligence, respiration arrested, the blood stagnant, a cold and lifeless object—we perceive that he is dead. Yet, in spite of our senses, with the loved object before our eyes—sad evidence of death!—we are told this being lives. We may here ask the question in sober earnestness, whether "Seeing is believing?" That which we recognized as the living man is but too surely dead. We behold another intelligent creature, inhaling the same atmosphere, the vitalizing fluid circulating through its veins; it performs all the functions of life, and exhibits evidence of mental phenomena, such as memory, reflection, judgment, though a being of an inferior order—to wit, some favourite animal. We look again, and behold it is dead. We have the same evidence of intelligence, life, and death, as in the case of our fellow man. Again the question rises to our lips, whether "Seeing is believing?" We can perceive no difference in the facts of dissolution; in either case, the body, unless cared for, becomes a loathsome mass of corruption. Why then should we believe in the continued existence of the spirit of the one and not in that of the other creature? A mere tyro in philosophy, I ask with the simplicity of the child, on the death of a favourite pony, "Where is that gone that made poor Kitty live?"*—why the subtle spirit that can take

* *Vide* Eccles. iii. 18, 19, 20, 21.

cognizance of the senses, and direct and control the voluntary and involuntary motions of life in the lower animal should be extinct, and the same spirit in man should continue to exist? The body and the life constitute the being we recognize, whether it be the dog or the horse, why not the being man? Why should the body and the spirit be separate entities in the one case and not in the other? When any other animal than man dies, no one imagines it exists in another sphere; neither have sense-impressions hitherto given us any real experience of the existence of man out of the body. If it be said, "True, the man is dead, but his spirit is an immortal being;" I answer, then, in that case, it is something else, and its identity is at an end! When we lose consciousness of personality, it is much the same as if we *were not*, either as regards a former or a future state of existence.

In support of the existing affinity between brutes and man, we quote the following from a paper by Horace Moule, on the Science of Language.

"The claims of brutes may be stated very strongly indeed. Brutes can see, hear, taste, smell, and feel; they have, that is to say, five senses, just like ourselves, neither more nor less. Brutes have sensations of pleasure and pain; they have memory, for they remember their masters and their homes; they are able to compare and to distinguish, and they have a will of their own. Brutes also show signs of shame and pride, of love and hatred, as any one knows perfectly well who has had anything to do with horses or dogs. We are, in short, forced to admit that brutes have sensation, perception, memory, will, and intellect, in a certain low degree. We are now told, moreover, that the anatomical distinction between man and the brutes may be reduced to a single fold in the brain, a single angle of the skull. Where, then, is the line of demarcation, if, indeed, after all these admissions, there is any line yet to be found? It is fearlessly asserted that the one great barrier between the brute and man is *Language*. This is the Rubicon which no brute has ever yet been able to pass. This is the charter which proves man to be something higher than a more favoured beast, something generically different from an unusually accomplished ape." To this it may be replied, that, doubtless, animals have a language of their own, though they may not converse either in French or English, Greek or Latin, even though there be such a thing as *dog-latin*.

A French horse accustomed to the word *allons*, would not at first, without the aid of the whip, comprehend the English impulsives *gee*, and *come hither, whoy;* but it is evident, by culture, both horses and dogs can be taught to associate ideas of things and actions with sounds. Because we do not understand their language, it is no reason that they cannot communicate with each other; on the contrary, we have ample evidence that all social animals do so communicate. Of this we have many instances, especially amongst birds and beasts; neither must we exclude the social habits of the insect tribe, as in the ant and bee.

"It must not be overlooked, that though the psychologists have agreed in neglecting the intellectual and moral faculties of brutes, which have been happily left to the naturalists, they have occasioned great mischief by their obscure and indefinite distinction between intelligence and instinct, thus setting up a division between human and animal nature which has had too much effect even upon zoologists to this day. The only meaning that can be attributed to the word *instinct*, is any spontaneous impulse in a determinate direction, independently of any foreign influence. In this primitive sense, the term evidently applies to the proper and direct activity of any faculty whatever, intellectual as well as affective; and it therefore does not conflict with the term *intelligence* in any way, as we so often see when we speak of those who, without any education, manifest a marked talent for music, painting, mathematics, &c.

"In this way there is instinct, or rather, there are instincts in man, as much or more than in brutes. If, on the other hand, we describe *intelligence* as the aptitude to modify conduct in conformity to the circumstances of each case—which, in fact, is the main practical attribute of *reason*, in its proper sense—it is more evident than before that there is no other essential difference between humanity and animality than that of the degree of development admitted by a faculty which is, by its nature, common to all animal life, and without which it could not even be conceived to exist. Thus the famous scholastic definition of man as a *reasonable animal* offers a real no-meaning, since no animals, especially in the higher parts of the zoological scale, could live without being, to a certain extent, reasonable, in proportion to the complexity of its organism. Though the moral nature of animals has been but little and very imperfectly explored, we can yet perceive, without possibility of mistake, among those that live with us and that are familiar with us—judging of them by the same means of observation that we should employ about men whose language and ways were previously unknown to us—that they not only apply their intelligence to the satisfaction of their organic wants, much as men do, aiding themselves also with some sort of language; but that they are, in like manner, susceptible of a kind of wants more disinterested, inasmuch as they consist in a need to exercise their faculties for the mere pleasure of the exercise." (When the dog recognizes its name and its master's voice, or whistle, it has no misgivings as to the individuality, or personal identity, either of itself or its master.)

"An attentive examination of the facts, therefore, discredits the perversion of the word *instinct*, when it is used to signify the fatality under which animals are impelled to the mechanical performance of acts uniformly determinate, without any possible modification from corresponding circumstances, and neither requiring nor allowing any education, properly so called."—*The Positive Philosophy of Auguste Comte. By Harriet Martineau.*

The five senses operate much in the same manner in all animals. Man requires no more refined or subtle spirit to enable him to perceive than the dog, and the dog requires *no less* subtle spirit; the manner of perception is the same, the sole difference is in the organization. Ignorance of this fact, coupled with an arrogant conceit that he possesses a higher spiritual nature, is the foundation of man's superstition. Man is probably the only superstitious animal in creation, and, while false notions of mind, soul, or spirit, are inculcated and indoctrinated by theologians, it ever will be so. Whether these be truths or not, they are as manifest to some minds as any of the phenomena termed spiritual can possibly be to the spiritualist. If they are not truths, let them be utterly exterminated, and I for one will, with heart and soul, wish Spiritualism God speed.

We cannot dissociate cause and effect. Wherever we perceive effects we know there must be a cause, although it be invisible; experience assures us of this fact, and like experience also assures us *that* cause must be material, because we have no knowledge of anything apart from, or independent of matter:—we can form no conception of, nor can we define nothing; as soon as we attempt to do so we make something of it. Thus we deny the assumption that mechanical phenomena can be produced wholly without mechanical or muscular agency—to pinch, for instance, requires the application of parts with a purchase or fulcrum, to the part pinched, as with the finger and thumb, and whatever the instrument or contrivance be, it must be material. We deny the possibility of a purely mechanical act, such as a pinch, by purely spiritual hands. If science, together with our senses, is to be ignored, of what use is either knowledge or existence? Far better that we had never been born.

The predilection shown by the spirits (?) for the guitar and the accordion in particular, is very significant; how is it they never exhibit their musical powers on the pianoforte? an instrument to be found in almost every home of any pretensions—and with which we should have thought them to have been far more familiar when in the flesh. When we behold the keys of the piano manipulated upon, and hear music cleverly executed by spirit hands visible or invisible, possibly our scepticism may waver: until then we fear we shall remain sceptical, or in that state of mental darkness so much compassionated by Mr. Howitt in a letter to Mr. T. P. Barkas, published in the "*British Controversialist,*" Aug. 1861.

Before I am open to conviction I must be sure I am not the subject of deception either through the abnormal condition of others or that of myself. I believe that either in the notes annexed to the letters of several correspondents of the "Star," or in the matter contained in the Appendix, I have shown that phenomena parallel to the whole of the manifestations recorded may be induced without the aid of disembodied spirits. Ecstacy is admitted by all physiologists to be a departure from the normal state, and so far it is disease; we have yet to learn that man exalts his nature by prostrating his reason at the feet of visionists, male or female. It is no use beating about the bush, the facts I have mentioned are involved in the question, and must be ventilated; the present phase of spiritualism is the offshoot of the older spiritualism, and they must exist or fall together. I am one of plain speech; but this is a subject that needs not the flowers of rhetoric, nor the inspiration of the poet, nor much classic lore; I have therefore purposely abstained from attempting any reply to Mr. Howitt, contenting myself with stating that which perhaps is needless, but of which, nevertheless, I am sensible that "I am no orator as Brutus is." Yet am I fully sensible of the importance and magnitude of the question, "*Is it true?*" For if shown to be false, it involves the downfall of supernaturalism; while, on the other hand, if it can be made manifest that man has an *immortal* soul, what more weighty subject can engage our attention? although I must observe that the demonstrations hitherto made, are not such as to give us any very exalted ideas of the transcendent knowledge of the life beyond the grave. As nothing can be put in comparison with life, unless it be our belief in truth and justice; so nothing can equal the value of an immortal soul; therefore all honour is due to Mr. Howitt for the propagation of his faith, while equal honour is due to those who as faithfully promulgate that which they as sincerely believe. Supposing for one minute the possibility of the spirits of our departed friends being in close proximity to our persons, we have no means of identifying them in the absence of a medium, and it is somewhat singular they never perform the impish tricks of which we read but in the presence of a medium, who seems absolutely essential to the exhibition of their powers.

Christ himself, after his resurrection, appeared in the body to his disciples ; and when "they were terrified, supposing they had seen a spirit, he said unto them, why are ye troubled ? behold my hands and my feet, that it is I myself ; handle me and see, for a spirit hath not *flesh* and *bones* as ye see me have. And he showed them his hands and his feet, and while they believed not for joy, and wondered, he said unto them have ye any meat? and they gave him a piece of broiled fish, and of an honey-comb, and he took it and did eat before them." Luke xxiv. 36—43.

Thus the founder of Christianity confounds the affirmations of the spiritualists, who assert that muscular and mechanical phenomena can be produced (without the aid of bone and muscle or other mechanical contrivances), such as pinching and grasping legs, (*calves*, rather, I should have said, but from respect for the honoured names of those who are said to bear testimony to the facts, I forbear), by "invisible beings possessing the attributes of intelligence, affection, and volition, themselves claiming to be

human, and giving rational grounds for belief in the truth of their claims." Much of the phenomena detailed are of such a puerile nature as to give us no very exalted notions of the spirits' intelligence—to wit, pulling skirts, and pinching legs, under tables, savours more of the indelicate than the sublime. We do not ignore the "spiritual element," if by that is meant the forces of nature; but we do most emphatically deny that the witnessed phenomena are the vagaries of disembodied intelligences. Herein lies the fallacy of Modern Spiritualism—that mind can exist apart from, and yet perform the functions of organized matter. These visitors neither speak nor eat—physical operations far too gross for their spiritual nature; though they can exhibit feats of superhuman strength, such as dashing "iron bound, lunatic-defying tables" to fragments, &c., evidently the organs neither of speech nor deglutition are wanting in those who affirm these things; whatever the spirits lack in that respect, they assuredly possess the latter faculty to perfection. By the bye, we have heard of the spirits being present at dinner tables laden with wines and dessert, but we have no remembrance of their having been invited to partake of anything: could the indignity thus offered them, occasion the subsequent thrusting away and demolishing of said tables?*
A propos of dessert, we will e'en give these gentlemen another nut or two to crack. Having quoted from the New Testament, it is only reasonable that

---

* Doubtless the hand that could offer a glass of water could take a glass of wine!

we should quote the Old. And we will cite Job as an authority on the subject, whose experience of the evil one's existence was scarcely as agreeable, or so great a gain, as it would seem to be to Mr. Howitt. " As the waters fail from the sea, and the flood decayeth and drieth up ; so man lieth down, and riseth not; till the heavens be no more they shall not awake, nor be raised out of their sleep." Job xiv. 11, 12. Also what saith the Preacher? "Then shall the dust return to the earth as it was. And the spirit shall return unto God who gave it." Again, " For the living know that they shall die, but the dead know not anything." Eccles. xii. 7; ix. 5. One other such quotation, and we say *quantum sufficit.* " His breath goeth forth, he returneth to his earth, in that very day his thoughts perish." Psalm cxlvi. 4.

We know not what the Spiritualists will make of this, they will carp at it, we have no doubt—but it is Holy Writ—and we know on whose side the truths range. Even Mr. Andrew Leighton, who attempts to pooh-pooh the admirably written and very logical article of Mr. Charles Bray, extracted, by permission, from the August No. of the "*British Controversialist,*" admits that the spiritual agency is invisible to all but clairvoyant and natural seers. Knowing the hyper-excited state of the brain in these cases, this fact of itself ought to exclude the belief in the revelations coming from any other source than the subject or medium's own mind or that of persons, either absent or present, with whom he or she is brought by means of some material object *en rapport.*

I extract the following from "*Somnolism and Psycheism,*" (by Joseph W. Haddock, M.D., 1851), and bearing upon the argument contained in this paper:—"In ordinary vision, the *mind* does not *directly* behold the outward visible object; but it has a *perception* of that object as existing in the *imagination*. By imagination is not here meant *mere fancy*, as is sometimes done when the term is used, but the *image-forming faculty*, or the general power of the sensorium to form images *within itself*, of objects that are *without itself*. Imagination is, therefore, considered as a true and proper faculty of the psyché, or animal mind, and thence, as a distinct mode of sensation *above* the ordinary senses of the body, and to which they are subservient. For it is by the outward senses, which depend on nervous influence, and their connection with this image-forming faculty, that mind and matter are brought into mutual relationship and connection. Whether, therefore, it is by ordinary sight, by cerebral lucidity, or by the suggestions of another's mind, that the ideas of the objects are transmitted to the sensorium, they are alike *subjects of the image-forming faculty when there*, and, *as subjective perceptions*, they are equally real." The observation already made, that animals have no other mode of perception, will at once strike the reader—we shall see by what a gross perversion of terms our author tries to wriggle out of the dilemma. He says, "It will form no objection to our general statements of the spiritual nature of man, that brutes possess an image-forming faculty, and hence, it may be concluded, something analagous to the human animus. There is little doubt but that all animals possess something of the nature of a soul, and that hence they have their peculiar psychological development. But they want the *Pneuma*—the purely spiritual and rational essence, which gives man his essential character, and by which he is enabled to contemplate his Maker, and from which he derives his title to immortality. This, however, is not a subject for discussion in these pages, and the writer would only further remark, that he was not a little surprised to find one of our best and most popular physiologists using the terms of the apostle, and yet in a sense just opposite to that of the inspired writer; for he attributes to animals the possession of a *pneuma*, and to man the supposed higher faculty of the *psyche*,—thus exactly reversing the apostle's statements."

A more glaring instance of the blinding influence of preconceived opinions on men's judgment than this, can scarcely be conceived. While giving to brutes an image-forming faculty, psychical or mental phenomenon, he denies them the possession of the *pneuma*, which is, to all intents and purposes, the animal spirit or soul—the breath of life. Or are we henceforth to extract an additional entity from the animal organism, besides those of spirit, soul, and body—Spiritus, et anima, et corpus? Thus, it is our author that reverses the order of things to suit his own notions of man's immortality, founded on a forced and erroneous construction of the 7th verse of the 2nd chapter of the book of Genesis. And thus it is that all experience, all nature, and science, is set at nought, and man's reason led captive to mere dogma and blind faith. He, forsooth, thinks brute creatures "have *something* of a soul!" Such is not the language of the inspired Psalmist, who says —" Thou hidest thy face, they are troubled: thou takest away their breath, they die, and return to their dust. Thou sendest forth thy spirit, they are created: and thou renewest the face of the earth." Psalm civ. 29, 30.

I conclude with the remark that views derogatory to the creature are no less so to Him "in whose hand is the soul of every living thing, and the breath of all mankind." Job xii. 10.

We have an admirable illustration of the sagacity evinced by the feathered tribe, in the following anecdote of the thievish, or, in modern language, *kleptomaniacal* propensities of the crow.

" The crows are the flying thieves of the place; and no article, however unpromising its quality, can with safety be left unguarded in any apartment accessible to them. They despoil ladies' work-baskets, open paper parcels to ascertain their contents, will undo the knot of a napkin if it enclose anything eatable, and have been known to remove a peg which fastened the lid of a basket, in order to plunder the provender therein. The following *ruse* seems almost beyond corvine craft :—One of these ingenious marauders, after vainly attitudinising in front of a chained watch-dog that was lazily gnawing a bone, and after fruitlessly endeavouring to divert his attention by dancing before him, with head awry and eye askance, at length flew away for a moment, and returned bringing a companion which perched itself on a branch a few yards in the rear. The crow's grimaces were now actively renewed, but with no better success, till its confederate, poising itself on its wings, descended with the utmost velocity, striking the dog upon the spine with all the force of its strong beak. The *ruse* was successful; the dog started with surprise and pain, but not quickly enough to seize his assailant, whilst the bone he had been gnawing was snatched away by the first crow the instant his head was turned. Two well-authenticated instances of the recurrence of this device came within my knowledge at Colombo, and attest the sagacity and powers of communication and combination possessed by these astute and courageous birds."—*Tennant's Ceylon.*

"As for the study of animals, its use has been vitiated by the old notions of the difference between instinct and intelligence. Humanity and animality ought reciprocally to cast light upon each other. If the whole set of faculties constitutes the complement of animal life, it must surely be that all that are fundamental must be common to all the superior animals, in some degree or other: and differences of intensity are enough to account for existing diversities;—the association of the faculties being taken into the account, on the one hand, and, on the other, the improvement of man in society being set aside.

If there are any faculties which belong to man exclusively, they can only be such as correspond to the highest intellectual aptitudes; and this much may appear doubtful if we compare, in an unprejudiced way, the actions of the highest mammifers with those of the least developed savages.

"It seems to be more rational to suppose that the power of observation and even of combination exists in animals, though in an immeasurably inferior degree;—the want of exercise, resulting chiefly from their state of isolation, tending to benumb and even starve the organs. The extreme imperfection of phrenological science is manifest in the pride with which man, from the height of his supremacy, judges of animals as a despot judges of his subjects; that is, in the mass, without perceiving any inequality in them worth noticing. It is not less certain that, surveying the whole animal hierarchy, the principal orders of this hierarchy sometimes differ more from each other in intellectual and moral respects than the highest of them vary from the human type. The rational study of the mind and the ways of animals has yet to be instituted,—nothing having been done but in the way of preparation. It promises an ample harvest of important discovery directly applicable to the advancement of the study of man, if only the naturalists will disregard the declamation of theologians and metaphysicians about the pretended degradation of human nature, while they are, on the contrary, rectifying the fundamental notions of it by establishing, rigorously and finally, the profound differences which positively separate us from the animals nearest to us in the scale." — *Comte's Positive Philosophy.*

Much also, that is both interesting and instructive will be found in the chapter on Instinct, in Darwin's "Origin of Species."

Professor Huxley states, "The roots, as it were, of the great faculties which distinguish man, and confer on him his immense superiority over all other created beings, are traceable far down into the animal world. No one who has at all carefully observed the faculties of animals can doubt that they possess in many cases a distinct power of reasoning, and of observing the connexion between cause and effect." With the mass of evidence before us of the existence of mind and soul in the whole animal world, I inquire wherein consists Man's sole claim to immortality?

LETTERS ON SPIRITUALISM.

FIRST SERIES.

FIRST SERIES.

A WORD WITH "BLACKWOOD," AND OTHERS, ON SPIRITUALISM.

Blackwood's Magazine has a paper entitled "Seeing is Believing," devoted to the discussion of the phenomena which are known by the name of "spiritual manifestations," to which so large a share of attention has been attracted by a recent article in the *Cornhill Magazine*. The writer is evidently too strongly animated by hostile prejudices to be qualified for the treatment of a question which should be examined in a calm philosophical spirit. Much of his reasoning is extremely weak, and the entire contribution is characterised by transparent special pleading. The topic is one which cannot be too thoroughly ventilated; but essays pervaded by a vehement spirit of partisanship are not likely to bring us much nearer to the truth.—*Star and Dial.*

I.

"Quel Dieu est assez Dieu pour protéger ce qui n'est autre que la pensée de Dieu même?"—MICHELET.

"Those that to confute their credulity desire to see apparitions, shall, questionless, never behold any. The devil hath them already in a heresy as capital as witchcraft, and to appear to *them*, were but to *convert* them."—SIR THOMAS BROWNE'S "Religio Medici."

SIR,—Allow me to say a few plain words, and to advance a few plain facts on the subject of spiritualism. In doing this I shall not seek the protection of the anonymous, for the assertion of truth needs no disguise. Let those who attack spiritualism have the candour and the courage to do the same.

The English press is just now getting into a fuss on this subject. The article in the "Cornhill Magazine" has had the effect of a ferret in a rabbit warren. It has roused journalists into a paroxysm of terror and indignation. But these gentlemen would have done well to consider that this battle has been fought with all heat and ability already by the press in America; and with what result—the extinction of spiritualism? On the contrary; the immense augmentation of inquiry, the increase of spiritualists, from a few thousands to upwards of three millions, from the publication of one or two spiritual journals to the publication of seventeen journals. Do the gentlemen of the press here hope to do what the 'cute Yankees could not do? Do they think that Brother Jonathan has not men as clever, as learned, or as logical as old John ? and that he has not "five hundred good as these?"

Sir, I have just now had "Once a Week" and "Blackwood" sent to me. As to "Once a Week," I shall only say that the anonymous writer's diagrams are very amusing and very useful, because thousands in this country know the facts of spiritualism thoroughly, and are therefore qualified to laugh at the folly of these pretended explanations. Let the writer go on and explain in the same way how Mr. Home floated about the top of the room as mentioned in the "Cornhill Magazine," and as numbers of persons in London saw him do on another occasion. There are plenty of Martin Korkys still alive. Martin, in Galileo's time, declared that telescopes were all very well for looking at things on earth, but that they were delusive when applied to the heavens, and he was not going to give up his planets for that Italian fellow. The Martin Korky of "Once a Week" is quite welcome to his planets and his diagrams.

As for "Blackwood," as the main part of the anonymous article again is wasted on Mr. Dale Owen's "Footfalls on the Boundaries of Another World," I will not meddle with that. Both Mr. Dale Owen and his book are admirably able to take care of themselves. But there is one assertion which I wish to notice, and for which I have but one term —it is a gross and notorious untruth, as I will at once show. The writer confesses that he has been amongst spiritualists as an impostor, and yet he expects the public to believe him as a true man. He says:—" If the believers of spiritualism were really anxious to have their hypotheses investigated, according to strict scientific methods, there would soon cease to be much difference of opinion. Unhappily, while they all claim the right of scientific inquiry, invoke scientific freedom, and scatter scientific formulæ over their statements, they all *resist* and *evade* scientific enquiry."

The italics are the writer's own. I shall not follow him into the courtesy of his charges of " scoundrelism" and " imposture," but simply ask, what are the facts ?

In the earliest days of modern spiritualism in this country, Sir David Brewster and Lord Brougham expressed a desire to witness and examine the spiritual phenomena, as developed through Mr. Home. Was their desire resisted or evaded by Mr. Home ? Quite the contrary. Mr. Home had two meetings with these learned and scientific men, at one of which Mrs. Trollope was present, and was thoroughly convinced of the *bonâ fide* truth of what she saw. Dr. Maitland, F.R.S., and F.S.A., a distinguished clergyman of the Church of England, and a well-known author of a capital little book, styled " Superstition and Science," says:—" I have now before me a newspaper containing a letter from Sir David Brewster to Benjamin Coleman, Esq., and dated so recently as October 9, 1855, in which he says, ' At Mr. Cox's house, Mr. Home, Mr. Cox, Lord Brougham, and myself, sat down to a small table, Mr. Home having previously requested us to examine if there was any machinery about his person: an examination, however, which we declined to make. When all our hands were upon the table, noises were heard—rappings in abundance: and finally, when we rose up, the table actually rose, as it appeared to me, from the ground. This result I do not pretend to explain.'"

Now, sir, I have nothing further to do with this fact, on this occasion, than to say that it is in direct contradiction to the assertion of the writer in "Blackwood," "that they all resist and evade scientific inquiry." What is more, it is well known that it has been the practice of Mr. Home, on all occasions, to accept any invitation by gentlemen and Christians to display the phenomena which come through him. He has exhibited scores of times before the Emperor of France, and in presence of any scientific men that the Emperor has chosen to name. Mr. Home has done the same at almost every court and capital in Europe, and possesses the most unequivocal testimonials to the reality of his demonstrations from numerous crowned and learned heads. If there be one thing more than another conspicuous in Mr. Home, it is his readiness to meet and oblige all respectable inquirers. During his late sojourn in London, he has repeatedly visited—on one occasion for a whole fortnight—Lord Lyndhurst, and has been the medium, at his lordship's house, of most striking phenomena, to the entire satisfaction of that great lawyer and his family. Now, surely, Lord

Lyndhurst is a highly scientific man, in the science especially essential to such inquiries, that of shrewdly examining and taking evidence of facts. Mr. Home has displayed similar phenomena in the houses of literary, artistic, parliamentary, and scientific people in London during the whole last season.

Mr. Faraday, we all know, wished to see table-turning, and he propounded a theory to account for it. But his theory of involuntary muscular action in the persons who put their hands on the table, was immediately stultified by the tables rising up far out of the reach of all hands. Mr. Faraday, I know, has since been repeatedly invited by a scientific friend of his to witness those more decided demonstrations. But a burnt child dreads the fire, and Mr. Faraday so dreadfully burnt his fingers by deciding in a hurry, that he has steadily persisted in refusing to go near tables that rise up to the ceilings of lofty rooms.

Dr. Ashburner is a highly scientific man, the translator of "Reichenbach." He desired to examine these phenomena; he found no resistance nor evasion; he saw them repeatedly, became convinced of their reality, and, with a noble daring, rare in this age, publicly avowed his conviction; and I could give you numerous instances of scientific men who have wished to examine them, and are believers; but they, like the correspondents of "Blackwood," and nearly all the correspondents of the journals, have their prudential reasons for preferring the anonymous.

There is one instance of this most remarkable. A

distinguished physician and editor of one of our scientific journals, has for several years made a stout fight against spiritualism. He went to Mr. William Wilkinson, solicitor, of 44, Lincoln's-inn-fields, and said, "You talk in the 'Spiritual Magazine' wonderful things: I challenge you to let me see them." Mr. Wilkinson accepted the challenge, and took Mr. Squire, a well-known American medium, with him to this gentleman's house. The learned doctor invited a learned Cantab and secretary to a scientific society to meet them. They spent a whole day, and parts of two other days, with these gentlemen, allowing them to make every examination that they pleased. In the course of this visit, many astonishing things were done; a heavy table was flung from one end of a room to another. A table constructed scientifically, to defy the efforts of the most raging lunatics, and which had defied them, was, at the particular desire of the doctor, though it was strongly clamped and bound with an iron rim, torn to fragments. All this the doctor, thoroughly convinced, as well as his friend, declared that he would publish in the "Athenæum" and the "Lancet" with his name; but he was advised, from obvious motives of prudence to himself, by Mr. Wilkinson, not to do it. However, he drew up the exact account, had it verified by his friend, and sent it to the "Spiritual Magazine," where it appears in the number for April of this year.

This, I think, is pretty well in England; what in America? I could, did space allow, give you voluminous proofs of the utter falsehood of the assertion of the writer in "Blackwood." I will content myself with two remarkable refutations. Professor Hare, one of the most scientific men and greatest electricians of the age, called the Faraday of America, desired to witness and examine, in the terms of the "Blackwood" writer, "according to strict scientific methods," these phenomena. He met with no resistance or evasion whatever. All circles threw themselves open to his research. He pursued this enquiry thoroughly, and so far from finding these phenomena the wretched product of machinery, trickery, or even clever legerdemain, he finally acknowledged their unearthly origin, and published boldly his conviction. In this conviction he lived and died.

Judge Edmunds, one of the most distinguished American judges, so famed for his professional acumen, that, contrary to the custom of England, he has retired from the bench, and returned to the bar, where his countrymen assure me his practice is worth £5,000 a-year; also desired to examine thoroughly these extraordinary phenomena, "according to the strictest" legal method. The result was the same All circles were thrown open to him, and so far from discovering a cheat or a fallacy, he discovered a great truth, and, like a brave, honest man, continues to proclaim it, by word, and pen, and press.

These, sir, I think, will be admitted " according to strict scientific method," to be a complete refutation of the statements of Blackwood and Co.; and, in conclusion, I will beg to remind these gentlemen of the press, that the very same things which they now assert of spiritualism, were said of Christianity, for above one hundred years after its appearance; ay, far worse things. The Christians were held by the Greek and Latin *illustrissimi,* not only as the grossest impostors, but as the most vile and degraded of men. The practices attributed to them were too revolting for modern language. Christianity was the "superstitio prava" of Pliny the younger; the "exitiabilis superstitio" of Tacitus: the Christians were the "homines per flagitiis invisos" of that historian. Every classical reader can lay his hand on these statements.

These are the calumnies which truth has, in every age, to endure. Take the very highest philosophical authority of Greece—Plato. He makes Socrates, in Euthyphon, say:—"And we too, when I say anything in the public assembly concerning divine things, and predict to them what is going to happen, they ridicule me as mad: and although nothing that I ever have predicted has not turned out to be true, yet they envy all such men as we are. However, we ought not to heed them, but pursue our own course."

How precisely identical are the truth, and the enemies of the truth, in every age of the world! Sir, I am a man who all my life has hated humbug, and has, at whatever cost, dared to expose it without hiding my head under the anonymous. In my early years I had my blow at priestcraft. I am not one of those who think it wise to jeer at what I do not take the trouble to examine. Some years ago I heard some very wonderful things of gold-finding in

Australia. I determined to go and examine how far these fine stories were true. I did not think the way to come at the truth was to shy an article at it from a journal without going near it. I got a real spade, and dug in real earth, and I and my sons found one of the finest gold fields in Victoria—Nine Mile Creek—in consequence of which, my son is at this moment heading a Government expedition of discovery in that colony. I got as much gold with my own hands as would have knocked any man down who should have said it was imaginary. Well, I am just as sure of the facts of spiritualism as I am of those of gold-finding. If I were to go to Lord Campbell and tell him that I knew more about the business of the Court of Chancery than he did, he would laugh at me; and if Lord Campbell came to me and said that he knew more about the phenomena of spiritualism than I do, after years of examination, I should laugh at him; and we should both laugh on the same good grounds at the other talking of things that he had not thoroughly sifted, to a man who had.

I have sifted these things for five years. I have witnessed nearly all the varieties of extraordinary things seen in this country, and often in private houses of the highest character, where no professional medium was present. The facts of spiritualism are, therefore, to me, common-places, and as positive as a stone wall. Let the opponents, instead of blustering and talking the sheerest nonsense, sift these things for five years, and then they may cavil if they please. The writer in "Blackwood" thinks spiritualism "the disgrace of the age;" I, on the contrary, think the disgrace of the age is the want of faith in peoples' own senses, and the want of courage to make use of them.

Of the higher and more sacred teachings of spiritualism, and its numerous phases, for this movement of tables is but one, and one of the least, I could say much, but I confine myself here to the refutation of a most transparent calumny.—Yours, &c.,

WILLIAM HOWITT.

II.

SIR,—I have read Mr. Wm. Howitt's letter, which appeared in your number of this date, with considerable interest, and I beg to ask Mr. Howitt, through the same medium, if much unbelief would not be staggered or entirely removed by some practical and really serviceable experiment? For instance, might not some information be obtained, to be privately communicated to Mr. Slack, of Bath, who has so assiduously devoted himself in the fearful and mysterious case of the Road child-murder, by which he might be assisted to prosecute further investigations? I do not mean that any magistrate would commit, or any jury convict, on the unsupported evidence of spiritualism; but, in such a case as this, surely some table might be persuaded to furnish a clue for transmission to him, by which the mystery should be unravelled, and the act be brought legally home by customary evidence to the criminal or criminals. This, if done, would make more converts to Mr. Howitt's views (spite of "Blackwood" and others) than any results, in themselves perfectly useless, and prove that there is a reality about the professed communications which may be turned to the good purposes of deterring from, or detecting crime.

      I am, yours obediently,
Reading, Oct. 6.   Jas. N. Buckland.

III.

SPIRIT-RAPPING.—THE COCK-LANE GHOST.

Sir,—An apology is due from me for this attempt to intrude on your valuable space, by a few remarks on the subject of spiritualism, in the hope of their being of some slight interest, though from the pen of a novice in supernatural mysteries. I had heard little of the facts or doctrines of spiritualism until enlightened by that talented legerdemainist, Anderson, to wit, who not only arrogated to himself the title of "Wizard of the North," but claimed to have, by means of his very clever electrical rapping machine, cured thousands of what he termed "this delusion." I must own I stared in my ignorance at hearing of myriads, where I had only expected scores. The Cock-lane ghost I had read of; it is noticed in grave history as an instance of successful trickery, imposing on the aristocratic circles of London, and even on the credulity of the great Dr. Johnson himself. The ghost was then, as now, invisible, indicating its presence and intelligence by the usual significant knocks. It is added, that the imposture was found out to be the contrivance of a woman.

What would that chronicler say now? The direct communion with spirits seems held by a multitude to be not only within possibility, but actually achieved, and achievable at will. I am only a sceptical spectator, yet as such I witnessed on two occasions some facts which I would willingly learn the explanation of on natural principles. They occurred at my own house, and were incidentally and involuntarily originated by myself, at that period a sincere unbeliever. A small party was assembled after tea on a plot of green sward in my garden, sitting, standing, reclining, walking, talking, as it happened. Relaxing manly gravity, I was endeavouring to amuse the younger part of the company by some boyish juggling feats with two hats, &c., when a young lady, not an adept, if I recollect right, proposed an attempt at hat-turning, and seizing one accordingly, she was joined by another lady, a believer, and kneeling together on the grass, with the hat on a hassock between them, they grasped its rim, according to art, and awaited the result. No movement followed, however, beyond that produced by several of the others playfully pitching into it wine-glasses, fruit, &c., with an occasional tuft of grass. With the view

D

of aiding the tardy or reluctant spirit, and easing the two sorceresses, I brought out a little table, hitherto guiltless of all turning, save now and then an innocent, if not harmless overturn, and the hat was transferred to it. Still it gave no sign; general patience was ebbing fast, when it was proposed to try the table. The proposal was approved by acclamation, and all present surrounded and placed hands or fingers on the table, giggling for the most part as they joined in this novel round game. I should add that a summer twilight was setting in. After a moderate lapse of time, a slight but unequivocal movement of the table occurred. The mirth of all, save one lady, instantly subsided. I looked under the table, not a foot was near it. Our lady medium, then, in the most polite terms, requested "the spirit" to signify, by three knocks, if willing to answer our questions —three deliberate gentle uprisings, and as many gentle, yet audible, footfalls ensued. All were silent. I felt impressed; so did the others evidently, except the laughing lady, who still indulged in her mirth. My age was asked (I am said to bear my years lightly); a concatenation of knocks followed five times as long, if not as tedious, as the longest moaning of the "Big Ben" family—with a very little tap for the fraction of a year, thus giving me the full measure. I could not gainsay the account, and the rest took its accuracy on credit without the production of my baptismal certificate, which is strictly in accordance. The laugher's age was demanded. No response followed. It was then requested to give two blows if refusing to communicate the required information; they followed sharply, together with a hasty movement towards her, as if the table tried to push her away; other questions and answers followed, till increasing darkness put an end to the exhibition —the table thrice bowing, not ungracefully, to those around. A robust young unbelieving friend assured me, that on his holding the table firmly down, when about to answer, it commenced a lateral movement which caused him then to desist.

I must add that I never witnessed anything of the sort before, and but once since, when my impression decidedly was that trickery had been used. The answers were then absurd and inaccurate. An alphabet was used, the spirit selecting the letters for its answers. These were disgracefully spelt. Example:—

Question: Will you tell me Mr. B.'s age, &c.?
Answer: Somebody has lost a black dog.
Question: Who?
Answer: Find out.

The spirit or fiend also declared its angry intentions, thus: "I will give you sutch a poak."

You may judge of the effect on me of such a manifestation; it repelled me back into the regions of incredulity.

Could I produce these effects in solitude and alone, I might believe. But I would not acquire faith at the risk of having the constant companionship of a disembodied spirit of equivocal character.

I enclose my card, and again apologising, am your humble servant, FABER.
Oct. 6.

IV.
THE SYSTEM OF SPIRITUALISM.

Sir,—The publication of William Howitt's letter on the subject of "Spiritualism," in the *Star*, may, I presume, be taken as an invitation to discuss that subject in your widely-extended journal; and should you deem this letter, from amongst the many you will receive, worthy of a place after that of the great historian of priestcraft, you have my full permission, not only to publish my name, but my address also; although I do not think either will in any way add to the value of the remarks which I may make. Indeed, I am one of those who consider that rational arguments ought to be weighed in the same scale, whether they proceed from the palace or the cottage —whether they are delivered by the philosopher or the peasant. When facts have to be detailed, we, undoubtedly, wish to know that they are related by a truth-teller; but the arguments and remarks of a story-teller should not be cast away on account of the source from whence they come.

When a number of facts are related by persons who cannot be suspected of a wish either to deceive themselves or others, the general rule is to believe that such facts really were observed by the narrators. The observer may account for the phenomena which he has seen and heard in one way; the listener may account for them in another. And it is in this difference of opinion that we frequently see the greatest acrimony of controversy.

If tables turn, or fly up to the ceiling—if hands appear—if voices are heard—if legs are pinched—or, I imagine, if brimstone was smelled or tasted, there would be, if there was no obvious cause for any one, or all, of these phenomena, several very different modes of explaining the possible or probable cause.

Such phenomena as those I have just referred to, except the smell and taste of brimstone, which I have not yet heard of, are accounted for by the spiritualists, through the presence, or active agency of some spirit; while others account for them in a material manner, and even suppose it possible that some undiscoverable trick may have been employed to impress the senses.

In any examination of this subject which is really deserving the name of philosophical, we must, however, admit the possibility of the senses being impressed with the image of things when the things themselves are absent. But the metaphysician can discover in the living being itself, in its immaterial portion, a sufficient cause for the phenomenon.

What are the ghosts of our sleep? What are those ghosts seen, in the apparently waking moments, by some? Not necessarily the spirits of the absent; for the individual mind has within itself the power to create images; and in the unconscious moments either of sleep, or that which is called wake, images do so impress themselves on our senses that the senses are obliged to believe in their existence. It is only when the reason gives to these images an erroneous source that there is danger to fear.

I have made no "attack" upon spirits, unless this metaphysical mode of accounting for them should be considered so. And as to "the system of spiritualism," I have no power of attacking it, for I have not been let into the secret of the system; but I have a firm impression, after a somewhat careful thought on all the manifestations which I have heard and read of, that this "system" is an endeavour to demonstrate that which the majority of thinking men deem to be undemonstrable—viz., the separate and individual existence of spirits apart from organization.

My only apology for saying these few words in behalf of that which I conscientiously believe to be the only rational explanation of spiritualism, must be that I have been studying anatomy and physiology for nearly thirty years ; and for the last eighteen or twenty years, have paid some attention to the science of metaphysics. These qualifications may not enable me to remove the convictions of your truly able correspondent; but they may serve to show that both body and spirit have received some attention from yours obediently,

WILLIAM ROBINS.

49, Oxford Terrace, W., Oct. 6.

V.

Sir,—I read in your impression of Saturday a letter written by a gentleman whose name has become a household word amongst us, and published with the intention of rebuking and controverting the writers in *Blackwood* and *Once a Week*, who have lately ventilated their opinions on the subject of spiritual manifestations, as exhibited spontaneously, or through the agency of a modern medium.

It does seem strange that, at this time, we should still be halting between two opinions on this vexed question, and that what one authority asserts to be a truth too absolute to admit of doubt, another, equally worthy of credence, as stoutly maintains to be a falsehood and palpable deceit.

Mr. Howitt says it would be well to remember that the battle between the pro and anti-spiritualists has already been fought with all heat and ability by the press in America, and asks if we can hope to do that which the 'cute Yankees found to be impossible? To my mind, the question of 'cuteness has nothing whatever to do with the matter, and it would be quite as absurd to admit as established fact that which our 'cuteness is unable to prove to be an imposition, as to swallow, without reflection, the marvellous stories of the modern wonder-workers. The question is, in fact, too grave a one to rest for an answer on the detection or non-detection of any trick, or series of tricks, and conviction of the truth or falsehood of it must, I am persuaded, come from within.

A wide field is opened up before us when we come to consider this matter of spiritual manifestations, bordered on one side by the sublime, and on the other by the ridiculous. "Then shall the dust return to the earth, as it was, and the spirit shall return unto God who gave it," said the old Jewish preacher when he spoke of the dissolution of soul and body, but not so says your modern spiritualist. The body may return to mother earth and resolve itself into its constituent atom, but the spirit shall wander about my drawing-room, shall rap out upon my table answers to my questions, shall scratch upon a slate, play a fantasia upon an accordion or piano, clasp the ancles of my friends, or play fifty other pranks which only the shade of a mountebank could be suspected of knowing how to perform. Is this fact, or is it not? If it is, our forefathers did not hang, burn, and drown old women for nothing, after all, and the tales of ghosts and banshee, which were wont to send me into paroxysms of childish fear, are likely to be true as the Gospel.

One might well be excused for asking what purpose all this can serve; surely there can be no high teaching in a dancing table, and no hidden meaning in a squeezing of one's legs; at least, if there is either teaching or meaning, I have not heard that any one has discovered it.

It is a high thought, truly, this—that if I die to-morrow, I may next evening help to break a lunatic-defying table, or carry Mr. Home, in a horizontal position, up to the ceiling; or, perhaps, as another ill-conditioned spirit is said to have done at Stockwell, bring utter ruin on some old lady's crockery.

Internal conviction, then, and a feeling that the spirits of the mighty dead are not intended to amuse or terrify an evening party, or afford satisfaction to a scientific *reunion*, compels me altogether to reject the modern theory of spiritualism, though should its votaries be at last divided into deceivers and deceived, I should (giving Mr. Howitt credit for as honest a conviction as my own) never think of classing him with the former.—I am, sir, yours, &c.

Hornsey, Oct. 8. LEX.

VI.

SPIRITUAL MANIFESTATIONS.

SIR,—A large section of the people will award its thanks to the *Star* for opening its columns for the ventilation of this curiously interesting subject.

With your permission, and for the convenience of those who are strangers to the subject, or who have been content to remain satisfied with the exposition of it as furnished by the Wizard of the North, I send you extracts from some very remarkable letters, and will conclude with a short account of my own experience.

Extract from Sir David Brewster's letter to Benjamin Coleman, Esq. :—

"At Mr. Cox's house, Mr. Home, Mr. Cox, Lord Brougham and myself, sat down to a small table, Mr. Home having previously requested us to examine if there was any machinery about his person, an examination, however, which we declined to make. When all our hands were upon the table, noises were heard, rappings in abundance, and finally, when we rose up, the table actually rose, as appeared to me, from the ground. The result I do not pretend to explain; but rather than believe that spirits made the noise, I will conjecture that the raps were produced either by Mr. Home's toes, which, as will be seen, were active on another occasion, or, as Dr. Schiff has shown, 'by the repeated displacement of the tendon of the *peroneus longus* muscle in the sheath in which it slides behind the external *malleolus ;*' and rather than believe that spirits raised the table, I will conjecture that it was done by the agency of Mr. Home's feet, which were always below it. It is not true, as stated by you, that a large dinner table was moved about at Mr. Cox's in the most extraordinary manner."

Sir David likewise stated that the table was covered with copious drapery, beneath which nobody was allowed to look. After disposing of, in a somewhat flippant manner, the other facts, he concludes by remarking :—

"I offer these facts for the spiritual instruction of yourself and Mr. Cox, and for the information of the public. Mr. Faraday had the merit of driving the spirits from above the table to a more suitable place below it. I hope I have done something to extricate them from a locality which has hitherto been the lair of a more jovial race."

The following are extracts from a letter written by Mrs. Trollope, the authoress (dated Florence), to a gentleman residing near London, at whose house she witnessed the phenomena in the presence of Sir David Brewster:—

"I declare that at your house, on an evening subsequent to Sir David Brewster's meeting with Mr. Home, at Cox's Hotel, in the presence of Sir David, of myself, and of other persons, a large and very heavy dining-table was moved about in a most extraordinary manner; that Sir David was urged both by Mr. Home and yourself to look under the cloth and under the table; that he did look under it, and that while he was so looking the table was much moved; and that while he was looking, and while the table was moving he avowed that he saw the movement."

"I should not, my dear sir, do all that duty, I think, requires of me in this case,, were I to conclude without stating very solemnly, that, after very many opportunities of witnessing and investigating the phenomena caused by or happening through Mr. Home, I am wholly convinced that, be what may their origin, and cause, and nature, they are not produced by any fraud, machinery, juggling, illusion, or trickery."

Another writer observes:—

"Such evidence has been produced as would give judgment in favour of spiritual manifestations in our courts of Westminster."

Another, under the signature of "A True Believer," writes:—

"The Great Wizard of the North makes raps and raises tables by an agent which cannot be concealed. The humble medium, who is neither wizard nor conjuror, makes raps, raises tables, and plays accordions by an agent which cannot be discovered. How is this? will Sir D. Brewster or any of your correspondents explain?"

Extract from a letter signed "Veritas:"—
"I am one of those who have seen a heavy table lifted bodily from the floor, and poised mid air, and I have seen various articles carried both above and below the table. I have seen the accordion played whilst held in a position impossible to be acted on by ordinary means. I have held it myself, apart from anyone, suspended in one hand, with the keys nearly touching the ground, and whilst so held the particular air I asked for was played throughout in the most perfect and beautiful manner. I have had intelligent communications of a family nature made to me, of which I was not previously aware, but which were subsequently verified. Let those who say these things are done by machinery, or by any other than by spiritual agency, prove it and expose the imposture."

The following is from the pen of one who signs himself "Rusticus." The entire letter is lengthy:—
"As far as I have read the history of 'the manifestations,' as occurring in America, nothing more effectually contributed to their diffusion than reducing the argument to the alternative of believing in the truth of the facts, on the one hand, or on the other, in the sudden impostures of men hitherto known to be honest; for, certainly, husbands and wives, sons and daughters, brothers and sisters, were more likely to believe a strange event to be supernatural than that they had become to each other from affectionate friends, a set of mutual unprincipled liars.

"It may be that the Roman Catholic Church has been too credulous in matters of this kind; it may be that the Protestant Church has been too incredulous. Even the existence of those inferior order of spirits who are said to indulge in musical performances upon various instruments, in jocular remarks, or familiar colloquies, is fully acknowledged in the Church of Rome; they take their place in their own proper scale of spiritual existence; while those whom Protestants would scoff and scout, the Roman Catholic Church would treat with solemn prayers and exorcisms, thus acknowledging the truth of that which a Protestant public might be likely to regard as a barefaced imposture. The time, however, seems to have come when all these questions must be reconsidered, without any bias, whether scientific, philosophical, or religious."

Extract from a letter signed "E. C."

"The last occasion when I saw Mr. Home, the company were at supper, and the raps were heard in several places on the table, and frequently, but faintly repeated, before much attention was paid them. They sounded on the table close to my own platter, and at the moment I mentioned the circumstance to Mr. Home, who sat opposite to me enjoying some nicely baked rice, a rap was forcibly made under my foot, so distinct and palpable that I knew it struck exactly under my heel. There was too much hilarity at the table to enter into conversation, but a few questions were asked by one or two persons, and proper answers returned. After a short interval, two or three louder raps were heard, as if by a different hand, immediately recognized by a lady present, as the token of her brother who perished at sea. As she mentioned this circumstance, the table began to move with that peculiar labouring motion of a vessel when it struggles through the troubled waters. I should say it was impossible for any human hand or machinery to produce such an effect. The table literally groaned and creaked, and in a few moments rose a little from the floor, and rocked like a ship, even the plush of the water along the sides of the vessel was imitated, and as this peculiar noise passed along by my own chair, and down by my side of the table, I am confident it was not produced by Mr. Home or any confederate. He could have had no confederates except one of the family, all of whom I had known too long and intimately to lay them open to suspicion." "There is something unmistakably peculiar in every sound and motion, and in many cases such a feeling of a spiritual presence, that it leaves the mind perfectly satisfied."

I proceed to give you an extract from a letter, published by myself, in February, 1856:

" In May last, being at the house of a gentleman of distinction, I met there an English lady, a visitor, whom I discovered to be what is usually termed a medium. I sat down with her to a large library table, on which we placed our hands. She inquired if the spirits were in attendance, and was answered by three very distinct taps that appeared to proceed from the centre of the table. She then put several questions, to which she received intelligent answers by means of the raps, and by the help of an alphabet and pencil. I asked the name of the spirit in attendance, and received for answer, 'Afflick.' I desired to know where a deceased relative had died a few months previous. The reply was 'Devonport.' As none in the room but myself knew this, I was certainly surprised. The position of this lady places her beyond the suspicion of any contrivance to deceive. About a fortnight after this, I met Mr. Home at the same house in the country. Mr. Home had only just then arrived from America. In the evening, Mr. Home proposed that himself, I, and a gentleman present, should go upstairs in the dark. We did so, and stationed ourselves in a tapestried chamber. We stood and joined hands, remaining some time in silence; at length, on being questioned by Mr. Home, 'the spirits' made us aware of their presence by very loud raps and thumps all about the room, on the furniture, oaken ceiling, and floor. We moved into the state drawing-room, our hands joined, and standing; there these extraordinary noises were more remarkable and more manifest. Scratching on the furniture, raps and thumps on the tables and ceiling, sounds as of many feet, which gradually approached us until we were literally encompassed with these tramping sounds. Mr. Home received a blow on the shoulder, and my companion on the thigh. We adjourned to the library, this time in the light, and numbering seven; two of the party, ladies, sat down to a large and heavy round table. Placing our hands on it, we heard loud raps from all parts of this table, and from the oaken book-cases. We spelt out that 'they did not come to hold conversation, but to make manifestations,' and they asked that 'we would investigate with fairness and candour.' I desired to know if they would give us some music. Reply: 'Yes.' One of the ladies brought a guitar, and placed it under the table; as the table was large, it was easily seen; presently the strings were faintly agitated, the sounds became gradually louder, and a tune was fairly played out by invisible means. I observed the instrument to move twice, but I am sure no one touched it. After this, the heavy table at which we were sitting gradually rose from the floor, our hands resting upon it; it rose at least six inches, and remained in a state of suspension some time, then tipped backwards and forwards; this was succeeded by a vibration in the table, that was communicated to our bodies and the chairs upon which we were sitting, as if some powerful fluid were escaping. The sensation as of the grasp of a hand was felt on the knee of two of the party successively, followed by very loud raps from the table. A little before twelve o'clock we removed to a room upstairs, and took our seats at a large square table; here we heard loud raps on the table and from some parts of the room. The lady to whom I have before alluded was sitting next to me, and we were both of us, with the chairs on which we were sitting, forced violently from the table nearly to the end of the room, and then drawn round. I tried to resist, but without success; the table followed us, leaving the rest of the circle behind. Our host, who is a learned and accomplished gentleman, watched the phenomena with a jealous eye, and he has since tested Mr. Home, and is satisfied that there could have been no trickery. He leaves it for science to explain."

Having read Mr. Howitt's letter in your impression of the 6th, I considered it my duty to forward you these particulars.

I am, sir, yours, &c.,

JOHN JAMES BIRD.

VII.

SIR,—In the first number of the "Spiritual Magazine," I gave, at the request of the editor and several friends, a short history of my personal experiences in the investigation of the phenomena—which, after hearing much, and after reading almost everything that had been published for and against—*I* call spiritual. Emboldened by the example of William Howitt, and by your wise determination to open your columns to a fair discussion of the subject, I desire to lay before your readers the result of my experiences, and I must necessarily repeat statements which are familiar to my friends but are not known to the public at large, and which will have for their verification whatever value may attach to my name.

At the outset permit me to say that I am not learned in the laws of physics, nor can I lay claim to any scientific acquirements; but on this account I hope it is not presumptuous to say that I think I am even a better authority for a plain matter of fact than the Brewsters, Faradays, and the lesser luminaries who lead public opinion, simply because I have no public reputation to support, no false theories to recant, no deep-rooted prejudices, nor hitherto wise dogmas to unlearn. I am simply a plain, practical observer, and I speak of facts, brought home to the evidence of my senses, which no learned theories nor subtle reasoning can set aside; whether the establishment of the facts shall lead in the main to good or evil it is not my province to decide. With that view of the question I have nothing to do. Every serious inquirer will be guided by the result of his own convictions; and for my own part, whilst claiming credit only for the perfect truthfulness of my narrations, I am ready and most willing to pay respect and deference to the religious scruples of those who would discourage investigation, because in their opinion these manifestations are anti-Christ, the agency of the devil, and therefore, as they think, ought to be avoided by Christian men and women.

It is for men like the writers in the several serials, who have recently taken up this important subject for the purposes of ridicule, that I have no respect whatever; men who can only see in it trickery and delusion, and who support their statements by transparent falsehoods and calumny.

Up to the period of my first introduction to Mr. Home, six years since, who was then staying with a neighbour of mine, I had no more knowledge of "spirit-rapping" than I had gleaned from the perusal of extracts taken from the American papers, and which I treated as most of your readers will, no doubt, be still inclined to do—with indifference, if not with a smile of incredulity. The thing to my untutored mind was simply "impossible," and, therefore, not worthy of further consideration. "Table moving" had been explained by Faraday, and satisfied in my ignorance of the folly of attributing the phenomena to any other than natural agencies, I did not trouble myself to seek for testimony, though it was manifold and irrefutable.

Invited by my neighbour to join his family circle, we sat, a party of twelve persons, around a large dinner table in the full light of lamps and candles. I there heard for the first time the "rapping" sounds on the table, on the floor, on the wall behind me, and on the keys of the piano in a distant part of the room, entirely out of the reach of all present. I had, in common with others of the party, a message given to me, purporting to be from a deceased relative, which, at the time, I was unable to attest, but which was verified by subsequent inquiry. Then, by no visible or human agency, an accordion was brought from a distant part of the room, and placed in my hand by being thrust up between me and the table; taking hold of the blank end of the instrument, as I was requested to do, and supporting my arm on my knee, I asked the spirit to play for me "Angels ever bright and fair," which to my astonishment was done in the most perfect and beautiful manner possible. The strong pull, as if by a human hand, necessary, in a large instrument, to produce the sounds, made it difficult to hold, and it was evident that fingers must have also manipulated the keys to bring out the air.

Now here was a fact which no theory could destroy, and which no rational explanation based either upon "*odic-force*," "electricity," "involuntary muscular agency," nor any other scientific solution would meet; and I was compelled to admit, since no better explanation could be given, that these phenomena were indeed effected by supermundane agencies, and I am happy to say I have always been bold enough on all suitable occasions to proclaim the fact and submit to the consequences, which, however, have not been very harmful hitherto, but, on the contrary, my open advocacy has led to most valuable friendships and to many interesting acquaintances, and, what is of much greater importance, my testimonies, in the first instance, and the opportunities from my intimacy with Mr. Home, Mr. Squire, and several "mediums" in private life, have enabled me to facilitate inquiry, and have thus been the means of converting many from rank infidelity to a full and openly-avowed recognition of a life hereafter.

Among other extraordinary facts which followed immediately after my first séance, I saw, in the presence of Mr. Home, a large-sized drawing-room table rise gradually from the floor, ascending steadily to the ceiling, out of the reach of all present but myself, and descending as steadily until it came again to the floor with no more force than if it had been a feather's weight. Following up the subject, after the departure of Mr. Home for the Continent, where it is known he was received by most of the crowned heads of Europe, as recorded in that very excellent journal, the *Spiritual Magazine*, I have since seen almost every phase of "spiritual manifestations," some of them transcending in their marvellous character even those of which I have spoken; and, in support of the writer of "Stranger than Fiction," published in the *Cornhill Magazine* of August last, which has created so much excitement, I here assert that I have seen all the phenomena of which he speaks, and much more; and on one occasion, where a party sat down to a table without any known "medium" being present, two of them—father and daughter—proved to be mediums, with a power at once so fully developed, that after obtaining a variety of messages of a very remarkable character, the table, when the whole party had left it, moved about most actively for an hour without any one being near it.

As Mr. Howitt, in his very masterly letter in your

paper of the 6th inst., has incidentally mentioned my name in connection with Sir David Brewster's, it may not be uninteresting to your readers to learn something of the cause of that learned gentleman's having written to me, and I venture to think the circumstances do in no way redound to his candour or to his professional acumen. After I had witnessed the phenomena first spoken of by me, I was informed by Mr. William Cox, of Jermyn Street, that Lord Brougham and Sir David Brewster had, by his invitation, met Mr. Home at his house, and that some of the most striking manifestations in broad daylight had taken place in their presence, at which they had expressed their great astonishment, and their desire to investigate still further, and as I had read an article recently written by Sir David, in one of the northern magazines, against spirit manifestations, I determined to compare notes with him, and in company with a gentleman at whose house Mr. Home was then staying, I called on Sir David, and found him quite disposed to talk upon the subject, and most anxious to see more of it. He said he had made up his mind that the phenomena was not the result of trick or delusion, but he was not prepared to admit the spiritual source, as that was the last thing he would give in to. He was invited to fix his own time to renew his investigation, and on the following day he went to my friend's house, and there met Mrs. Trollope and her son Thomas, who were on a visit, staying for several days under the same roof with Mr. Home, and witnessing hourly, as I know, manifestations of the most remarkable character. At this séance Sir David witnessed a great variety of phenomena, and was to all appearance most seriously impressed. He walked about the garden afterwards, talking over the subject with Mr. Trollope, and left the party with the conviction on their minds that, if he were not bold enough to recant his errors, he at least would never venture to assail spiritualism again.

Mr. Home, pleased with the success he met with, wrote to his friends in America saying that Sir David Brewster, Sir Lytton Bulwer (who had also fully investigated the subject), and others, were converted.

An extract from Mr. Home's letter was inserted in one of the American spiritual papers, and copied in the London *Morning Advertiser*, which, meeting the eye of Sir David, he not only wrote to deny, but he condemned the whole exhibition as a farce, and was restrained, he said, from saying all he desired "in deference to the feelings of the talented lady who was present."

This letter aroused the indignation of all who had heard Sir David's previous opinions. I wrote to him, and very stinging letters followed from Mr. Cox and Mr. Trollope. I asked him to be good enough to let us know how much he admitted, and how much he denied? In his reply he made the remarkable statement quoted by Mr. Howitt, and which, for the instruction of those who have recently adduced Sir David as an authority against the facts,

I may as well repeat. He said: "At Mr. Cox's house, Mr. Home, Mr. Cox, Lord Brougham, and myself, sat down to a small table, Mr. Home having previously requested us to examine if there was any machinery about his person, an examination, however, which we declined to make. When all our hands were upon the table, noises were heard, rappings in abundance; and finally, when we rose up, the table actually appeared to rise from the ground. This result I do not attempt to explain."

I asked Sir David what he meant by saying "the table actually appeared to rise from the ground?" It was a question of fact, did it rise?

The Rev. Doctor Maitland, in commenting upon Sir David's extraordinary letter, says, "Here is a philosopher who does not know whether a table under his own nose does or does not rise from the ground, and it is upon men so avowedly incompetent that we are asked to pin our faith in matters of physical science," &c.

Surely, after this, Sir David Brewster's authority against spirit manifestations can never again be seriously quoted; but if any one should be so disposed, let him inquire what are Sir David's real opinions now. I am not prepared to assert that Sir David admits the spiritual agency of these phenomena, since that " is the last thing he would give in to;" but I speak advisedly when I say that his opinions on this subject have undergone a material change since the date of that letter; and if he is now satisfied of the reality of the phenomena, as I have good reason to believe he is, why, may I ask, does he not in a manly manner, in the cause of truth, boldly proclaim it to the world, and, with the opportunities which are open to him of further investigation, help to place this much-vexed and most stupendous question on its proper plane?

Your readers are no doubt aware that, during the last six months, many hundreds of persons in all ranks of society, in London, have witnessed the phenomena under circumstances that admit of no doubt whatever of their reality, and I know more than one of high professional repute, who were present at the séances which Mr. Thackeray's "friend of twenty-five years' standing" has so graphically described, and who speak in private of what they saw, heard, and felt.

Their testimony ought to be forthcoming publicly in support of the facts. Let us first establish beyond a doubt that these things, of which so many speak, marvellous and astounding as they may appear, are not delusions. If they are, there is an end of the matter. If they are facts, they are too significant and too important to be lightly pushed aside. When we have established that point, the *cui bono* so eagerly demanded can, I am sure, be most satisfactorily answered.—I am, sir, yours, &c.,

BENJAMIN COLEMAN.

48, Pembridge-villas, Bayswater, Oct. 11.

[In admitting this and other letters on the same side of the question, we must not be understood to express any opinion of our own. We feel bound, however, to state our knowledge of Mr. Coleman's high character, and our conviction that his statements may be implicitly relied upon.—ED. *Star*.]

VIII.

SIR,—In Mr. Howitt's letter, which appeared in your columns a few days ago, he refers to Mr. Home as a medium upon whose *bona fides* he placed implicit reliance. Now, sir, there is a report about Mr. Home very current, which, if true, would go far to shake the confidence (even of the most credulous) in Mr. Home's spiritual accomplishments; and if untrue, should be at once contradicted. That report is this, that after several interviews with Louis Napoleon, the Emperor proposed that Robert Houdin should be present at the next séance—a proposal which Mr. Home declined.

Now, sir, if this be true, I see no satisfactory explanation of Mr. Home's refusal—except this—that he feared to submit himself to those tests which a professor of the "Science of Legerdemain" would apply to expose the tricks of legerdemain. If the "manifestations" were beyond the region of that art, why object to the presence of one acquainted with it, rather than to that of any indifferent person? It cannot be answered, because it would be an insult to the spirits, inasmuch as it would have been time enough for Mons. Houdin to have withdrawn when the spirits had in the usual manner displayed their resentment. Will Mr. Howitt do some gentlemen in the Temple, who are really desirous of investigating the truth, the honour of mentioning the name of some trustworthy medium, or afford them some other method of forming an opinion one way or the other on a solid foundation?—I enclose my card, and am, sir, your obedient servant,

A Barrister.

Temple, Oct. 11.

IX.

Sir,—Spiritualism is either a gross deception, or there does exist some positive communication between the beings of the other (and I trust the better) world and those of this transitory sphere.

Does Mr. Howitt expect to find Christians ready to believe in such communication, when evidenced by the turning of tables, and the rapping in reply to questions, frequently of a frivolous nature? Far be it from me to deny that the Great Unseen can, and may at any time, will to communicate with his creatures by means that may be seen as well as heard and felt; but I must see something superhuman in the object, as well as in the act, before I

can acknowledge agency, divine or devilish—before I can believe in the interposition of spirits, good or bad. When spiritualists can show, from their intercourse with the other world, deeds and objects worthy of such a source, they may find the present unbelieving generation more ready to examine their pretensions, but as long as they descend to the moving and rapping of tables, they will not find Christians very ready to believe in the divine, or even spiritual, origin of their associations.—I am, sir, yours faithfully, SENEX.
Brixton, Oct. 9.

X.

SIR,—In Mr. Howitt's letter on spiritualism, in your Saturday's paper, he mentions Professor Hare, of America, as having, after profound investigation, become convinced of the "unearthly origin" of the spiritual manifestations. Now, it is in America a well-known fact, that soon after Professor Hare devoted his attention to these subjects he went out of his mind, was confined in a lunatic asylum, and died mad. Mr. Howitt is doubtless unaware of this fact, or he would not attach much value to Professor Hare's testimony.

A LOVER OF THE WHOLE TRUTH.
October 10.

XI.

Sir,—The discussion now going on in your columns respecting "spiritualism" cannot but prove interesting, so, trusting that you will find room for them, I send the following few remarks:—In table-turning I am (from experience) a firm believer, but my belief is, that the revolution is unquestionably caused by involuntary action of the muscles of the actuators. When, however, not mere rotation, but tilting, and even elevation of the table result, the cause must be different. Here I cannot help remarking that the activity of tables has been progressive; at first they did respect the laws of gravity, and merely ran about on their feet; next they took to rather more violent exercise, and commenced kicking; finally, giving way to their emotions, they rise bodily from the ground, or even emulating the suicidal vagaries of certain star fishes, break themselves to pieces, and this in despite of iron bands—truly wonderful! Does not this look suspiciously like an exemplification of " practice makes perfect ?"

Why, too, is Mr. Home such an especial favourite with the spirits that they positively " chair" him like the successful candidate at an election ? It seems, though, that the spirits are getting shy, and so afraid that anybody should see as well as hear them, that they require the candles put out before elevating their medium. This carrying business is the largest and most trying mouthful to swallow, for if spirits are the active agents in this case, surely they are (or might be if they pleased) quite as invisible as when engaged in merely knocking a table or lifting it up, and, therefore, the darkening of the room appears rather superfluous. Perhaps Mr. Home is so much heavier than a table that they are obliged to use fleshy cushions to protect their spiritual shoulders from the hard edges of the chair. I will not allude to the musical tastes of these invisible gentry further than to suggest that if the "medium" were to supply them with a full brass band, instead of the mere accordion, they might, perhaps, give us poor mortals some strains of spiritual music, perhaps even a few bars of that which Milton mentions. In conclusion, I promise that, if Mr. Home will kindly send some disembodied postman to rap out the letters of my name with my own doorknocker (which I humbly submit is a more convenient instrument than a loo-table), I will become a disciple of his, and sign my recantation in the next *Morning Star*, with my name in full, instead of subscribing only my initials,

A. S. L.

XII.

Sir,—I am old-fashioned enough to believe not only in a real personal devil, but that there are legions of demons. I see no reason to doubt that if men in the nineteenth century wish to hold intercourse with them, such a desire may be gratified. Witchcraft and demon-possession were universally credited before Christ's advent. Sacred historians, as well as profane, cite numerous instances. Spiritualism, if it means anything, means devilism. Since the apostolic period this manifestation has been restricted. We may seek it, but it cannot exhibit itself to us without our consent. I say—do not open the door to admit an influence which you may not control.

All these exhibitions have been made within four walls and with a consenting auditory.

Mr. Howitt says a man floated in the air. Very likely; I do not dispute the fact. Let him float over London, and show himself to men who have not tried to unlock the gates of Hades, and then I will give up my theory that it is one of the deeds of darkness, to be frowned upon and reprobated by the wise and pure.

I am, yours, &c.,

A. S. Braden.

13, High Street, Islington,
Oct. 10.

XIII.

Sir,—In common with your correspondents on the subject of spiritualism, I beg a small space in your columns, to call attention to one point in relation to which I have not seen any observations other than those of Mr. Wm. Robins, in the *Star* of the 10th inst., viz., mental impressions.

It is a fact well known to all acquainted with what are termed electro-psychological or electro-biological phenomena, that the senses, under certain conditions, may be impressed with the image of things not present, such as a bird, a rabbit, or a snake, for instance; the sensitives or subjects, generally, being in a state known to mesmerists as the sleepwaking-state. But is it not just possible that, under the excitement attending the investigation, the investigators themselves may, from the very nature of the phenomena, readily become subject to the control, probably, of the most facile and powerful operator that has hitherto exercised this influence on the minds of men? Mr. Home, for aught we know to the contrary, may be a most skilful and powerful biologist and ventriloquist; he may, by a peculiarly abnormal existence, possess great muscular and vital power or magnetic force, irrespective of any extraneous agency, so much so, as to be able to overpower the imaginations of his audience. That they do not really see or feel the unearthly hand of which we read, I am tolerably well convinced; but that, by some artistic means, their senses may be impressed with various imaginary objects, so that they cannot but believe in their actual presence, I have ample personal experience, as everyone must have who has practised the above illusion. Mr. Robins very naïvely says :—" The metaphysicians can discover in the living being itself in its immaterial portion (by which I presume he means the mind), a sufficient cause for the phenomenon." He further says :—" What are the ghosts of our sleep? What are those ghosts seen in the apparently waking moments by some? Not necessarily the spirits of the absent. The individual mind has within itself the power to create images." Everyone who reflects upon this statement must be satisfied of its truth. I firmly believe animal magnetism, coupled with credencive induction, by some means or other, as yet only known to a few, will be found to be the medium of Mr. Home's astonishing feats and unrivalled success. This will perhaps scarcely account for all the phenomena of table turning, lifting, &c., of which we hear and read, but neither will spiritualism, I am certain. Perhaps Mr. Home himself will inform your readers, if the embodied spirit will not raise a man into the air, and enable him to float over the heads of his fellow men, how many disembodied spirits it requires to accomplish the feat? I have frequently experienced the sensation in my dreams, but never have I had actual experience of the fact when wide awake.

October 11. SCEPTIC.

XIV.

Sir,—Will you allow me to dispose of your three correspondents, "Senex," "A Lover of the Whole Truth," and "A. S. L. ?"

I would ask the first, if he has ever read something to this effect—"God has chosen foolish things to confound the wise;" and if he has, whether he does not consider it unphilosophical to reject manifestations, because they do not come up to his idea of what they should be!

To the second, I will give a little more of the article he loves. Dean Swift and Dr. B—— both died mad, but no one has ever dared to say they had not previously great powers of reasoning. Therefore, Mr. Howitt would not be justified in repudiating Professor Hare's opinions.

To the last I beg to say it is the opinion of sincere spiritualists, that the manifestations are intended to bring conviction to the minds of doubters and unbelievers in a future state, and not for the mere purpose of spelling his name.

Bayswater. W. S.

XV.

Sir,—Seeing the question of spirit-rapping, &c., is being discussed in your paper, I should be glad if any person acquainted with the subject will inform me that in raising a spirit of any person, the same can be made to appear at several different places at one and the same time—for instance, I have read in the American papers advertisements by certain celebrated adepts, offering to bring up the spirit of Washington or Napoleon, and other public characters who were in particular request, and must have been operated upon by many persons in different parts of the earth at the same time. I have not heard this question asked, or seen it touched upon. I should really like to know what account is given of it by those who profess to understand the thing. It would be a good thing if one of these mediums would call up the spirit of young Kent, to learn who murdered him. I have seen what is called electro-biology, and I think this and spirit-rapping to be the same thing. I cannot understand the difference between the table rising and various phenomena seen by persons operated upon in the system of electro-biology. In the latter the operator or medium—I can see no difference between the two characters—can make those under their influence believe anything. At one time they are persuaded it rains, when they fly for shelter; then that they are being charged by an enemy, the house on fire, that each had a child to nurse, that beautiful music was being played, that a tiger was running at them, that they were being shipwrecked; in all these cases, and many others similar, I have seen the persons act as if they believed they were in the circumstances so named; in fact, they really believed it as much as any one ever believed the table turned, or that an accordion was playing. How are we to know that persons who say that they have seen these spiritual manifestations are not labouring under the same delusion as I have seen in the above-named cases of electro-biology?—I am, yours, &c.,

October 12. A LADY.

XVI.

SIR,—I have a few remarks to make on this subject, and I hope you may deem them worthy of insertion.

I know personally some of the persons who uphold the so-called spiritualism. I do not doubt their honour or veracity, but I think they are either deluded or self-deluders.

There is a natural repugnance on the part of the dwellers in flesh to the disembodied; that is to say, we all naturally shrink from ghostly visitants. Now the three millions or more (of Mr. Howitt) in the

United States, and the three thousand or more in Europe, who profess communion with spiritual agents and agencies, exhibit no such shrinking.

They take this unnatural communion as coolly as they take their breakfast.

Take another remark. Of what use to anybody are these manifestations? Why, if there is spiritual intelligence that can aid us, should there be undiscovered murderers in Great Britain?

If there is to be no war in Europe between the Great Powers, why should our war taxation be so immense?

Except for the amusement of children in intellect, of what use, I ask again, are these manifestations?

Poets, statesmen, and philosophers have, according to the assertion of these spiritualists, given poems, opinions, and sentences. What person of decent education could have so utterly disgraced our language?

I think the subject, as it is presented to us, may e concluded under two propositions.

I. The pretended spiritual manifestations are ılse, and in that case no honest person should anction them.

II. They are really made, and in that case they are probably evil, and so no Christian should sanction them. It must be remembered that many of the pretended spirits are reported to have confessed themselves to be false, lying spirits.

Mr. Harris, and other spiritualists, have warne¹

their readers and hearers of the evil character of these pretended spiritual manifestations.

To those who are reverent students of Holy Writ I may just say that they know we are taught that in the "latter day" signs and wonders are to be wrought (by permission, of course) by evil agents.

It is not my purpose to dilate on this subject, but simply to call the attention of the thoughtful of our fellow-citizens to the two propositions I have stated.

Some years ago some folks met together every night to "raise the spirit" of the First Napoleon. This attempt at necromancy was practised in London. —Your obedient servant, M. D.

XVII.

Sir,—Notwithstanding the belief I have in Mr. Howitt's honour and integrity, I do not believe in this new "spiritualism," as it is called, and permit me to give two reasons for doing so :—firstly, because I never yet received a sensible answer to a plain question ; secondly, because hitherto I have been a match for the spirits, and prevented their rapping. I will give you a public case : About three years ago a gentleman delivered an address on the subject, with practical illustrations, at St. Martin's Hall, which I attended. After witnessing a great deal of rapping, I ascended the platform, and asked the spirit some questions, when, to my surprise, the medium informed me that the spirits would not answer my questions, or have anything to do with me; to which I replied, "that the spirits were very uncivil, and that I would stop their rappings," which remark was received with derision on the platform, and with applause among the audience. I instantly seized a table in motion and stopped it, and held it quite still nearly twenty minutes, in spite of the medium and friends, and all the "spirits" they could muster, although I was told that I stood in great peril, that the table might rise up and dash me off the platform, &c., which only served to amuse me. The end of it was that the medium apologised to the audience for the failure, and spoke of my great muscular strength as being the cause, which seemed to me very absurd.

In conclusion, sir, permit me to say that I do not consider private drawing-rooms, with closed curtains, lights put out, are proper places to test this question. Let Mr. Home engage some public place and exhibit himself "floating round the ceiling;" for, if he can do so in a drawing-room surely he can in St. James's Hall, or some other such place; and, leaving at home the frisky mahogany, let him demonstrate to us some means by which we can use this mysterious power for some useful purpose, such as the raising of heavy goods, blocks of stone, butchers' blocks, &c. By so doing he will gain more adherents than by all the letters in the world.

Apologizing for thus troubling you, I am, sir, yours respectfully,

ALFRED M. MITCHELL.

25, Skinner Street, Euston Road.

XVIII.

SIR,—"A Lover of the Whole Truth," whose communication appeared in yesterday morning's issue of the *Star*, asserts that Dr. Hare went out of his mind, was confined in a lunatic asylum, and died mad, and draws his conclusion from this, that his testimony is valueless. So one might infer from these facts. But the truth is that Dr. Hare did not become insane, was not confined in an insane asylum, and did not die mad. His mind was never clearer, never gave better evidences of its strength and vigour during the whole of his long and useful life, than it did after he became a convert to spiritualism. Like many other delvers in the mines of pure science, he was for many years a disbeliever in the immortality of the soul, and looked upon the truths recorded in the Bible as so many fables, and constructed several kinds of expensive and ingenious contrivances to prove spiritualism a delusion; but the tables literally turned against him, and, through the agency of his own experiments, he was forced to confess that he had made a grand mistake. I saw a letter which he addressed to Mr. Charles Partridge, of New York, a short time before he died, and no language could be freer from the colour of lunacy.

Some of your correspondents—opposers of the spiritual phenomena—suppose that investigations are usually conducted in the dark. So far as my own experience is concerned, this is an error. I have, I may say with safety, sat in circles more than two hundred times; I have seen chairs occupied by substantial flesh and blood glide over the carpet without visible aid; I have seen a table walk rapidly the length of a drawing-room and return, repeating the exercise several times with no apparent assistance, except one finger of a child lightly resting upon it. I have seen another table elevated in the air, freed from the floor, and moved several feet across a room, and that repeatedly, without even so much as the contact of a child's finger; I have felt a hand take hold of my own, and press for some minutes upon my knee, when all visible in the room had their hands upon the table; and I have heard bells rung, and musical instruments played upon, all in the clear light of day, or with gas or candles burning as brightly as usual. In my own experience, while investigating these phenomena, dark circles have been the rare exception. I do not now call to mind more than three or four occasions when the lights were ordered to be put out. I could mention several instances in which the benevolent tendency of these manifestations is unmistakeable, but I will not at

present intrude further upon the space given to them in your valuable journal.—Yours truly,
Oct. 13. AMERICANUS.

XIX.

Sir,—Mr. Howitt and others have been favouring you with their views on spiritualism. Without entering into the question as to whether the various phenomena we read of be *instigant Diabolo* or *Dei permissu*, I shall simply relate two facts—one witnessed by myself, the other related to me as having occurred at the house of a gentleman in Leicestershire. I myself witnessed a table tell the ages of a gentleman, his wife, and three children; and I know from an eye-witness that a table walked up and down the stairs of a gentleman's house. It is also a curious fact that Tertullian, speaking of the errors of his time, refers to table-turning; his exact words I cannot quote, not having his "Apologia" by my side, but it is something about *verteri tabulas*. Perhaps one of your correspondents would give us the quotation. Enclosing my card, I am, sir, yours faithfully, B. A., CANTABRIGIENSIS.
Manchester.

XX.

Sir,—Since you have so liberally opened your columns to the discussion of this very interesting subject, may I ask the favour of your inserting the following?

Spirit rapping, and spiritual manifestations, are now the subject of serious inquiry. Many are ready to accept them as the true emanations from disembodied spirits. Others are sceptical and are unbelievers; but among all the various defenders and disclaimers who have come before the public in your columns, I have not yet met with any one who calmly and dispassionately views the subject as one requiring deliberate and unbiassed investigation.

Let us have an opportunity of investigating the subject fairly, openly, and candidly, and we shall soon have a decided verdict either in favour or against spiritualism.

I have witnessed only a few instances of spiritualism, but I have seen and heard the usual manifestations: tables turning, tables rising, accordion playing, candle snuffing, rapping, &c.; and I must confess I have witnessed them with so much astonishment, that I am desirous to see the matter fully tested by proper persons, so as to complete the partial conviction already made upon my mind.

There are, however, some remarkable matters in connection with the operations which I would call attention to; and I trust the objections I name may be well explained away to the universal satisfaction of all. In the first place, I have noticed that all the circles have been formed round tables, and that all persons present were requested to sit round the same, of course the medium being always among the number. I have observed that the feet of the medium, as well as the others of the circle, are always under the table during the process of knocking. And it is incumbent (as is alleged) that the hands of all present should rest on the table. Now, sir, in this position, I submit, all the feet being under the table, any experienced person (especially if assisted by a second, as may be the case with some circles where there are two mediums present) could cause the vibrations by the movement of the feet under the table, and even raise the table from the ground, whilst it is utterly impossible for the persons seated round to detect the movement. To obviate this part, I suggest that a circle be formed of some few persons, whilst others shall remain out of the circle in such a position as to be enabled to see the feet of all those sitting at the table: if then the table shall rise, &c., I will admit there is something more "than my philosophy dreams of;" if, however, this test is refused, then the public may fairly set down the whole as an arrant imposture, and treat it accordingly.

I further suggest that it is quite possible, with the knees under the table, to make raps with the toes and heels of shoes, or of boots, varying in sound, according to the material the blow was given with. I have tried this, and with cork, wood, iron, and lead, so placed on the heel of the boot as to be acted upon when struck against the floor, I have made raps which have been distinctly different, and which seemed to come from different parts of the room.

I would suggest that any well-known medium shall meet a certain number of gentlemen inquirers in a place not to be named until the moment of investigation, where the usual manifestations shall take place, and let the shoes of all be examined, &c.

This would obviate anything like collusion or complicity, and a favourable report under such circumstances would do more for the advance of the cause than seven years' argument.—I am, sir, yours respectfully, J. BENNETT.

4, St. Ann's Gardens, Tavistock.

XXI.

SIR,—Perhaps you will allow me to offer a few remarks in reply to the letters of Mr. William Howitt and Mr. Bird, which recently appeared in your columns. I quite agree with you in your criticism of the article in *Blackwood*, for it is worse than useless to oppose with mere banter, ridicule, or party feeling such a movement as the present, which is exercising so deep and powerful an influence over a large section of the people of this country.

I have every possible respect for Mr. Howitt, whose talented writings have beguiled the tedium of many a long weary hour in my early life; and, therefore, it is with feelings of the sincerest regret that I find myself constrained to oppose what I believe to be his mistaken doctrines on the subject of spirits. It is true that there are many things far beyond our mortal comprehension, and that with all our vaunted progress in science and learning, we know but little of the nature of our being, whence cometh the spirit of life, or what form it assumes when our earthly body is given up to corruption and decay. These are secrets which we may never know, and which have baffled for centuries the curiosity and research of mankind, and have originated those ideas of the supernatural on which are based such doctrines as those propounded by Swedenborg and his followers. Few, however, deny that there are many strange, mysterious, and subtle influences surrounding us, and by their ofttimes invisible and unaccountable agencies, controlling our actions, and shaping our desires; nor will they refuse to admit that the all-merciful Creator may, in his far-seeing wisdom, permit disembodied spirits to wander unseen and unfelt, through this material world; but the very fact of our belief in these things causes us to doubt the truth and genuineness of the exhibitions of Mr. Home and other celebrated mediums. If the spirits evoked by the asserted influence of such mediums possess the power to lift and smash heavy tables, to raise elderly gentlemen up in their chairs, to support

Mr. Home in the air, to pinch and poke people's legs, to pluck flowers, pull coat tails, and the like, surely they could be enabled to make their presence known or felt by methods somewhat more dignified in their character. I am no juggler myself, and therefore I do not profess to accuse or detect jugglery in others; but I must state that, after a calm and deliberate enquiry into these things, I can arrive at but one conclusion, which is, that the effects known as "spirit rappings" have their origin in self-deception and imposture! In doing so, I admit that it is impossible on my part to pretend to be able to offer any explanation of the mode whereby the sounds and movements are produced, or to endorse the statements printed in "Once a Week," "All the Year Round," "Blackwood," &c.; but these facts do not in the least invalidate my conclusions.

In ancient times the discovery of the art of ventriloquism gave its professors an immense influence over the minds of their fellow-men, who were led to believe that the ventriloquists were enabled to hold familiar intercourse with unseen spirits, and even the most sceptical must have felt somewhat shaken in their convictions, when they found that they could not explain the supposed phenomenon by any of the scientific laws then known. No machinery was used, and no confederates were employed, hence the chances of detection were lessened; but although the art remained unknown to the generality of men, the pretended intercourse with spirits was not the less an imposture. As it was then, so it is now; and I feel convinced that the day will arrive when many a mind will experience regret at having yielded credence to a system which is utterly irreconcilable with religion, science, or common sense. I am not surprised at Mr. Howitt's energetic defence of the doctrines which have taken such a strong hold of his imagination, for I believe him to be truthful and sincere, but mistaken. All the force of Luther's character did not restrain him from giving credence to the most absurd fables respecting the existence of devils and spirits, and surely we may excuse the same failing in Mr. Howitt.

The mere number of believers professing a creed, is no proof of the soundness of that particular doctrine; on the contrary, any history of popular delusions will show that the larger the number of dupes, the greater will be the chances of deception.

Why should I be called on to believe that those who once held me in their fond and loving embraces —whose eyes beamed with pleasure as they gazed into mine, and who would have done all in their power to render life a joy and lasting happiness to me, but whom the cold, icy hands of death have reft from the land of the living, should make their presence known unto me by pinching my legs, or by plagiarising the exhibition of the " learned pig ?"

If their spirits be permitted to hold intercourse with us, might I not reasonably be expected to believe that they would enfold my form in their invisible and almost impalpable arms, or feel their shadowy kisses on my lips, or their soft feathery touch on my brow? Something like this would be more reasonable than jingling bells or pulling accordions under a table.

Again, if the supposed spirits have the powers attributed to them, how is it that those powers can only be exercised in darkened rooms? Why cannot they bear Mr. Home up to the ceiling of an apartment in the broad glare of day, as well as by night?

We all know the effect of darkness and fear upon the human imagination, and how the slightest illusion may be exaggerated and distorted, and therefore it cannot be surprising that I should be so sceptical of a system which requires the aid of darkened chambers to be successfully carried on.

When tables are lifted up in broad daylight, no human being near them; when persons sitting entirely aloof from others feel pinches, &c., in the legs and other parts of the body; when Mr. Home floats about the room in the honest open light of day; and when all the present seeming phenomena are produced by agencies which can be proved not to be of human origin—then I may be induced to change my opinion, but not till then.—Yours, &c.

JOHN PLUMMER.

Kettering, Oct. 11.

XXII.

Sir,—As I see your correspondents on the subject of spiritualism repeatedly appeal to me for an answer to their suggestions and assertions, allow me, once for all, to remind them of the plain statement in my letter of the 6th, that it was necessary, before persons entered into discussions on this great topic, that they should take the ordinary means of practically acquainting themselves with the facts of it. I stated that I had carefully sifted the subject for the last five years, and I advised them to do the same. If they would follow this simple course, there would soon be no need of discussion at all. Without such practical, and, in the first place, elementary inquiry, all discussion is futile, and a mere fighting with shadows. If a new comet were to appear, or a new eclipse were announced, would your readers send you a great number of letters to express their doubts whether such things were really in the heavens, or would they, like men of sense, go out and judge for themselves? There is, or was, an Australian animal in the Zoological Gardens called a wombat. Now, I put it to your intellectual acrobats whether it would be very rational to deny the existence of the wombat without going to judge for themselves? Really these gentlemen must excuse me saying that they are all beginning at the wrong end—putting the cart before the horse—repeating the thunder of the Royal Society in regard to Charles the Second's question about the relative weight of the water in the vase with the fish in it, or the fish out of it. Neither spiritualism nor any other science or mystery will ever be learned by beginning to talk before beginning to study. What would Professor de Morgan say to your correspondents, if they presented themselves at his class, and proposed, not to study mathematics, but to instruct him in them, before they had even taken the trouble to acquaint themselves with the simplest elements of arithmetic? Yet your correspondents have actually got upon the " *Pons Asinorum*" without even opening Euclid.

All this discussion is empty, useless, absurd, and in the highest degree beside the mark, because it *precedes* instead of following practical inquiry. If gentlemen think that spiritualism is a mere phantasmagoria—a thing without shape, or substance, or beginning or end; not based upon clear and eternal principles, it is not worth their troubling themselves about. " It will die of itself, if they'll let it alone." But, if it be a thing based on as express and operative laws as the universe itself, which it is, the only rational proceeding is to study those laws in reverence and patience before beginning to argue upon them. Solomon made a very pertinent remark on this head some thousands of years ago, in a book which I hope your correspondents read, and which is brimful of spiritualism from end to end—" He that answereth a matter before he heareth it, it is folly and shame to him."—Proverbs.

One writer, assuming the honourable title of "Senex," has actually, like thousands of others, suffered spiritualism in its modern development to pass its first decenniary, and to have made its millions of converts, without knowing that table-moving and table-rapping are only one out of numerous of its phases, and, indeed, but its most elementary phases. Every spiritualist knows that, in drawing, in painting, in writing, in music, in preaching, in communication of poetry of the noblest character, and in still higher and more surprising phenomena, spiritualism is operating throughout society. They who have arrived at these care little for any mere physical manifestations whatever. I have seen pencils laid down in the centre of rooms, on paper, and there write upon it. The Baron Guldenstubbé, in Paris, professes to have upwards of a thousand specimens of direct spirit-writing, some of which have been obtained by persons going into the first stationer's shop they came to, buying a packet of note-paper, putting their seal upon it, and never letting it pass out of their hands till they laid it down at a distance from themselves and the baron in open light and sight. Baron Guldenstubbé has published a book upon this subject, and given *fac-similes* of some of these communications. I have seen musical instruments play far from anyone's hands; I have seen ponderous dining-tables rise into the air, and move themselves to different parts of a room, all in full light; but I regard these, so far as I am concerned, as very gross and outward. Yet, it is through these elements that people who are outward themselves, and far removed from that spirit of faith which should have been in the world after nearly nineteen centuries of the preaching of Christianity must pass. And, for this reason, I regard the request of "A Barrister" to become acquainted with some trustworthy mediums, as the most rational proposition yet advanced in this discussion.

And yet, is not such a demand surprising? Has not the barrister heard ever and anon of Mr. Home, and Mr. Squire, and Mrs. Marshall? And has he not seen their trustworthiness over and over attested by gentlemen of character and veracity? Must we not answer him as the blind man who had just received his sight answered the Jews—"I have told you once already, and you would not believe." Yet, as he appeals to me, I can only say that I regard these mediums as all trustworthy; and I could name numbers of mediums in private life, did the customs of society permit, and I may add, were it quite prudent to do so. For I think all must allow, that after the conduct of the press, after the example of "Blackwood," charging honourable spiritualists with "scoundrelism" and "imposture;" after conduct which many of us have seen in private circles, by those calling themselves gentlemen, families of respectable status and refined habits, may well hesitate to open their doors to inquirers, except under special introduction. This is certainly a barrier to free inquiry, raised not by spiritualists, but by their taunters and opponents. Still I aver, whether "A Barrister" knows this or not, mediumship and spiritualism are surrounding him in and through the whole mass of society. There are thousands of families who, in their own quiet circles, and in a spirit of reverence and thankfulness, are sitting down in the evening to their table as to a family altar, and there learning daily that the oracles of God, which have in all ages spoken to the patriarchs, the prophets, the apostles, the fathers, the saints, have no more ceased than the sun to shine, and the earth to yield its harvests. For my own part, spiritualism has been to me, to my whole family, and to a wide circle of relatives and friends, through whom it has radiated, the most substantial blessing of existence. Before its luminous facts, knitting up the present with the sacred past, binding up the life of to-day with the spiritual life of the great-souled and great-hearted in all ages and all quarters of the world; of Plato with Moses, of Zoroaster with Bacon, every doubt, nay, every uncertainty of Divine revelation, and of the immortality of man, has fled as the shades of night before the morning. Do men still ask the *cui bono* of spiritualism? Is it nothing for men—and there are thousands of such, who would have given the one-half of their souls for the positive assurance of the infinite security of the other—to feel the deadly talons of doubt loosened from their spirits by facts as palpable to their senses as the sight and touch of their daily environments? to have the fiendish whisper of a blasting modern Pyrrhonism chased for ever from their bosoms?

Now, with all possible desire to see really earnest people seize hold on these advantages, I can merely bid them follow the direction of our Saviour— "Seek, and ye shall find; knock, and it shall be opened unto you."

But people say with "A Barrister," "What shall we seek?" I reply with Sir Christopher Wren from his urn, "Si quæres monumentum, circumspice." There is no absolute need for great and popular mediums. Spiritualists have no monopoly of this great agent; it is a principle of the universe, as much the heritage of all mankind as the imponderable and invisible agent of the telegraphic wire or of the galvanic battery. Spiritualism, like electricity and magnetism, lies all around us and within us. The earth, the air, the vital frame, and the soul of man are all permeated by it—all saturated with it. It needs only evoking to perform its marvels, and like the angel before Manoah, "to do wonderously"—to bring its solemn messages, not from the ends of the earth merely, but from the innermost depths of Heaven.

But where shall we begin? it may be asked. Just where I myself, and where millions of people have begun, by sitting down with your families and friends, in patience and in reverence, in pure faith and sincere prayer, desiring that the wonders and the teaching of this great gift of God may be opened up to you—opened, not for mere curiosity, far less for any selfish or worldly end. Whoever approaches the Ark of the Covenant to-day, with unhallowed hands, will suffer, more or less, as Uzza suffered in the days of David. We have all our faculties for all worldly purposes, and if we attempt to desecrate the teaching of spirits by applying it to mere secular and sensuous ends, we degrade this divine power into necromancy and sorcery. Let those who say it is of the devil, take care that they do not unite the devil with it. Let those who approach it remember that there is no half thing which has life in all creation. Spiritualism is as God has made it, and as He has made the world and the human soul; it has its two sides, its night and its day; its dark and its luminous hemispheres. Woe to those who seek to turn this night into day, this day into night; to confound the sacred limits of nature; to pollute the Holy place with the sacrifice of devils! To the pure all things are pure; to the impure all will become impure; for like inevitably attracts its counterpart. Where a door is opened to the angels of God, the emissaries of the devil will assuredly thrust themselves in, if possible. The devil did not fear to confront the Divine Majesty, to stalk into the very presence of Christ, and tempt him in all impudence.

What I say, therefore, to all who wish to learn spiritualism practically, and not to waste their time in words without knowledge, is, to form circles amongst themselves, as millions before them have done. At the same time I solemnly warn them of the dangers as well as of the benefits. Whoever expects to walk through London and not to be elbowed by thieves and prostitutes is just as simple, and no more, than the man who expects to traverse the spirit-thronged highways of pneumatology without, like Bunyan's Pilgrim, encountering Apollyon and his snares. But there is a sure bulwark and talisman against all these—it is the Cross, and an humble but firm trust in that Cross. Whoever does not enter into this inquiry in that trust, and with the clean heart and hands of a man seeking the truth for itself, had better serve God, as Milton says he may—

"They also serve, who only stand and wait."

Amongst a number of assertions founded in mere empty rumour, there have been two advanced in the *Star*, which I would passingly notice. One is that of "A Barrister," regarding Mr. Home's declining to meet Robert Houdin at the Tuileries. Whether he did or not, Mr. Home may perhaps inform us; but of this I am sure, from what I have seen of Mr. Home, that he no more would fear to meet Houdin, or any master of legerdemain, or any real sorcerer, than Moses did to encounter Jannes and Jambres before Pharaoh. The other is the assertion of "A Lover of the Whole Truth," who states that "in America it is a well-known fact that Professor Hare, after embracing spiritualism, went mad, was sent into a lunatic asylum, and died mad." He kindly supposes that I am not aware of this fact. I certainly am not. I have heard a great deal about Mr. Hare and his life, both from friends and enemies, but never heard "of this well-known fact." Hare, like many other spiritualists, both in America and in this country, was declared to be mad because he was a spiritualist. To satisfy myself, and I trust others too, on this head, I yesterday put these questions to two different Americans, perfectly acquainted with American affairs :—" Was Professor Hare ever confined in a lunatic asylum ?" " Never." " Did he die mad ?" " Certainly not." They added, " Had such been the case, it would have been too good a thing for the anti-spiritualists not to have been trumpeted throughout the whole world." What next ?

Having made these plain statements, I must, once for all, say, that I am a very busy man, and cannot undertake to answer all the appeals and challenges which may be made to me: for the simple reason that they are unnecessary. There is a great tribunal open to all men on this question—that which I resorted to myself—practical examination. The means are in everyone's hand, let them employ them as so many thousands have done. I satisfied myself on all these points before I saw a single public medium. If people wish to inform themselves, let them read the *Spiritual Magazine*, which they can procure at Pitman's, in the Row, for 6d. every month. If they read that in a proper spirit, they will not long be ignorant. I have just sent to the editor an article, entitled "An Apology for Faith in the Nineteenth Century," which, if they did me the honour to read it, would show that what they are, many of them, imagining to be a new delusion is a truth as old and as inextinguishable as the earth.—Yours, &c. WILLIAM HOWITT.

XXIII.

"Non sine lumine."

Sir,—Philosophical belief or disbelief is a condition of mind entirely beyond the will or control. Our convictions are the result of evidence received. It is impossible to close the senses after they have been once impressed with palpable physical phenomena. The first stage of intellectual existence is marked by the total occupation of the senses with the detached phenomena of isolated objects, the rapid succession of novel impressions, the delight of childhood in the ever-changing scenes of the great phenomena of nature; and it is only when this delirium of the senses has been calmed and satisfied, that reflection is awakened by the multiform relation of surrounding objects. Now it is that differences and similarities, antecedents and sequences, arresting attention, furnish new materials to the newly-born intellect. Things are classified, arranged, and order established—new phenomena are observed—new comparisons instituted—new relations discovered, until the superstructure of science, with all its imposing grandeur and accurate proportions, stands forth revealed—a mighty truth.

"Man, the servant and interpreter of nature, understands and reduces to practice just so much as he has experienced of nature's laws; more he can neither know nor achieve."

What is the law of nature? On this subject there is a general error, which even exists among men of science. A conventional theory is surely no " law of nature," nor is it an original principle established by the fiat of Omnipotence. He who has the temerity or hardihood to examine its validity is charged with questioning the order of nature itself. It was for this crime that Roger Bacon was excommunicated by the Pope, and imprisoned ten years, accused of dealing with the devil.

At that same period, the thirteenth century, professors in some of the universities were bound by an oath to teach the dogmas advocated by Aristotle.

Even in this vaunted age of electric telegraphs and railroads, the same intolerant unphilosophical spirit is manifest, not content to be as children in the search after truth. Some men assume the attribute of gods, and dictate how, when, and where, she shall present herself! Until "the conditions" essential to produce results are known, how can we expect to witness phenomena, when the very first condition of success is absent?

If it requires a certain frame of mind, calm, dispassionate, free from bias, in order to arrive at correct mental deductions in the ordinary vocations of existence, how much more requisite in the humble desire to have revealed new truths, "apparently," in contradiction to our preconceived ideas of what constitutes a law of nature, where the most learned in science are only on the verge of knowledge, as to the great principles which regulate and govern the universe.

It is now some twenty years since I first made the discovery, that persons could be influenced in the "waking condition," so that false impressions could be produced on the mind. I extract from a work published by me in 1843:—

"Mental hallucination can at any time be produced on persons in the waking state, who are recipients to the agency. I have made persons, when perfectly awake, to believe themselves to be partaking of a good dinner: they would in their own minds be filling their plates from empty dishes. I could successively change the nature of their food; making potatoes turn into apple dumplings, a turkey into a leg of mutton, water into brandy, sugar into aloes—a piece of wood into candy. In one instance, I took four persons, pressed their thumbs; they all immediately commenced reeling as if intoxicated; I then restored them in an instant; would obliterate from their memory the occurrence which had just transpired, and again bring it back vividly to their recollection—cause them to scream with agony on placing a piece of money in their hands—they (imaginatively) feeling all the torture as if hot metal had been placed upon their skin. I made two persons, at the same time, believe themselves to be bottles of ginger beer; they distinctly heard the fermentation within, and desired me, with all earnestness, not to pull out the cork, for that would kill them. I made a man fancy himself a general officer, a locomotive, &c. In fact, I know not a single condition of mind but what may be brought about by the mind of the operator."

This state was subsequently, absurdly enough, denominated "electro-biology." Being the original discoverer, and knowing the conditions essential to produce this state of brain, I can conscientiously declare that the "spiritual manifestations"—as recently witnessed, heard, and felt by myself—have nothing in common, or even analogous to that of "induced mental hallucination."

Until yesterday, I had endeavoured to explain all mental phenomena as material physiological states of the nervous system. I do not condescend, nor would I degrade myself, to answer that class of men whose only weapon is to scoff, ridicule, or resort to low jeers, ribaldry, or abuse.

The arrogant and self-conceited continually ask this most stupid of all questions—

"If they do this, why do they not do that?" This is begging the whole question. We must, if we do not wish to remain in ignorance, receive truth as she presents herself, and not dictate terms and conditions.

If these, the conditions of success, were known, uniform results would be obtained; there could be no such thing as failure as long as the requisite conditions were observed. If, as we are aware, it is essential to the successful exhibition of any phenomena connected with chemistry, or any other department of science, to observe certain conditions, otherwise no satisfactory results follow, then how much more necessary must it be not to disturb or do anything calculated to destroy the mental condition of the "medium?"

Let the most sceptical give to what he suspects to be fraud, deceptive trick, full play; error will soon expose itself if left alone; but truth, on the contrary, will manifest itself so powerfully, even at moments the least expected, as to leave a lasting impression on the mind.

Yesterday (now not yet twenty-four hours have elapsed since) I had tangible, positive proof that effects have been produced which, according to preconceived opinions, are incompatible with any known laws. What I am about to relate I cannot expect to be received without incredulity, for, had any person yesterday morning told me what I now know to be a reality, I should not have received his narration as a fact; therefore, I can afford to be charitable. All I ask is, that others shall investigate for themselves with an honest desire to obtain truth.

I was accompanied by a lady to the house of the "medium," where we found a party of four ladies and one gentleman sitting round a table about three feet in diameter. On our entrance, all being entire strangers, and not being expected, we asked permission to form part of the circle, which, after some hesitation, was granted, "the spirits" having been consulted as to the advisability of our being allowed to participate, which was affirmatively replied to. I would here state that, prior to our arrival, no manifestation of a marked character had been elicited. After some few minutes a young lady, whose scepticism had induced her friends to cause her to witness these things, said, "I feel some one pulling my dress." I looked at her with great surprise, and I said, "Are you in earnest?" when she jumped up, screaming out, and answered, "Yes, something took hold of my leg." The lady who accompanied me, who is not in the least degree imaginative, said, "Some one is pulling my dress." The "medium," whose hands were on the table—every part distinctly visible—said, "Will the spirits raise the table?" Judge of my surprise when the table raised up some two feet above the floor, and swinging full twenty seconds without support from any person present, and this by some invisible agency. I paused when the medium said, "Will the spirits take the table to the door?"—a distance of some twelve feet. The reader will imagine my utter surprise when the table jumped some two feet high, and three feet at a time, until the door was gained in four efforts, when there it leaped up and made a blow at the door with great violence; this was repeated twice.

The table being returned to the same place from where it started, we all sat round, and placed our hands on it again. The gentleman took down a guitar, gave it to the young lady first referred to; she placed one hand on the table, the other on the end of the instrument, in the vicinity of the keys, not touching any of the strings, the whole body of the guitar being under the table. To me it was wonderful, for the strings were played on, and the unknown fingers ran across it, producing sounds as loud as I ever heard with a guitar, though no tune was executed. I then whistled the " Sailor's hornpipe," when the table commenced dancing to the same tune in accurate time. When I whistled " Yankee Doodle," the tune was responded to by loud raps. It was now that, for the first time, I felt something or some one pulling and jerking at the bottom of the left leg of my trousers; instantaneously I looked down, but saw nothing; remember, at this time every hand was on the table. I then felt a severe pinch of the left leg—felt an apparently palpable hand and fingers grasping the calf of my leg forcibly, and this continued for some minutes, when I had to cry out from the pinches received. I then said, " Pinch me so as to leave a mark."

I then experienced as violent a pinch as it was possible to make; I felt all the consequent pain, but on going to the window, for it was five P.M., there, sure enough, the mark existed fresh made, and is now quite discoloured, showing the indentation of the thumb and two fingers. Of course all present came forward to see it. I have shown it to several persons at my house last night and this morning.

I could occupy many columns with a detailed account of what was presented in the short space of one hour and a half, and on some future occasion will avail myself of your liberality in so doing. I have purposely abstained from recording all the phenomena which were presented, as they referred to private matters, the relation of which would not be interesting to the public, though convincing to myself. In conclusion, allow me to remark that if these " spiritual manifestations" demand the obedience of certain conditions of mind to ensure their presence, it is most unphilosophical and unwise for persons to expect the presentation of phenomena when their own violent antagonism thwarts the very object they have in view. I am particularly impressed with this fact, in consequence of having devoted my life to the investigation of subjects of a kindred nature, when disturbing influences have rendered every effort to obtain satisfactory results abortive.

I will promise a faithful account of the " manifestations," from time to time, as I have now commenced the investigation, without fear of going to wherever the truth may lead me.

   Yours respectfully,
    ROBERT H. COLLYER, M.D.
Beta House, 8, Alpha Road,
 St. John's Wood, Oct. 12.

[Dr. Collyer is too well known to render necessary any guarantee of ours for the good faith with which the extraordinary statements contained in his letter are made. In order to convince us of the truth of one of his assertions, Dr. Collyer exhibited to us the bruise made upon his leg. We feel bound to say at the same time that we still remain incredulous, and venture to submit to him the conjecture that he has been the subject of a mental hallucination similar to those which he describes himself to have produced in other persons some years ago. We may here state that we have a perfect deluge of letters on this subject, and that henceforth we shall only be able to give insertion to such as are short, contain something quite new, and are guaranteed by the permission to publish the name of the writer.—ED. *Star.*]*

* I can endorse Mr. Grimes' views (author of "Phreno-Philosophy of Mesmerism") on the subject of "credencive induction." He says, "It has long been known that very susceptible subjects may be deluded and willed into almost any state of mind; but it has not before been known that it requires less susceptibility to perform these experiments than any other. It has not been known that it is on this principle that most of the successful experiments in Neurology, Pathetism, and Hypnotism, also the so-called Electro-Biology, and Electro-Psychology are performed." What is induction but an induced state of entire passivity or abstraction from continued watching, in which the mind becomes lost in vacuity, and is unable to resist the slightest impression? An assertion is all-powerful, and as the operator gains ascendancy over his subject, a mere whisper, or the unexpressed will is sufficient to influence the patients in the most extraordinary manner. Thus "It is a fact, capable of being easily demonstrated, that nearly all subjects can be made to believe anything, or to assume any character, or to conform to the wishes, expressed or implied, of the operator; and this can be done when they are affected in the least degree, while they are wide awake, and appear to know what they are about." This is in entire accordance with Dr. Collyer's own experience, and it does appear extraordinary to me that he cannot imagine Mr. Home or others having an influence over him under somewhat similar circumstances. Thought reading is no new thing, and much of that which is marvellous may be explained by it. "If the organ of wonder be large," says Mr. Grimes, "and especially if, what he terms, the conforming socials are much developed, and the governing socials are small, there is a tendency to the most unbounded credulity, and a total want of independent judgment. In this case a large intellect does not prevent credulity, but rather searches for arguments to fortify it; for it should be remembered that the intellect is the mere servant of the larger impulsives; the intellect does not control the propellers, it only directs them to the objects which they desire."—[*Note by Compiler.*]

XXIV.

Sir,—Perhaps you will allow me to add my experiences on this subject to those of your numerous correspondents. At the same time, allow me to express my regret that none of those gentlemen whose names have been repeatedly mentioned, such as Sir Lytton Bulwer, Sir D. Brewster, Mr. Bell, &c., have had the courage either to contradict or to express their concurrence in the opinions attributed to them by your believing and unbelieving correspondents.

I will only relate the result of one evening's trial. The "operators" were my sister, a Cambridge friend, and myself. The table was a small chess table, with spiral pillar to support it; it rested on three carved claw feet. The first question asked was the age of a friend, which no one in the room except the gentleman himself knew. A correct answer—twenty-three—was received. The age of my brother was also correctly told. Encouraged by these successes, we asked if it was acquainted with the Rev. Mr. M——, the respected clergyman of the parish in which the experiments were being made. The answer was, "Yes, I know him very well." "Is he married?" "No." (We knew this to be false.) "Are you sure of that?" "Yes, Wolfdog." It then commenced rolling about in the manner which your other correspondents have described, and it was some time before we could resume the conversation. We then asked, "By what agency do you tell us these things?" The strange reply was, "Dewil." The answer was several times repeated. No cross-examination could induce it to alter the middle letter. A painful occurrence was the immediate result: the lady, who was before an avowed sceptic, was so overcome that she had to be removed from the table, and she is still very nervous if the subject is mentioned in her presence.

It would only be tedious for me to go through the many other questions given, and answers received, of which I was an auditor, and at which I assisted. I need hardly say I am not aware of any of our party being "media." The subject was taken up as an amusement more than anything else.

I will only trouble you with one more circumstance, which, occurring as it did close upon the last-mentioned one, was very remarkable.

I have in my possession a curious plaster cast taken from a figure in Lincoln Cathedral, with which many of your readers are no doubt acquainted. It is said (with what truth I know not) to represent his sable eminence. One of the company fetched this grotesque figure from an adjoining apartment. The immediate result was, that the table, which had hitherto been comparatively tranquil, seemed as though its "feelings were too many for it;" at all events, it was greatly "moved" at its appearance, signifying its displeasure by violent plungings and kickings of an unusually turbulent nature. On inquiry in the usual manner the table refused any more communication until the offensive piece of plaster was removed.

I can only leave these extraordinary manifestations for others to explain if they can. Of the facts it is impossible I can be deceived. They are too remarkable to be treated in the flippant manner of some writers on the subject, who, I fear, are among those " who would not be persuaded though one rose from the dead."

Sir, I have seen hats, chairs, tables, &c., move about the room in the most extraordinary fashion: it was, indeed, but last week that my hat and that of a friend, temporarily residing with me, were, in this way, hung up on the pegs, in the hall, which are regularly assigned to them.

Allow me, in conclusion, to add my thanks to those of the previous writers in your columns, to you for opening your paper for a discussion of these questions, which, it appears, no other London paper has the manliness to do. This is one of the advantages of a cheap and independent press.

Enclosing my name and address, not for publication, but as a guarantee of good faith, I have the honour to subscribe myself, sir, with much respect, your obedient servant,

ONE WHO HAS TRIED THE SPIRITS.

City Club, Oct. 15.

P.S.—It appears to me that the absurdity of answers received is no proof of trickery, but an indirect one to their correctness, as, if any one wished to deceive his friends, a plausible reply would at least be given.

XXV.

Sir,—On the day Mr. Howitt's interesting communication appeared in your columns a friend of mine handed me a letter, which he had received from the curate of Montgomery church, in answer to some inquiries he had addressed to the rector of that parish. As this reverend gentleman's letter seems to be an indirect corroboration of the "system of spiritualism" so ably defended by Mr. Howitt, it and the subsequent remarks are at your service, should you deem them worthy a place in this discussion. The letter explains itself, of which the following is a copy:—

"Montgomery, Sept. 11.
"Sir,—I am sorry I have not been able to write to you sooner, owing to the rector's absence, but I have at length opened his letter. The man whose grave you speak of was executed here in the year 1821, for highway robbery with violence. He acknowledged the robbery but denied the violence, which made his offence capital, and at his trial he prayed that the grass may not grow upon his grave for one generation, at least, in proof of his innocence of the violence for which he was hanged. There is now a

portion of ground about six feet long, and about four inches wide, over his grave, quite bare, although the grass grows all around quite luxuriantly. The bare part was much wider some years ago, but has gradually been becoming narrower. Not only have grass seeds been sown on it, but it has been turfed over, and even that has died away.

"Our late clerk, who held the office for more than forty years, told me that the weather on the day of execution was remarkably fine, and the sky cloudless, but a violent thunderstorm came on very suddenly and dispersed the spectators. There were two witnesses upon whose testimony the man was condemned, and of these, I am told, that one was killed at a lime rock, and that the other died away, appearing to waste gradually.

"An interesting little pamphlet has been written upon this subject by the late Mr. Mostyn Pryce, and if I can procure a copy I will send it you, and shall be happy to answer any further questions.—Believe me, yours very truly,

"J. LLOYD JONES, Curate of Montgomery."

If the phenomena adduced by Mr. Howitt and the advocates of spiritualism be accepted as evidence of some invisible and supernatural agency under the control and volition of certain mediums, I certainly think we have no reason to doubt the extraordinary and unnatural occurrences referred to in Mr. Jones's letter. Previously to such a conclusion, however, we ought to be sure that what there is of reality and fact about these exhibitions and traditions cannot be explained upon natural grounds alone; otherwise we open the flood-gates of history for the imagination to revel upon much that is ignored at the present day by all our scientific teachers. The testimony of the witnesses named by Mr. Howitt, Mr. Bird, and Mr. Coleman is sufficient to challenge a searching investigation. If this be accorded I am strongly impressed with the belief that what Riechenbach calls the "Od-force," *i.e.* animal magnetism, the "nervous influence" of other writers, will be found to unravel all that at present transcends our comprehension in this system of spiritualism. There is much, I confess, adduced that seems incomprehensible upon ordinary scientific grounds—if the testimony of the witnesses is to be relied upon— such as a table constructed so as to defy the efforts of raging lunatics, iron-bound and strongly clamped, being torn to fragments; music discoursed by some unseen power, from accordions and guitars, &c. Assuming these to be proven facts, I would not necessarily conclude they are caused by what are termed disembodied spirits. Natural causes alone have hitherto accounted for all that was considered above or beyond nature by our forefathers. As in the past, we have every reason to believe it will be with the present and the future.

Somewhere about the year 1843 there lectured in the Manchester Mechanics' Institution a gentleman (named Hawes, I think), from Greenwich, upon "Animal Magnetism." This gentleman brought with him a subject named "Jack," who appeared to be about 18 or 19 years of age, to prove demonstrably the truth of clairvoyance, *i.e.*, that what we term matter was no impediment to the vision of persons in such a mesmeric condition. The lecture hall was crowded, a large number of medical gentlemen being present. Previously to introducing Jack, the lecturer informed us he had operated upon him at his hotel, from the difficulty he experienced of inducing the clairvoyant state in him before a promiscuous audience. After his introduction, the lecturer requested some medical gentleman to step forward and bandage Jack's eyes with court plaister, strictly stipulating, however, that the plaister was not to cover that portion of the forehead termed by phrenologists "individuality." This was done by Mr. Williamson, surgeon—now Professor Williamson, of Owen's College. During the time he was doing so, the late Dr. Dunn, who was sitting on one of the front seats, cried out, " I beg to direct attention to a quivering of Jack's eyelids, whether it be voluntary or involuntary I will not now say." This remark was received with manifest signs of disapprobation by the audience. Dr. Dunn being a great sceptic of mesmerism, hypnotism, phrenology, &c., and at previous lectures had frequently given public expression to his scepticism. When Mr. Williamson had concluded, some other medical gentleman was requested to cover Jack's eyes with white plaister, to make doubly sure there was no imposition. This being accomplished, a third was directed to cover the whole with a folded silk handkerchief. Could precautions have been more carefully taken for preventing imposture? Most certainly the audience in general thought not. Here were three medical men, well known in scientific circles in Manchester, in the presence of great numbers of their medical brethren and fellow-townsmen, testifying that, in the ordinary condition of life, it was impossible for any person to have visual cognisance of external objects. The audience were now requested to test the powers of "Jack's" vision. This they did in a multiplicity of ways, some holding watches, others keys, and some uncommon articles they happened to have in their possession at the time, all of which were accurately described, to the satisfaction of the owner of each article, and the audience generally. Never was an exhibition more successful. The only perceptible difference between the vision of Jack and that of common mortals was, that while they looked direct at the objects they wished to see, Jack always bent his head towards the object, like one of the Ruminantia when about to make use of its horns. Few left that hall unconvinced of the reality of clairvoyance.

A short time elapsed, and public placards announced that Dr. Dunn would lecture in the theatre of the Manchester Athenæum, upon mesmerism, with more particular reference to Jack's performance at the Mechanics' Institute. The theatre was crowded. As before, a large body of medical men were present, as well as our lecturer and his boy Jack from Greenwich. After explaining, upon natural grounds, many of the wonderful phenomena exhibited by itinerating lecturers upon mesmerism—such as their professed power of suspending at will the circulation of the blood, raising and lowering at will the temperature of the body, he at length explained the apparently wonderful manifestations of the clairvoyant Jack. The first of these, I may just observe, he showed us could be accomplished by any person pressing the inner side of the arm against the walls of the thorax in such a way as to arrest the circulation of the blood in the brachial artery, which runs down the inner side of the arm and supplies the radial arteries at the wrists. Of course, if the blood is arrested above, it cannot pulsate below. The other he illustrated by placing the globe of a thermometer in his mouth. When this was in close contact with the cheek and tongue it indicated the natural heat of the body. When he wished it to indicate a lower temperature he simply inspired a current of air, and removed it from its former position.

Previous to giving an exposition of Jack's performances, he read an account of the same as related in the *Manchester Guardian*, which was agreed to be a very correct report, and explained that, although he was thoroughly convinced of the imposition of the assumed clairvoyance of Jack, yet that he had never gone through the ordeal he was about to submit to that evening, and might possibly fail in his endeavour. Whatever was done on his part, was without fraud and trickery, and he had every confidence he would succeed.

He then requested the medical gentlemen who had bound up Jack's eyes, to perform the same offices for him, Mr. Williamson covering his eyes with court plaister, and the other gentlemen with white plaister and the silk handkerchief. When all was pronounced analogous to Jack's condition, watches and sundry articles were presented for Dr. Dunn's inspection. Bending his head, *a la* Jack, he, after a little time, accurately described whatever was put before him. In explanation of how this was accomplished, he said the quivering of the eyelids, to which he had directed attention when Jack's eyes were being bandaged, prevented the court plaister from adhering, as was intended. Of course, the white plaister put upon the loosened court plaister added nothing to the sight difficulties; neither did the silk handkerchief. The restriction with regard to the organ of individuality, enabled him, by contracting the muscles of his forehead, and adapting his eyes for that object, to see from the inner corners of each eye whatever he desired. The refutation was complete, and Jack was stamped at once as an impostor.

These, sir, and kindred exposures are sufficient to make thoughtful men pause ere they conclude the phenomena witnessed at these séances, through the agency of "mediums," are of supernatural origin. There is much to distrust in these exhibitions. It seems to me a remarkable circumstance that "the spirits" never talk by verbal utterances. If they have the power to pinch people's legs, and splinter iron-rimmed and clamped tables, surely they have the power to speak, like the Ghost in Hamlet, in their own mother-tongue. The "spirits" of our forefathers used to talk audibly, and surely the race has not degenerated. The statement made by "A Barrister" that Mr. Home refused to perform before Mr. Houdin, and that of Mr. Mitchell, who asserts that he stopped the manifestations at a public exhibition at St. Martin's Hall, are sufficient to create and sustain the belief that there is some sleight-of-hand work in these séances. And when we know that electro-biologists, in public, make our friends to forget their own names, believe that water is brandy, that their clothes are on fire, and a thousand other illusions, it is but common prudence to demand that every care be taken that we are not imposed upon by any clever art in legerdemain or the development of any psychological phenomena.

Yours respectfully,
WILLIAM SMITH.

Mumps, Oldham, Oct. 13.

XXVI.

SIR,—In Mr. Coleman's letter of the 11th inst., he gives his opinion that the gentlemen who were present at the meetings recorded in the "Cornhill Magazine," under the head of "Stranger than Fiction," should confirm or confute the statements made in that article. I was one of the persons present at the evening meeting. The other gentlemen were a solicitor in extensive practice, and two well-known writers of solid instructive works—not writers of fiction—who, by-the-bye, appear to be so used to inventing that they cannot believe that any one can possibly be employed in stating facts. It will be seen that the joke about "fools of fashion" does not apply to the gentlemen alluded to, but that we were all workers in callings in which matters of fact, and not of fancy, especially come under observation. Further, it may be useful for some persons to know that we were neither asleep, nor intoxicated, nor even excited. We were complete masters of our senses; and I submit that their evidence is worth a thousand conjectures and explanations made by those who were not present. Scores of times I have been much more agitated and excited in investigating a patient's case, than I was in observing what occurred at the evening meeting in question.

With this state of senses at the time, and revolving the occurrences in my mind again and again, since that time, I can state with the greatest positiveness that the record made in the article "Stranger than Fiction," is, in every particular, correct; that the phenomena therein related, actually took place in the evening meeting; and, moreover, that no trick, machinery, sleight-of-hand, or other artistic contrivance produced what we heard and beheld. I am quite as convinced of this last as I am of the facts themselves.

Only consider that here is a man, between ten and

eleven stone in weight, floating about the room for many minutes—in the tomb-like silence which prevailed, broken only by his voice coming from different quarters of the room, according to his then position—is it probable, is it possible, that any machinery could be devised—not to speak of its being set up and previously made ready in a room which was fixed upon as the place of meeting only five minutes before we entered it—capable of carrying such a weight about without the slightest sound of any description? Or suppose, as has been suggested, that he bestrode an inflated balloon, could a balloon have been introduced inflated large enough to hold in mid-air such a weight? Or could it have been inflated with hydrogen gas without being detected by ears, eyes, or nose?

It seems to me a much stronger sign of credulity to believe either of these suggestions, with our present knowledge, than to adopt the wildest statements or dreams of what is called spiritualism. Let it be remembered, moreover, that the room was, for a good part of the evening, in a blaze of light, in which no balloon or other machine sufficient for the supposed purpose could be introduced; or, if already introduced, could remain unobserved; and that, even when the room was comparatively darkened, light streamed through the window from a distant gaslamp outside, between which gas-lamp and our eyes Mr. Home's form passed, so that we distinctly perceived his trunk and limbs; and most assuredly there was no balloon near him, nor any machinery attached to him. His foot once touched my head when he was floating above.

Then the accordion music. I distinctly saw the instrument moving, and heard it playing when held only at one end, again and again. I held it myself for a short time, and had good reason to know that it was vehemently pulled at the other end, and not by Mr. Home's toes, as has been wisely surmised, unless that gentleman has legs three yards long, with toes at the end of them quite as marvellous as any legion of spirits. For, be it stated, that such music as we heard was no ordinary strain; it was grand at times, at others pathetic, at others distant and long-drawn, to a degree which no one can imagine who has not heard it. I have heard Blagrove repeatedly, but it is no libel on that master of the instrument to say that he never did produce such exquisite distant and echo notes as those which delighted our ears. The instrument played, too, at distant parts of the room, many yards away from Mr. Home, and from all of us. I believe 1 am stating a fact when I say that not one person in that room could play the accordion at all. Mr. Home cannot play a note upon it.

To one whose external senses have witnessed these things, it is hard to increase the insufficiency of those attempted explanations which assert the use of tricks and machinery. As I said before, it requires much more credulity to believe such explanations than to swallow all the ghost stories that ever were related. I may add that the writer in the " Cornhill Magazine" omitted to mention several curious phenomena which were witnessed that evening. Here is one of them. A distinguished littérateur, who was present, asked the supposed spirit of his father, whether he would play his favourite ballad for us, and, addressing us, he added—" The accordion was not invented at the time of my father's death, so I cannot conceive how it will be effected; but if his favourite air is not played, I pledge myself to tell you so." Almost immediately the flute notes of the accordion (which was upon the floor) played through "Ye banks and braes of bonnie Doon," which the gentleman alluded to assured us was his father's favourite air, whilst the flute was his father's favourite instrument. He then asked for another favourite of his father's, "which was not Scotch," and "The last rose of summer" was played in the same notes. This, the gentleman told us, was the air to which he had alluded.

I have thus borne testimony to the truthfulness of the facts related by the writer in the "Cornhill Magazine," whom I recognize as having been my neighbour during the meeting. And I have endeavoured to show that, as regards the principal and most wonderful phenomena, there could have been no contrivance by trick or machinery adequate to produce or account for their existence. How then, were they produced? I know not; and I believe that we are very, very far from having accumulated facts enough upon which to frame any laws, or build any theory regarding the agent at work in their production. Intelligent phenomena, such as the music played at request, point to intelligent agents; and spiritual beings that have quitted fleshly bodies may be at work. I, for one, wish that it were proved to be so; for a more solemn discovery than that of a means of communication between embodied and disembodied sentient beings cannot be imagined. It giddies the brain to think of the possible result of such a discovery. But, whilst I obstinately stand up for the integrity of my senses during my observation of the wonders above related, my inner senses cannot but observe many gaps that must be filled up before the bridge between the spiritual body's life here in the flesh, and its life elsewhere out of the flesh, can be finished. Meantime the facts must be patiently and honestly accumulated, and enthusiasm must be banished from the minds of the inquirers. And, as regards the denials, and abuse, and jests of the non-inquirers, let it be remembered that scurrility and laughter never discovered or disproved anything whatever in the world's history.

Respecting the purely physical phenomena, such as the raising of weights, whether of human bodies or tables, it *may be* that we are on the verge of discovering some physical force hitherto undreamed of: who shall say that we know all the powers of nature? Here, too, dispassionate inquiry must go on, regardless of the noise outside; regardless, too, of the ignorant and malicious prejudice which would blast the reputation of those who inquire in a direction opposite to that prejudice.

Inquirers, unlike routine people, must be prepared to rough it among their fellow-creatures. And I suppose that I, for having asserted that I have five senses as yet unimpaired, and for having testified to what the majority disbelieve, shall come in for my share of pity or abuse. Let it be so, if it helps on a truthful search.—I am, sir, yours faithfully,

Malvern, Oct. 14.   J. M. GULLY, M.D.

XXVII.

SIR,—Great surprise is expressed that such a man as Mr. Howitt should, by an open avowal of his belief in table-rapping and other ludicrous impositions of spiritualism, risk his hitherto well-deserved reputation as a writer and instructor of the people; and with Dr. Gall we might exclaim, "Is he a fool or an impostor? or is there a particular organization which imposes in this form on the human understanding?" It would be but Christian charity to give Mr. Howitt and all those that think with him the benefit of the latter proposition. Fools they cannot be, for such persons are deficient in their intellectual faculties, and could not, therefore, be deep thinkers; impostors they cannot be, because they gain nothing by their adherence to their new belief; on the contrary, risking their worldly prospects thereby. Therefore, being neither fools nor impostors, we come to the conclusion that their own understanding imposes upon them, and through them such portion of the world as may be similarly organised, for Sir Walter Scott observes, " No man ever succeeded in imposing himself on the public as a supernatural personage, who was not to a certain degree the dupe of his own imposture." What, then, is the moving cause of this imposition? Hitherto the world, when disturbed by these fantasies of the brain, gape on, shrug their shoulders, and, sagely expressing their belief that the upper stories are cracked, pass on their way, trusting to time to show the utter absurdity of the doctrine or teaching thus attempted to be imposed upon them. It never strikes them that for such things to happen so continuously in the world's history, there must be a natural cause—a something that impels men thus to sacrifice their reputation for the sake of a crotchet, a myth, a dream, and there must be a "natural cause" to induce thousands to look up to such men as their leaders and advisers. That there is such a natural cause I will endeavour to prove, and trust thereby to warn my fellow-men to beware of false teachers.

Tasso, the Italian poet, firmly believed that he had a "familiar spirit," with whom he held, in the presence of visitors, conversations. Manso, Marquis of Villa, was present upon one occasion, and thus describes what took place:—"In the meantime, Tasso began to converse with this mysterious being. I saw and heard himself alone. Sometimes he questioned — sometimes answered, and from his answers I gathered the sense of what he had heard. The subject of his discourse was so elevated, and the expressions so sublime, that I felt myself in a kind of ecstacy." In fact, had he lived in the present age, what a "medium" Tasso would have made!

Swedenbourg was a spiritualist, and yet his biographers describe him as a man of unquestionable sincerity. Dr. J. Stilling was a doctor in medicine, moralist, journalist, divine, therefore an intellectual man; yet a firm believer in apparitions, upon which subject he wrote a book. Cromwell may also be included in the spiritualist list, along with Shakspeare, Sir Walter Scott, Kepler, Newton, Davy, Dr. Samuel Johnson, and other great men of the bygone ages—all men of learning and great repute in their different walks of science, and yet inclined to the belief in supernatural agency. How was this? He would be a bold man in the present day who should assert they were either fools or impostors. Surely there must have been a "natural cause" for such "spiritual" effect. Observe the populations of the earth: in every portion of its inhabited surface spiritualists are to be found, who can be amused with fictions, tales of wonder, and miraculous occurrences; in every passing event they find some extraordinary circumstance, some "special providence," as many describe it. "How many thousands are disposed to believe in dreams, sorcery, magic, astrology, in the mystic influence of spirits and angels, in the power of the devil, in second sight, and in miracles and incomprehensible representations of all sorts," inquires a departed philosopher. Why should all this be, and yet men refuse to acknowledge the cause, and thereby endeavour to modify or keep the effect within a safe compass! I now begin to tread upon dangerous ground, and yet truth must be asserted, when men's minds are apt to be led astray into the paths of superstition by those who should show them the realms of light. The fact is, God has provided us with a particular faculty, called by phrenologists the "organ of wonder," and it is more or less active in individuals and entire nations. The great men I have named were more or less under its influence for good purposes. When this sentiment is not in excess, it assists the promulgation of religious truth, and is essential to faith and refined religion. Legislators of antiquity made frequent use of it to bend their fellow-men to conformity with their laws. By using the name of angels or of supernatural beings, or the name of the Most High, they were, by the universality of this faculty, enabled to do as they listed with the peoples over whom their superior intellect raised them as rulers, and in numerous cases, to their honour be it spoken, they used this power to elevate mankind. But when this sentiment of wonder is in excess, the results are most lamentable, and parties in whom it is largely developed may really be said to be affected with a species of insanity; and under such influence Joe Smith the Mormon, Irving, Mahomet, &c., and many of the spiritualist leaders of the present day, may be considered to have been and to be. The misfortune we have to guard against is, that when the faculty or sentiment of wonder is largely developed in such persons as above-named, whose object is in many cases the desire to be "known to the world," to be "talked about," the impression then excited is mistaken by the ignorant masses as direct communication from heaven, and however absurd, or wild, or wicked the theory broached may be, implicit credence is given to it, and reason is blindfolded. Hence it is that table-rapping, table-moving, dancing, or by whatever name it is called by its friends, finds no difficulty in drawing after it a crowd of admirers, consisting of those who love the marvellous—of those too lazy to form a judgment of their own—and, finally, of the richer classes, whose lazy mode of life has enervated both body and mind, making them willing votaries to be led by the ears for the sake of a new sensation.—Hoping you will kindly find space for the insertion of this, I am, sir, your obedient servant, W. E. A. HARPER.

17, Liverpool Terrace, Islington, Oct. 15.

XXVIII.

Sir,—The discussion going on in your columns respecting "spiritual manifestations and table-turning," will be incomplete if the phenomena of this

description which present themselves in China and Japan attract no attention. I find that Dr. Macgowan, in his lectures, so popular among the educated classes of the country, adverts to these points. In yesterday's morning lecture (12th inst.), delivered in this town, he treated the subject in a general manner; but his paper on spiritual manifestations and table-turning in China, published some years ago in that country, and republished in one of Chambers's works, describes the practices in detail. Those of your readers who are in search of information corroborative of the pretensions of spiritualists, will discover nothing in Dr. Macgowan's writings or lectures very satisfactory: he regards the whole affair as an illusion. In the matter of table-turning, he says that, in this, as in many other things, the Chinese go by contraries, the table performing its gyrations with its legs pointed towards the ceiling.
—Yours, &c. LEAM.
Leamington, Oct. 13.

XXIX.

SIR,—On Wednesday last Jane Wilson was brought to the Warneford Hospital, Leamington, as an in-patient. She was very ill with diseased kidneys, but in no immediate peril of life. She was accompanied as far as the Leamington station by her brother, and parted with him there. On Thursday evening, the 11th October, she went to the closet, but soon returned in the extremest terror, and trembling all over. She declared she saw her brother lying dead in the closet. From that time she became worse, and died last Saturday, 13th. Meanwhile, on Friday 12th, tidings reached the hospital that her brother had met with his death by hanging; but, owing to her weakness, the news was kept from her, and she died without any confirmation of her apprehension.—Yours respectfully,

N. W. WYER.

Bute House, Leamington, 15th, 10th.

P.S.—My authority for the above statement is my brother, O. F. Wyer, who is house-surgeon to the hospital. He was writing the register of her death when he told me of this curious case.

XXX.

SIR,—" Cantabrigiensis" asks for the quotation from the Apology of Tertullian. It is not exactly as he supposes, the words *vertere tabulas* not occurring in it. But in the twenty-third chapter of the Tertulliani Apologeticus, are the words " Si et somnia immittunt habentes semel invitatorum angelorum et demonum assistentum sibi potestatem, per quos et capræ et mensæ divinare consueverunt." They are thus rendered in the translation of the Rev. Temple Chevalier:—"If they inspire dreams, too, by having the powerful assistance of the angels and demons once invited to attend them, by whose means even kids and tables have been made the instruments of divination." A little further on in the same chapter occur the following words:—"Let any one who is confessedly under the influence of demoniacal possession be brought out here before your tribunal. If the spirit be commanded by any Christian to speak, he shall as truly confess himself to be a demon, as in other places he falsely professes himself to be a God. If they do not confess themselves to be demons, not daring to lie to a Christian, then shed the blood of that most impudent Christian upon the spot. What can be plainer than such an appeal to facts?"

In your paper of Friday last, "A Barrister" writes: —"That after several interviews with Louis Napoleon, the Emperor proposed that Robert Houdin should be present at the next séance—a proposal which Mr. Home declined." As you have opened your columns to a serious discussion of this interesting subject, it becomes a duty to set right some of the errors into which inquirers fall, and having the pleasure of calling Mr. Home my friend, I wrote to him at Paris to know if there were any truth in this statement. I find that there is none. So many falsehoods have been circulated about Mr. Home that he has made a rule of never refuting any of them. Had, however, the statement been true, it would not, in my opinion, have gone for much, for I can conceive other explanations of Mr. Home's refusal than that of conscious imposture. Is it certain that a conjuror is as proper a person as a bishop to investigate spiritual phenomena? According to the etiquette of courts, an Emperor's request is a command, and I should think that Napoleon would not have brooked a refusal. I believe, further, that he has too much sense to make such a proposal.

However, still further to satisfy "A Barrister," I can tell him that M. Canti, a conjurer, almost as well known in Paris as M. Houdin, was present one evening with about thirty persons, in the apartments of H.I.H. Prince Napoleon, and that he was accidentally chosen with seven others by Mr. Home to witness the phenomena occurring in his presence. M. Canti informed the Prince "that he could in no way account for them on the principles of his profession," and he published a letter to that effect.

I see that Mr. Howitt and others have disposed of the erroneous statement as to Professor Hare, made by "A Lover of the Whole Truth."

If any of your readers are on sufficiently intimate terms with the Queen of Holland, the Emperor of Russia, or the King of Bavaria, I can affirm, with truth, that they will each testify to the phenomena which have repeatedly occurred in their presence through Mr. Home. Prince Adalbert of Bavaria is himself a medium; so is Prince Luigi, the uncle of the King of Naples.

I have myself seen nearly all the phenomena described in the "Cornhill Magazine," and those described by Dr. Blank in the April number of the "Spiritual Magazine."—Your obedient servant,

W. M. WILKINSON.

Hampstead, Oct. 17.

XXXI.

Sir,—As I expected, Mr. William Howitt's letter has called forth many replies, and, with your permission, I will tell you why I cannot agree with him. Let me first, however, brush away one fallacy which all modern prophets are fond of advancing in favour of their own pretensions. I have seen it so often put forward that it ceases to have any influence. The Spiritualists tell us that " the very same things which they (the unbelievers) now assert of Spiritualism were once said of Christianity.". It is very possible that if Christ were to appear upon earth in this year 1860—I speak with all reverence—He and His followers would be treated as impostors, madmen, cheats, and what not? But just look at the difference. Christ had a new doctrine to impart; the spiritualists confessedly have none. He raised the dead, cured the sick, healed the paralytic, fed thousands, gave sight to the blind; Mr. Home (or the spirits at his call) make tables dance, play accordions without hands, throw furniture about rooms, and do a number of things that *primâ facie* are merely ridiculous, and I don't know that even the demonstration that they were done by spiritual means would render them otherwise. In the Christian miracles there was a direct and palpable appeal to common sense. Can we fancy an apostle arguing thus:—"I come to preach a new gospel, to reconcile man with God, and my credentials are, that in a darkened room you shall see me floating above you in the air, that bells shall ring, and notes be written without hands?" I need not go further to show that there is no parallel between the unbelief of the Jew and the incredulity of persons like myself, who think that the bearers of a revelation from Heaven should have other credentials than childish tricks that may be imitated and are often surpassed by a clever conjurer.

In your paper of the 10th, Mr. John James Bird gives us some very wonderful "experiences"—a bad evidence—for any quack doctor can bring as many to vouch for the miraculous powers of his pills and lotions. But, accepting these so-called facts, as for argument sake I am willing to do, I ask, what do they prove? I see tables dancing without the (apparent) aid of human hands; I hear bells ringing and accordions playing in the air. I can see no material cause for these things, and am I therefore to believe in an immaterial cause?—that spirits, and not mortals, are at work? Is it logical, because I cannot see or discover any other cause for a table's jumping, to conclude that spirits are moving it? What do I know of spirits? They are invisible, I am told, and yet have power to move heavy furniture and pinch women in the leg. I shall be told that heat, galvanism, electricity, are invisible yet real powers; but I see no analogy between these and the spirit of Washington, which comes into a room and plays me impish tricks. The soul or the mind of man acts through and is only known by that action through the organs of the body, and much as I am inclined to believe in an intermediate state between death and judgment, I must be excused if I refuse to accept the spiritualistic carnival described by Mr. Bird as a fact. I would much rather believe in the purgatory of Romanism.

I think, then, my friend William Howitt is too rapid in his conclusions when he brings in a spirit world to account for phenomena that may be accounted for in a more logical manner. Any hypothesis that will apparently account for certain phenomena is not necessarily the true hypothesis. It must work in with others, be consistent with analogy, and so forth. The "spiritual" hypothesis breaks down in many places. The spirits never appear but in the presence of certain persons, in private rooms which are sometimes darkened: they never do ought but foolish things, never bring us any "gospel" which we did not know before, and manifest a very singular taste for furniture. The development of the mania (if I may be allowed the word) is rather remarkable. First, we had raps, then the tables turned round, then they began to tilt up; now they either float in the air or suicidally dash themselves to pieces. In all this I see what more resembles the progress of legerdemain than the action of the spirits of our departed friends. I need not say that I do not ascribe these upholstery freaks to Satanic influence, for there is to my mind no more evidence of the one than of the other.

It has been said that one failure cannot tell against a thousand successes; but if the power employed be supernatural, surely a single failure must be fatal to its universality of power and knowledge. Spirits are invoked to furnish certain information: part of it is true and part false. How are we to distinguish, and what is the nature of the spiritual power that thus deceives us? I quote a case which came to my knowledge last week, and for which I am prepared to give my proofs. Mr. A——, a spiritualist and worker with the *planchette,* called at a newspaper-office the other day and asked for the names of the fine arts and theatrical critics. He was asked why he desired to know their names? He replied that a spirit, through the instrumentality of the planchette, had, in answer to his inquiries, written down the name of the editor (whom he knew) and of the two contributors, and he wished to know if they were correct. The editor's name was rightly given: the other two were entirely wrong. Now, if the spirit knew the editor, how was it he did not know the contributors, both well-known men, and one of them connected with the office for many years? The fact is, that the planchette, guided unconsciously by Mr. A——'s hand, wrote what he wanted it to write, and could not write what he did not know. Either the spirit was a very bungling one—I do not remember what name he answered to—or Mr. A—— is self-deceived. One thing is plain: it knew what the medium knew, and no more.

I do not feel justified in using the terms imposition and fraud, although these are cases which seem to merit such stigmas. I would put the "professors" in the same rank as M. Houdin or Wiljalba Frikell; but the amateurs are, I think, the victims of self-deception, not even excluding Mr. B. Coleman. With him and with William Howitt I cordially agree that the whole matter deserves investigation; but we must be allowed to cross-examine the witnesses and to see the miracles performed in open day. The adepts must be prepared to submit to the test of some crucial experiment, and not excuse themselves, as I understand they are perpetually doing, because the objects will not appear or exert their power while there are infidels in the room.—Yours obediently,

CALMAN BURROUGHS.

3, Truro Street, Haverstock Hill.

P.S.—Since writing the above I have seen William Howitt's second letter, which adds little to his first, beyond the re-asseveration of his own firm belief in spiritualism. He says the "laws" of spiritualism are as sure as the universe: where am I to find these "laws," as spiritualists give us only "facts?" These I accept, the former I dispute, as being

K

illogical deductions. I study my "Euclid" and ask what it proves. Are these "oracles" all of God, seeing that Mr. Howitt allows the possibility of Satanic interference? When he and Dr. Collyer speak of the good faith, &c. of the mediums, are we to forget the good faith of Irving and the miracles he wrought, and the unknown tongues spoken by persons of unimpeachable character in his congregation? The history of the human mind is full of these "pious frauds." Men begin by deceiving themselves and end by deceiving others. Amongst women there is a notorious inclination to play tricks —it partakes of the nature of a disease, and the more the men approach the mental nature of women, the more easily do they become deceivers and deceived.

XXXII.

Sir,—One of your learned correspondents has alluded to an expression of Tertullian with respect to what he terms table-turning. The most interesting vestige of this curious mode of incantation which has come down to us from antiquity, is that mentioned by Ammianus Marcellinus, towards the latter end of the fourth century, under the Emperor Valeris. The twenty-four letters of the alphabet were arranged round a magic tripod or table, in the centre of which was balanced a moveable ring, which, under spiritual influences (as was, of course, supposed), pointed in certain directions, so as to spell out particular names or words; and the persons implicated in the great conspiracy of Antioch thus ventured to predict that the next emperor's name would begin with the four letters Th-e-o-d—a premonition singularly fulfilled, by the accession of Theodosius the Great.—Amm. Marcell. Histor., lib. xxix., cap. 1, pp. 552-3 : Paris edit., 1681.

Interested as I am, with, I suppose, ten thousand others, in the investigation of spiritualism, simply as an honest inquirer after truth, and only desirous of keeping the windows of my mind open in all directions for its reception, at whatever labour, and at whatever cost, I beg to tender you my most grateful thanks for the generous and impartial manner in which you have offered your valuable columns to both sides of a subject which can only fail to be profoundedly interesting to the fool, the infidel, or the scoffer. I have not been able to come to any satisfactory conclusion myself, and am therefore only an observer at present in the sense of wishing to be always a learner. But if it would not be thought presumptuous, I would just add, that the phenomena of biology seems sufficient to explain a good deal, although by no means all, of what has been written. The famous Friar Bunguy, in the fifteenth century, could cover the wall of a room apparently with fruit, through simply acquiring a biological influence over the spectators. Some of the exhibitions made to Lord Macartney, in China, by the jugglers there,

may be accounted for, I think, in the same way. What the lookers-on behold, ceases under such circumstances to be objective; in other words, they become subject for the time to impressions analogous to those of somnambulism, without, however, actually falling asleep.—I beg to remain, sir, your obedient servant, MATTHEW BRIDGES.
Chester-hill, Stroud, Gloucestershire, Oct. 16.

XXXIII.

Sir,—Your amiable correspondent, William Howitt, urges the doubters of spiritual manifestations to inquire and judge for themselves. Sir, if you will allow me space, I will give your readers the result of my investigations. A friend, whom I had known for years, requested me to pay a visit, in company with him, to a celebrated medium, one that Mr. Howitt believes to be above suspicion, and endowed with the power of producing extraordinary results. I accepted the invitation, and promised I would form my opinion from the result of the manifestations produced at this meeting. I, accompanied by my spiritual friend, and another who was sceptical as to the new faith, arrived at a house in the neighbourhood of Red Lion Square. We were shown by my conductor upstairs to a second-floor front room. The apartment was large, and dimly lighted by a single candle. Seated at a round table were an elderly lady, an old gentleman of respectable appearance, and a younger one, a friend of his The table was a common old circular tea table, supported by a single pillar and three claws, one of which was shorter than the others, and consequently gave a sloping inclination to the top of the table. We were afterwards informed that the shortness of the claw resulted from a piece having been broken off by the spirits, who had served the table the same way more than once. After some general conversation on the subject, the party were requested to form a circle round the table, with their hands placed on the top. I was requested not to join, as also was my sceptical friend, who provided himself with pencil and paper to take down the spiritual communications. I followed his example, in case of any dispute about the words. At this period a young woman entered from the adjoining room, and took her seat at the table, placing her hands on it like the rest, and I then discovered that this young lady was the medium; there were now sitting round the table, with their hands on it, the elderly female (who was the mistress of the house), the young lady medium, the old gentleman, the young one, and occasionally my spiritual friend. The medium having asked if spirits were present, and received an answer in the affirmative, by the table being tilted twice or three times, the old gentleman was requested to put a question, when he asked the spirit to spell his name, and the young man, his friend, was asked to point out the letters on an alphabet pasted on cardboard, the table tilting when the letters were pointed out. After a great deal of going back, various mistakes, and substitutions of one letter for another, the table signified that the whole of the name was spelt; on referring to my notes I found the following as the result (Jememea). The gentleman said it was neither his Christian nor surname, his Christian name being Jeremiah, upon which the elderly female said it was evident that the spirits were trying to spell it. The table now went on to spell his surname, and on putting the letters tilted out together, produced (Amike), which the old gentleman declared had no resemblance whatever to his name. This was voted at once a failure. I was now asked to put a mental question, which I declined to do, but produced two sealed envelopes which I had numbered severally 1 and 2, and requested that the spirits would answer the question contained in the envelope marked No. 1, the answer to be taken down both by my spiritual and sceptical friends. The table, after some considerable fencing, proposed to read my question instead of answering it. I agreed to this, but took good care the envelope should not be put out of my sight. I was then requested to point out the letters of the alphabet, which I objected to; but the table, on being consulted by the medium, would answer no one but me. I then took especial care to time myself in pointing out the letter, so that no particular emphasis should be made on one letter more than another. After a great deal of trying back again, and questions asked if the spirits did not mean some other letter than the one the table tilted at, it was indicated that the whole question was read, and on putting the letters together, the following sentence was made: —" By them all, you wil soon be con in the next world;" which my spiritual friend interpreted as— " By them all, you will soon be converted in the next world." I then opened the envelope, and read the question it contained, which was, " Where is my deceased son buried?" The medium and company present admitted it was a failure, and said they were unfortunate that evening. The medium then proposed to bring up the spirit of my son, which I at once declined. During the time the words were being tilted out (for there was no rapping), every attempt was made on the part of the table, spirit, or medium, to draw attention from the matter in hand, by raising the table several inches from the floor, to the great astonishment of the old gentleman, the delight of my spiritual friend, and disgust of myself. There were several persons with their hands on the table and their feet beneath it, and I really attributed the lifting motion to material aid rather than spiritual endeavour. I was determined not to be juggled, and rated the table for not behaving itself in a more seemly manner and finishing its task. The old gentleman, admitting the utter failure of the answers, asked me if I could account for the rising of the table, when my sceptical friend replied that it was done by one of the ladies, much to their horror. They immediately challenged him to do it, which he readily undertook, and placing his hands on the top of the table, and his foot at the base of the pillar, between the claws, raised the table easily. Of course they denied they had adopted any such means, but they failed to convince me of the truth of their assertion. I preferred the rational material explanation to the spiritual one. The old gentleman then told me that he had seen that table go about the room with the fingers of some persons scarcely touching it. I immediately attempted the same feat, and requested the company to observe my hands and wrists, not a muscle or sinew of which showed signs of action, and yet I propelled the table all over the room, apparently without effort, much to the gentleman's amazement, who wished to make a medium of me, which honour I at once repudiated. Thoroughly surprised at the credulity and superstition of the believers, I left the house, astonished indeed that men, apparently in their senses, should be so easily imposed upon, and be ready to assist in imposing on others. In conclusion, I challenge all the mediums, Mr. Home included, to answer six questions which I will enclose in sealed envelopes. Till they can do this, I do not think the wonderful statements made worth consideration.—I remain, sir, yours, &c.

JAMES HOPPEY.

18, Gresse Street, Tottenham Court Road.

XXXIV.

Sir,—To me it is a matter of astonishment, that in England and the United States—nations which pride themselves on the study and knowledge of the Holy Scriptures—there should be so many persons who do not see that to consult the dead, to seek the truth from the dead, to evoke departed spirits with a view to obtain a sensible manifestation of their presence, and a sensible response to questions proposed, or even to intend and to attempt to do this, though without any visible result, is a very grievous sin. It is, in fact, the sin of necromancy. The word itself, as every Greek scholar at once sees, expresses exactly the very thing which is now disguised under the name of spiritualism, and which is now gaining so awful an extension. Now, is there any sin more severely denounced and punished in the sacred writings than this sin of necromancy? Let us see:—

"Neither let there be found among you any one . . . . that consulteth soothsayers, or observeth dreams and omens, neither let there be any wizard.

"No charmer, nor any one that consulteth pythonic spirits, or fortune-tellers, or that seeketh the truth from the dead.

"For the Lord abhorreth all these things, and for these abominations he will destroy them at thy coming."—Deuteronomy, xviii. 10, 11, 12.

I quote the Douay version. The Anglican runs thus : " Or that useth divination, or an observer of times, or an enchanter, or a witch, or a charmer, or a consulter with familiar spirits, or a wizard, or a necromancer. For all that do these things are an abomination unto the Lord ; and because of these abominations the Lord thy God doth drive them out from before thee." The Vulgate expresses the sin thus—" aut qui quærat à mortuis veritatem." The Septuagint—" interrogating the dead."

So much for the denunciation ; now for an instance of the punishment. Saul was condemned for the crowning sin of consulting the witch of Endor—in modern parlance, a medium ; and for desiring to evoke, through that medium, the departed spirit of Samuel ; thus violating the law which he himself, in the former part of his reign, had rigorously enforced, of " cutting off those that have familiar spirits and the wizards out of the land." I leave aside the disputed point whether it was really the spirit of Samuel which by Divine permission appeared, or otherwise. The fact of Saul applying to a " medium" to communicate with the dead was his crime. The Scripture expressly says so :—

" So Saul died for his iniquities, because he transgressed the commandment of the Lord which he had commanded, and kept it not ; and moreover consulted also a witch.

" And trusted not in the Lord : therefore he slew him, and transferred his kingdom to David, the son of Issai." — 1 Paralipomenon (Anglican version "Chronicles"), x. 13.

The Anglican version has:—" So Saul died . . . . also for asking counsel of one that had a familiar spirit to inquire of it, and inquired not of the Lord; therefore he slew him."

What else then are we to deduce from this testimony of Holy Writ but the sinfulness of necromancy, and " of interrogating the dead?" And what are we to think of the multitude of strange facts—for one cannot but admit that some are facts, and not tricks of legerdemain—which seem to give evidence of the presence of the departed spirits? Are they really the acts and communications of the souls evoked? Not a bit of it. The departed spirits are in the hands of God; either for beatitude or punishment; and not at the beck of presumptuous man. It is all the work of Satan and his angels—the "spirits of wickedness in the high places"—" the rulers of the world of this darkness"—of the "business that walketh about in the dark"—" the invasion and the noon-day devil." It is the work of those fallen angels who are constantly occupied, by Divine permission, for our trial, in deluding, deceiving, and tempting mankind. In short, I say it boldly as a Christian priest, it is diabolism. Many, likewise, are the internal evidences of its diabolic origin; such, for instance, as the ridiculous character of the manifestations—rapping and dancing of tables, &c. Is this a Divine or spiritual, or even a serious mode of giving or receiving a message from the awful world of the future? Then, again, the practical denial of hell; for, as far as I have read of these manifestations, all departed spirits are more or less happy. The spirits of men whose morals have been very questionable, and whose lives have been anything but Christian, perhaps not even their belief, are all supposed to be at liberty to come and have a chat with any medium who gives them an invitation. Very different was the rich glutton; "he died and was buried in hell." He was neither permitted himself to come, nor was Abraham allowed to send Lazarus to his "five brethren, lest they also come into this place of torment."—Luke xvi. 28. But these modern necromancers say, "Nous avons changé tout cela."

JOHN WILLIAMS, Catholic Priest.
Arno's Court Reformatory, Bristol, Oct. 16.

XXXV.

"The mind of man is like an enchanted glass, full of superstitions and imposture, if it be not delivered from them."—LORD BACON.

SIR,—I do not think the "spiritual manifestations" have made much way into the region of facts since we discussed them, several months ago, before; and all sensible people had arrived at the conclusion that what is true in them, possibly the larger portion, is the result of subjective impressions on the consciousness, and what is factitious and fictitious is no more worthy of serious notice than the feats of Houdin, or of the acrobats one is pained to see occasionally on the top of poles in various parts of London. There is a flunkeyism all through the present discussion at one side that is very unpleasant. What Mr. Home, or Mr. Canti, or the Man in the Moon said to his Imperial Highness the Prince Napoleon or the Grand Turk must be a natural law; as, also, that Prince Adalbert of Bavaria has settled it all, as, like the lady at Red Lion Square, he is a medium of undoubted virtue. Mr. Home evidently understands electro-biology, and mixes it up clumsily with Houdinism, and men like my esteemed friend, Mr. Howitt, are unable to perceive (from want of medical education) where one comes in to the aid of the other. Anybody with a thimble-full of chloroform, and one-tenth of his Houdinism, might do all that he (Mr. Home) says. Anyone a perfect master of mesmerism or electro-biology would succeed without the chloroform. Allied to this flunkeyism is the table-talk of peculiar, quaint men, who mystify themselves and others, as your correspondent at Malvern, about the laws of spiritualism, Baconian inductions, and sesquipedalian pedantry of that kind. What laws do the acrobats in the streets off the Strand bother themselves about? Yet they do as marvellous things as Home or Houdin. If we could remove out of the present debate this omne-ignotum-pro-magnifico grandeur, spiritualistic laws and mystification, which is most desirable, there would be still a great deal of a most interesting nature to discuss. There is not a dozen men in London, however, like Mr. Lewes, of the *Cornhill Magazine*, Dr. Carpenter, Mr. Faraday, Dr. Brown Sequard, Sir B. Brodie, who thoroughly understand the nervous system and the principles of subjective and objective consciousness; consequently, such shallow unscientific triflers as those in *Punch* and *Once a Week* merely put the cart before the horse; they excite idle curiosity, and are the best means of spreading "Houdinism." The article in "Blackwood" is better, but one can see it is violently one-sided, but admits it is puzzled. To remain neuter in such controversies, as your paper does, as admirably observed by Locke, is the proper condition of the understanding. If there be a natural fact or truth in question it will vindicate itself. I think, too, be it said with reverence, we might get rid of Tertullian, Sir David Brewster, Lord Brougham, and Deuteronomy, in the discussion. It is highly probable that you could get three or four baronets or lords to sit round a table, and before fifteen minutes have them mesmerised by staring at any single thing on the table. They need only hold their breath, keep up a fixed stare, and be told to fix their mind on what is well known in medical works as a "prominent idea." That idea would be that a certain spirit would appear. Forthwith the spirit would appear and float about, but whether a subjective or objective vision, as I explained it to Mr. Howitt, not

one of these puzzled non-medical baronets or Tertullianists could tell. Such persons once partially mesmerised would be unaware of it themselves, and you might play any tune on an accordion to them exactly as to a somnambulist. They would hear it, but could not see it.—Yours,
     Charles Kidd, M.D.
Sackville Street, W., Oct. 19.

XXXVI.

Sir,—Thanking you for the insertion of my letter in your this day's impression, I think you must agree with me, after perusal of Mr. J. M. Gully's, M.D., communication, that that portion of my letter not published should have been allowed to appear.

Mr. Gully writes:—"We were complete masters of our senses," in proof of which he proceeds to inform us that at one of the spiritual meetings he was witness to the sight of "a man between ten and eleven stone in weight floating about the room for many minutes!" and indignantly denies the suggestion that mechanical or other means were applied to effect this deception; and yet, a few paragraphs further on, he states "that even when the room was comparatively darkened, light streamed through the window from a distant gas-lamp outside, between which gas-lamp and our eyes Mr. Home's form passed, so that we distinctly perceived his trunk, and limbs, &c. His foot once touched my head when he was floating above."

So then the mystery is solved. For what purpose was the room "comparatively darkened," it having previously been in a blaze of light? If Mr. Home could really float round a room suspended in mid-air, why not do so in a "blaze of light," so that his admirers could have seen his gracious countenance smiling benignantly down upon their up-turned faces? Why only let them see "his trunk and limbs?" They only saw the "trunk and limbs" because the head was vainly trying to make its way through the ceiling, by the natural affinity of hydrogen to escape upwards. Here we have a gentleman "complete master of his senses," in a "darkened room," actually mistaking a balloon figure of a man, inflated with gas, for the ten or eleven stone weight Mr. Home, in *propria persona*. Many years since the gamins of this metropolis were highly delighted by the sight of such a figure floating over the house-tops, having ascended from one of the public gardens on the occasion of a fête the reverse of spiritual. Gentlemen of the jury, after the evidence given by the preceding witness, it would appear needless to carry the case further; he has been imposed upon by the substitution of an inflated figure of a man to represent solid flesh and blood. The verdict was—"We find that the deponent has been imposed upon by the undue development of a particular organization commonly called the 'organ of wonder,' or 'love of the marvellous.'"

As to the "accordion trick," although no one in the room could play it, yet some one outside the room could; and a certain proof of this is supplied by his own words in describing the music, "It was at others distant and long-drawn," "the instrument played, too, at distant parts of the room many yards away," &c.; in fact, just as would be produced by a performer playing the instrument while walking up and down a room underneath that in which the "nervous" gentlemen were being mesmerised. Did this occur in a "comparatively-darkened" room? As to the gentleman whose deceased father was partial to the tunes of "Ye banks and braes," and "The last rose of summer," it is wonderful how he could keep his countenance during the performance. Perhaps in the "comparatively-darkened room" the merry twinkle of his eye was not observed. The scene must have been rich. Would that I had been there to have noted the expression on the faces of the actors and audience who " were complete masters of their senses!"

I perfectly coincide with Dr. Gully, that we may be, and probably are, on the point of making many wonderful discoveries; but of this be assured that, " From the sublime to the ridiculous there is but one step" down which the gentlemen who supposed themselves "complete masters of their senses" have fallen.—I am, sir, your obedient servant,

W. E. A. HARPER.

17, Liverpool Terrace, Islington, Oct. 17.

XXXVII.

" We talk of a credulous vulgar without always recollecting that there is a vulgar in credulity which in historical matters, as well as in those of religion, finds it easier to doubt than to examine, and endeavours to assume the credit of an *esprit fort*, by denying whatever happens to be beyond the very limited comprehension of the public."—SIR WALTER SCOTT. *Introduction to "Fair Maid of Perth."*

SIR,—Your correspondents are upon such full cry against the poor spiritualists, who, notwithstanding, do not stand in any awe of them, that I fear they are in too headlong a chase to pause, and just look at one another. They could not readily see a more diverting spectacle, nor how completely they are verifying the old adage, " Give a man enough rope," &c. Now, spiritualism can be but one thing, but your "musical pack" have made it out already to be a dozen different things. With one, it is nothing at all; with a second, it is the—devil; with a third, it is Reichenbach's od-force, and a very odd force it must be, if it be half the things they say it is; with a fourth, it is only the result of the organ of wonder; with a fifth, it is nothing wonderful at all; with a sixth, it can smash tables and carry human bodies of upwards of a hundred weight all round the ceiling of a room; with a sixth, it cannot even lift a chair or a stool, but requires human legs and feet to do it; with a seventh, it gives surprising messages; and with an eighth, it cannot even stammer out "Jeremiah;" with a ninth, it is all the imagination; and in the tenth, it is all the toe-joints, and the *peroneus longus;* an eleventh says, it has no laws; and a twelfth, that it has no facts; a thirteenth, attributes it to trickery; and a fourteenth, to familiar spirits that peep and mutter, and are forbidden by the Scriptures.

Can spiritualism be all these, or the half of them? If so, the organ of wonder may well be excited in its Islington advocate, and he must be converted by it into another

"Katerfelto with his hair on end
At his own wonders, wondering."

Sir, I gave you a little warning of what would happen if you admitted to the discussion men who were utterly ignorant of the subject. Until this discussion is disencumbered of the class so happily styled by the Americans "Know-Nothings," it is impossible to elicit the simple truth. For my part, I shall pass all the crowd of Know-Nothings, guessers, supposers, and assumers, without ceremony; and as they have, happily, buried themselves under whole waggon-loads of verbiage, without one real fact amongst a dozen of them, the most charitable thing is—there to let them lie.

Such men as Mr. Wilkinson, Mr. Coleman, Dr. Gully, and Dr. Collyer, speak from observation, and no mere imaginations can answer their actualities.

There are others who have seen a little, though this is sometimes but a mere potsherd at the door of spiritualism. Those deserve their share of notice. Such is Mr. Hoppey, who has been to a medium, whom, he says, I deem trust-worthy, and could not get "Jeremiah" stammered out by the alphabet. I am sorry for him: he was unfortunate. I myself have been to public meetings, and the House of Commons, and have seen embryo orators able to stammer out quite as little; but that did not abate my faith in the existence of such speakers as Bright or Gladstone; and I would venture, from what I have seen, in hundreds of instances, to suggest to Mr. Hoppey whether he might not have himself to thank for his disappointment. If he or any of his comrades were in a cavilling spirit, not candidly desirous to see what would come, we are pretty certain of what he got. There are laws, as every one knows who knows anything of spiritualism, which regulate all these phenomena, as everything in the universe is regulated. Those who will violate these conditions must not complain of disappointment. Our Saviour could not perform many miracles at Nazareth because of unbelief. I have seen plenty of *séances* rendered abortive by such ignorant conduct. Let Mr. Hoppey go to a glass furnace and pass a cold air over the metal, when in the act of puration into some vessel, and see what the consequence will be. If he have seen one failure, thousands have seen the most splendid successes. Will Mr. Hoppey's abortion annihilate all that thousands and tens of thousands have seen? Let him not believe it.

I will now give him a simple fact, occurring at my own table. A distinguished physician, living upwards of a hundred miles from London, who had witnessed some few demonstrations, and was desirous further to test spiritualism, entered my room unexpectedly. I expressed my surprise to see him there. He said, "I have run up to town on most pressing business; I have not an hour to spare, but I would like to ask a question through your little table." We sat down. There was immediate evidence of spirit presence. "Can I put my question," asked the doctor, "mentally, so that I myself only shall know it?" "By all means," I replied. He was silent for a moment, and then said, "I have put my question." Immediately was read out through the alphabet, "Jesus Christ has taken little David to his rest."

On learning this, the physician started up in much agitation, exclaiming, "God forbid!—No, truly! no, that cannot be true!" I said, "Of that I can, of course, say nothing, knowing nothing of what you have asked." He then said again, "Good God! I have been attending a little patient whom I would give anything to save. His death would break his parents' hearts, and blast a thousand hopes! But there was a favourable turn in his complaint; I had business of the most vital importance in town; I thought I might run up for a few hours, and now this answer says he is dead." "Whether that be so," I observed, "you can quickly learn from the iron telegraph; but I have no doubt you will find this spiritual telegram quite correct." He pressed my hand in silence, took the railway, homeward, in haste, and found, on his arrival, that the child had died an hour or two before he put his question at my table.

That is but one out of millions—I may say millions—of facts equally extraordinary and equally truthful. Will Mr. Hoppey's laughing at the mediums set aside that one fact? And what is the use of talking of od-force or organs of wonder, in the face of such daily facts? A word about od-force. This is the forlorn hope of those who, after blustering about the non-reality of spiritualism, when they see more, and feel the ground of their unbelief slipping from under them, clung to, as the last twig, the last straw, of physicism left them; the Jonas gourd that, springing up in a single night for them to cower under, is sure to be smitten to the earth by the first glow of morning. Od, or odalic force, is, as I read Reichenbach, a simple, imponderable element, or igneous atmosphere, as the name in Greek imports, which, like electricity and magnetism, performs certain essential functions in that organism by which matter is made co-operative with mind. But Reichenbach nowhere pretends that this fire is anything more than a blind element. Spiritualism is— an intelligence. In all communications through the table, this intelligence displays itself as forcibly, as palpably, as ratiocinatively, as the soul in the human body. It has its will as positive as the human will. It tells things which no one present knows, as it told the physician his secret request. It brings messages from the dead, so full of the stamps and tests of truth, that a man would, indeed, be mad not to believe them. These intelligences everywhere—over mighty continents and amongst multitudinous peoples, operating at the same moment—declare themselves everywhere to be spirits. What right have we, or has anyone, to disbelieve them? What right have we or anyone to set them aside, thus speaking from day to day and from year to year with one persistent voice, and to enthrone odforce, or automatic action, or any other blind and dumb force, in their places? If they tell us the truth, as they have done in thousands and tens of thousands of cases, shall we not rather believe them than the miscellaneous and mutually-conflicting mob of Know-Nothings, who show themselves so utterly ignorant of what these intelligences are that they attribute to a score of vague causes? When the clamour of know-nothingism has barked itself out, and "the still small voice" of reflection is again heard, these divine intelligences will yet be standing their ground, and give ample proofs of their verity to those who seek in earnest.

Dr. Gully is one of those who deserve respectful attention. He admits the facts from personal observation, but he thinks that there requires yet many links of the chain to be added before we can pronounce upon the causes. That is true of Dr. Gully's present position on the spiritual plane. When he advances he will find that all these links have long been affixed to the chain by innumerable experiments. Spiritualists, well advanced, do not involve themselves in the labyrinth of guesses and speculations. They make a short cut to the facts. They see spirits. They do not need to ask the cause of this or that: there stand the causes palpably before them. Extravagant as this may seem to the gross and outward who have, perhaps, burst from the chrysalis state of know-nothingism, but are yet only on the steps of the portico of truth, I and hundreds know persons who all their lives have seen and conversed with spirits as they do with men. They give the most incontrovertible proofs of it. One of these is the lady who saw the apparition at Ramhurst, in Kent, and detailed to Mr. Dale Owen the names of these spirits, the day and year of the male spirit's death, as given by him, before any one in the parish or neighbourhood knew that any one of that name had ever lived there. Mr. Owen went down; by much labour (see his "Footfalls") discovered all that had been related by the spirits, and to his astonishment discovered in the papers in the British Museum, connected with this family, the date given by the spirit, of his death, verified to the day. Another is the lady on whose evidence, also related in Mr. Owen's book, combined with the evidence of another person unknown to her and far away, yet equally derived from a ghost, the War Office had to correct the return of Captain W——'s death.

These are hard nuts for this material age to crack,

but they are immovable facts. And, now, the Catholic priest, Mr. John Williams, comes to the rescue. He does not think spiritualism is od-force, or any such blind, deaf, and dumb thing: he boldly proclaims it to be the devil. I thank you, reverend sir; you have at once bridged over Dr. Gully's chasm, and landed us face to face with a spirit, though it be a devil. As I had occasion to say once before on this subject, that is a great advance—a real substantial gain. Grant us a devil, and you grant us the whole question. You admit, at least, that it is spiritualism, though of a dusky hue. How many thousands, philosophized out of all faith in Christ—men believing themselves wise, who have gone back to materialism—in other words, to something more dark than paganism, would rejoice if they could have proof of a devil! Oh! to them what comfort in a devil! for, if they found a devil, they would know that God and his angels were not far off, as sure as there must be a sun before there can be a shadow.

But why should the Catholic priests take all the good angels to themselves, and give us all the devils? The Catholic Church has been believing in spiritualism, from the first hour of its existence till this moment. Open its many and ponderous volumes of the "Lives of the Saints"—there is not a page in them which is not crammed with saintly miracles. Spirits descend to others as well as St. Cecilia, and whisper science to them, and support them in trying emergencies. The saints walk on water, quench fires, raise the dead—do many wonderful things. What! and when we acknowledge this power, and declare that we participate in its benefactions, shall they treat us rudely and say, "Stand off, heretics! ours are angels, yours are devils?" It would be hard to persuade us that those saintly inspirations which, through Dominic, and Loyola, and others, preached fire and annihilation to Protestants—which, under that precious Ferdinand II., exterminated a whole nation in Bohemia, came from God or his angels! Let us not reproach each other; let us to our own Master be content to stand or fall.

But Mr. Williams quotes a great deal from the Scriptures—(see his letter of the 15th)—to show us that all communications with the spirits of the dead were forbidden to the Jews, and made death by the law. We grant him every word of it. There is nothing more notorious than that the Jews, ever given to idolatry and necromancy, were forbidden this intercourse; there is nothing so notorious as that Christ himself restored this intercourse, and abrogated this law of Moses, as he abrogated many other Jewish institutions. Oh, Mr. Williams! "art thou a master in Israel, and knowest not these things?" Hear, then: it is not the first time that I have had to demolish this flimsy sophism. And let the reader especially note this, for it is the most remarkable case in the Sacred history, because it demonstrates, and no doubt was planned by our Saviour, to demonstrate, the express abnegation of the Mosaic law regarding the spirits of the dead.

Christ abrogated this law by himself, seeking the spirit of Moses, the very promulgator of that law, and leading his disciples to do the same. Christ conducted his disciples, Peter, James, and John, up into the Mount of Transfiguration, and introduced them to Moses and Elias, both spirits of the dead. Christ might have summoned Moses to appear before him; but no: as if the case were carefully studied, this law against "seeking to the dead" was to be abolished. He goes to, seeks to the spirit of the great dead, to Moses, the very man who prohibited such an act by the law in question, and there on the Mount, broke the law before his face! Nay, more, by his example, he taught his disciples, the future proclaimers of his new law to the world, to do the same. It must be confessed that there is no such complete, pointed, and striking abrogation of a law in any history, sacred or profane. The Lord of Life, who was about to become the prince of spirits of the dead, broke this law, and in no other presence than in that of the promulgator of that law, who had long been a spirit of the dead, and again in the presence of those selected by Christ to teach this great act to posterity. And the disciples found it so good for them, that they desired to build tabernacles, and remain with those illustrious dead. Let Mr. Williams stand up face to face with this fact, and in a manly spirit confess that it is a stone of testimony rooted in the eternal ground of the Gospel.

A new order of things was established by Christianity: our departed friends were allowed to come to us, and to minister to us of God's spirit and the Divine favour. In proof of this, at the Crucifixion, the spirits of the dead arose and went into the city, and appeared to many. And to show that they are spirits of the dead, who come as those witnesses to whom the Catholic Church has dedicated a particular day as the Festival of all Angel Guardians, we have St. John, in the Apocalypse, declaring that such was the spirit who showed him those glorious visions in Patmos :—"And when I had heard and seen, I fell down to worship before the feet of the angel which shewed me these things. Then saith he unto me See *thou do it* not : for I am thy fellow servant, and of thy brethren the prophets." — Rev. xxii. 8 and 9. And mark, here, there is no escape from this ; the last essential words, showing that the angel had been a man and a prophet, are most literally translated from the original. We claim, therefore, as much as the Catholics, the mediumship of good angels. We ask with St. Paul, "Are they not all ministering spirits, sent forth to minister for them who shall be heirs of salvation ?" We appeal to Christ's own test of the nature of those ministrants. " By their fruits ye shall know them." What are these fruits? Not the persecution of other churches, not bigotry and hardness towards one another ; not saying to our neighbour, as the Jews said to Christ, "Thou hast a devil;" but doing that which all churches and all mere arguments have failed to do, convincing and converting to Christianity numbers of atheists, deists, materialists, and indifferents by the foolishness of these despised phenomena.

Lord Bacon, in his time, had well considered this subject of investigations of this nature. In his "Essay on the Advancement of Learning," he observes:—

"It is otherwise (that is, not dangerous) as to the nature of spirits and angels; this being neither unsearchable or forbid, but in a great part level to the human mind on account of their affinity. We are indeed forbid in Scripture to worship angels, or to entertain fantastical opinions of them, so as to exalt them above the degree of creatures, or to think of them higher than we have reason; but the sober inquiry about them which either ascends to a knowledge of their nature by the scale of corporeal beings, or views them in the mind as in a glass, is by no means forbid. The same is to be understood of revolted or unclean spirits; conversation with them, or using their assistance, is unlawful, and much more in any manner to worship or adore them; but the contemplation and knowledge of their nature, power, and illusions appear from Scripture, reason, and experience to be no small part of spiritual wisdom. Thus says the Apostle:—"*Stratagematum ejus non ignari sumus.*" And thus it is as lawful, in natural theology, to investigate the nature of evil spirits, as the nature of poisons in physics, or the nature of vice in morality."

Sir, I must apologise for the length of this letter, but, as I am one against a host, I cannot notice everything in a few lines. Having, however, slain another hecatomb, I will just lay myself down, draw up my legs a little, and—wait for more.—Yours, &c.,

WILLIAM HOWITT.

XXXVIII.

SIR,—The question which naturally suggests itself to the mind—on mature reflection—after having witnessed, heard, and felt the spiritual manifestation, is this—Was there even the remotest chance of having been deceived? I have critically and severely examined the subject in this point of view; and, to make assurance doubly sure, have attended since, on no less than four occasions, at different houses, and under circumstances which would render it inconceivably more difficult to explain away, by any supposed deception, than to admit the truth, with all its apparent incongruities.

It has been naïvely remarked that I was the victim of my own discovery—"induced mental hallucination." I must, therefore, in justice to myself, state that my conviction has not been a sudden one, for it is now over eight years since I first saw the first table-turning in San Francisco, California, by Dr. Young of that city. I attributed the "tapping" of the table to involuntary muscular action, and the supposed conversation I had with the spirit of Dr. Franklin I explained as the reflex of the operator's mind. Though I witnessed this on several occasions, it made no serious impression, and was soon dismissed from my thoughts.

Being in New York, in 1853, several gentlemen at the hotel and myself called at the house of a medium—Mrs. Cohen—who received us without any formality, when we all were desired to take our seats round a large table. On this occasion no attempt was made to produce any physical manifestations. We heard a very small tapping, as if proceeding from the under surface of the table—very much like that produced by striking with the end of a pencil-case. Each one took his turn to have communion with some supposed departed friend. My turn came about the fourth, when I mentally desired that a friend of mine, who had died in Sacramento, California, in 1852, should appear. The alphabet being on the table, I was desired to point to each letter, when his name was correctly spelled. I then said, " Dr. Yearly, what did you give me in California?" The word " pillow" was given, also the word " pipe." This was correct; all present declared that the responses were equally so in each individual case. I was impressed with the coincidence, but ascribed the phenomena as a wonderful example of " thought reading."

My friend Mr. Coleman met me in the city of London some four or five years since, and narrated some of his experiences in spiritual manifestations. I smiled at his credulity; all he said appeared to me as simply preposterous — though I had the most implicit confidence in his integrity, and that he would be the last man to relate that which he did not believe to be true.

I have written and lectured on the modes of producing the feats of the Egyptian magicians, the fakirs of India, and know how most of the wonderful tricks are performed by noted conjurers; therefore, allow me to state that no man is less liable to be imposed upon than myself.

I remember, some two years since, seeing in Paris an automatic exhibition of an extraordinary character. One figure, that of a child, was made to raise itself up in the cradle, move its eyes and arms, and open its mouth and cry, "Mama, mama." There was a duck which plunged its head into the water, swam about and opened its bill, and made the sound of "quack, quack." So with a sheep. Had any of these figures been placed in their natural accustomed localities without any intimation that they were mechanical contrivances, no ordinary superficial observer but would have declared he had seen a real child, a living duck, or a sheep—they were really fine imitations—but this does not follow that there are no children, no ducks, or sheep. Yet this line of argument is attempted to be used, that because some adroit acts of legerdemain evade ordinary detection these spiritual manifestations are deceptions. The real diamond exists, though imitations are so fine that it requires a close examination to distinguish the true from the false. A forgery or imitation pre-supposes a real genuine coin.

Since my last communication, I have witnessed these manifestations over and over again, under such circumstances that trickery would have been impossible—that is, supposing the phenomena explainable on any such grounds. I have myself held with one hand an accordion by the valve end, my feet against those of the medium—her hands and my other hand on the table—the keys of the instrument being downwards. I cannot perform in the least on any musical instrument, but the most beautiful plaintive air was played that I ever heard in my life—the notes brought forth were of the most silvery, attenuated character, then the deep bass, executed in a style rarely if ever excelled! I felt the pulling and pushing up of the instrument as distinctly as I know of any other fact; besides, it was done in the presence of some dozen persons, in the house of a clergyman of the Church of England, and this was the first time that any such things had been done there. As to preparation or contrivance, this was entirely out of the question, for I had pre-arranged some of the experiments, if I may use that word, prior to my arrival, unknown to any one save myself.

A curious and quite unexpected circumstance occurred at a meeting on Tuesday evening, at the house of a gentleman in St. James's Street, Piccadilly. The glasses on the sideboard, away from persons several feet, all were struck and jingled together. At the request of persons present, they also responded intelligently to several questions put; besides, very loud knocks on the wall were made, at an elevation of at least nine feet.

A gentleman present asked the spirits to put three shillings into a tumbler, which was placed under the centre of a very large loo table, at least five feet in diameter. After a few minutes we all heard one of the shillings dropped into the glass, then the other, and after four or five minutes, the third. I took the glass from under the table with the three shillings in it; this being replaced, the spirits were requested to shake the tumbler with the money in it, while a gentleman played on the piano; it was done in tune to the music.

> "Can such things be,
> And overcome us like a summer's cloud,
> Without our special wonder?"

The communications, so far as my experience goes, were unexceptional, and worthy of respect. I give two, purporting to be sent to me by the spirit of a beloved relative :—

"All sinners will see the salvation of mankind through the instrumentality of us—the spirits."

Next—"Be calm and collected, and all things will work together for good.—R. M."

As to the cause or philosophy of these manifestations, I have no doubt it will be revealed, when we have collected and observed the facts, under various conditions, as I mentioned in my last letter.

No question but that violent antagonism destroys or disarranges the nervous state essential to success, it being imperatively requisite to produce marked results, and also that the most favourable mental atmosphere must be present.

What would be thought of a person who expected to have the various beautiful phenomena of electricity and electro-magnetism exhibited when the delicate apparatus necessary had been broken by a clownish sceptic, who demanded that these experiments should be performed independent of the conditions? Of course failure would follow : but the professor would not, therefore, be called an impostor. Still, how often has it happened that the absence of some condition has prevented the anticipated phenomena in our colleges and universities?

Impostors, charlatans, necromancers, have existed in all ages of the world, but from that circumstance we do not reject the discoveries of Euclid, Archimedes, Newton, Franklin, Galileo, Harvey, Jenner, though they had to contend against the obtuse disposition which marks the introduction of any discovery.

Had Sir Isaac Newton announced to the world, when he first saw the falling of an apple, that that simple fact was connected with the laws which govern the universe, he might have been asked, "What use are these investigations?"—also, when he announced that the diamond was a combustible substance, because it refracted light—though above a century elapsed before his inductive reasoning was verified by the agency of the hydro-oxygen blowpipe. Every one is aware that nearly half a million was expended in the construction and laying an electric cable across the Atlantic. Messages were exchanged between her Majesty and the President of the United States, though thousands of miles intervened. The conditions of success then existed; but subsequently, from a want of these conditions, no result followed, it became a failure. No one accuses all concerned in this enterprise of being impostors and dupes in consequence of this failure. Had any one only twenty years since announced the possibility of such an achievement, would he not have been denounced as a madman or a fool? Yes; the very notion of conveying ideas in a few moments under the ocean to America, and holding intercourse, is, *a priori*, more absurd than anything that may be said of the spiritual manifestations.

In the meantime, your numerous correspondents require—demand that the development of a new truth to man, should come, like Minerva, from the head of Jupiter, full-grown and armoured with all the perfected conditions, laws, and circumstances for its perfect and uniform manifestations! 'Tis true the great volume of Nature is open to all, but few are vouchsafed to interpret the great truths therein contained.

There is, truly, one undulation only from the sublime to the ridiculous. Those whose writings indicate a preference for the latter course are merely reflecting the impotence of their own powers, which they have no right to impose on the world.

Any man of the very lowest order of brain can torture the most splendid truth of science into a jest to make the unthinking laugh. It is only by constant application and the collection of facts under a great variety of circumstances, that the most favourable conditions to produce the spiritual manifestations will be ascertained. Then, and not till then, will results be produced, before which everything yet attempted will pale by its comparative insignificance. More anon.—Yours truly,

ROBERT H. COLLYER, M.D.

Beta House, 8, Alpha Road, St. John's Wood, October 19.

XXXIX.

SIR,—I am rather amused with the contents of a letter, signed "James Hoppey," in your impression of yesterday.

Certainly if the credibility of spiritualism depended upon such a poor and feeble investigation as that which your correspondent has described, it would have little chance of making converts of sensible people. If I had never seen anything more satisfactory than what was exhibited in Mr. Hoppey's presence, I, for one, would never have become a believer; but as, during a very minute and laborious investigation, now extending over a period of more than six years, I witnessed all, or nearly all, the manifestations narrated in the *Cornhill Magazine* and the *Spiritual Magazine*, I was compelled, in spite of my prejudices and scepticism, to accept spiritualism as a great fact.

I would recommend your correspondents to learn a little modesty and moderation in the expression of their opinions. I did not venture to say in public what I thought of spiritualism until after I had studied the subject practically and patiently for eighteen months. Wretched phenomena, like those described by Mr. Hoppey, came under my notice almost daily. I will make the sceptic a present of them, and also of all the other manifestations that can possibly be explained away. The great and overwhelming phenomena will still remain to demonstrate the truth of spiritualism. These, however, appear only on special occasions, and under conditions which are rarely complete.—I remain, sir, your obedient servant,

NEWTON CROSLAND.

XL.

SIR,—As the above subject is now attracting some attention, the following facts may, perhaps, prove interesting to a few persons.

You are aware that I have long been deeply interested in the Arctic question. Now, the first time that question came strongly before me, was at the end of 1849, while I was in the United States. Owing to other occupations engrossing my mind, I had previously paid but little attention to the subject. But on the return of Sir J. C. Ross's unsuccessful relief expedition, my thoughts reverted to our unfortunate fellow-countrymen and their sad fate. It struck me then, as it has always since done, that there was more in the whole matter than met the public eye, or that men who were not deep thinkers and close observers, could conceive. In my life I had witnessed too many instances of remarkable coincidences, and singular results, to doubt, even had I otherwise been a sceptic, the mysterious working —as we must yet call such working—of divine power. Consequently, I felt, as I have all along felt, that we in this land who profess a faith in what God teaches us in various ways, had, in the matter of the Franklin business, set at naught His teaching, and, in a manner, mocked Him. Instead of the real, the practical, the sincere, we were again at work upon the old system of subservience to the great, the powerful, or the wealthy.

I did not then know anything of Dr. King's admirable plans; but it seemed to me that the relief of the Franklin expedition would become another lesson to us, even as God himself so often says that "not by the great or the mighty" shall many things of a peculiar nature be accomplished.

I need not point out how literally this has been proved in the Arctic business. The simple fact is clear. Had Dr. King's offers been accepted, as they ought, undoubtedly this lost expedition would have been saved, and the country not have had to pay the million of money so uselessly wasted.

But, reverting to myself, I, thinking of the missing ones, almost instantly, as it were, had them all before me, exactly as we now know them to have been. The locality where they could be found; their route thither; and their after-wanderings were so strongly pictured to my eye, that, almost without preparation, I sent a plan of search, based upon geographical science and reasoning, which I felt would save the struggling remnant then existing. That plan is patent to the whole world; and, whatever may be said of it or its author and his ideas, there it is, and here I openly state the fact upon which it was produced. In the Parliamentary Arctic Blue Book for 1850, at the latter end, will be found my letter to Lady Franklin, and any examiner may soon find how correct it was.

But, yet more. In three days after a notice I received to join an expedition in England, I was on my way thither, still deeply impressed with what had so strongly come before my fancy.

In June, 1850, we sailed from Aberdeen for the locality I was so anxious to search. The night prior to our departure, a lady, well-known to public fame, called me to her room, and communicated what to me then appeared even more extraordinary than my own waking dream on the subject. She requested me to put down in my note-book the particulars she gave me. I did so. They are here before me, as written that very night. They can be proved by the note-book still being entire, with consecutive leaves having many memoranda relating to our fitting out.

The purport of those particulars is as follows :—

A person had informed this lady that the lost expedition would be found in a direction south of a passage of water with the initials B. S. (Barrow Straits). One ship had no men in it. Two vessels looking for the Franklin crews were going the wrong way (probably the Enterprise and Investigator, then bound for Behring Straits). Other information could be gathered from the initials E. T. (Erebus and Terror), S. J. F. (Sir John Franklin), N. F. and Victory, G. W. and Victoria, and from an outline of the whole locality which was furnished, and of which I hold a *fac-simile*.

Such was the strange information given to me the night before I sailed. How far it has been singularly verified everyone conversant with Arctic matters can tell. The Erebus and Terror were south of Barrow's Straits, and not north, as most persons strongly believed. They were in Victoria Channel, and at Point Victory a record giving information concerning them had been deposited.

Respecting the other initials, I can give no idea. I but relate the facts as they occurred in 1850, and refer to what we now know in 1860.

But, yet more. In August of the same year in

which we sailed, we were not far from the locality here referred to. Only about 250 miles divided us from the place I had so strongly before my eyes. Unfortunately, it was determined to turn back. I entreated permission to go on with some volunteers who came forward from the crew in a boat. My request was refused, and as I was only second in command, I had to yield. But I saw then, as I have seen ever since, the sad story of the hapless ones in that neighbourhood, where we now know that even at that time, when we were so near, some might have been saved.

In the account of that voyage, which I published on our return, the particulars I have just referred to will be found; and in many parts of the book allusions are made which bear out what I am saying. It was no idle thought which I uttered when, as can be read, I stated that, " I see in fancy some *hundred* or more human beings, stretching out their arms to us, that we might snatch them from their misery." Neither is it a mere whim, or interested feeling alone, that has kept me, and still keeps me, urging for renewed search.

In 1853, a gentleman at Sydney tried an experiment upon me, by what, even now, I do not understand. I was informed that mesmeric influence had been used, and that I had stated some particulars about the Franklin expedition, which I have long ago forgotten, except that the chief himself and some of his officers had died, but several still survived.

The same as to my present feelings on the subject.

No one can accuse me of not going into figures and facts; for, in my late pamphlet on the last Polar expedition, I have given pages of hard, solid, earthly matter, leaving entirely aside the constant "fancy" in my brain. Nevertheless, if I do get up there again, search will be made in certain places which that "fancy" has ever pointed out.

I could give some other singular instances, had I permission to use names and particulars; and I might have referred to the desire I have expressed of remaining for a time amongst the Boothian Esquimaux. This desire not only applies to the last expedition, but to science. The magnetic pole and the magnetic currents are mysteries which, to some minds, cannot be other than deeply attractive.

Very possibly what I here write may serve to do me more harm. But these remarks of mine will explain to many who know me how it is I have so often been misunderstood. A "dreamer," a "visionary," are terms frequently applied to me. But what are dreamers and visionaries? I could name one or two men of note with whom I have been closely acquainted who were greater "dreamers" than ever I could be, and who made their "dreams" and "visions" of benefit to their fellow-men. "A dreamer," a "visionary!" Bah! The noblest intellects in the universe require to "dream"—to have "visions"—to sleep and be abstracted from the world in which they live, ere they can see any of those brilliant truths, or imbibe those god-like beauties of the mind for which their names afterwards become noted.

No; a man is not a dreamer or a visionary, in the bad construction of the term, who, by practical tests, brings his "dreams" and "visions" to some real and tangible good. But it is he who by dreams and visions of a disordered fancy, or of a base mind, starts ideas as facts, without daring to apply those tests of science and experience which God has given us to gradually learn and know His partly-hidden mysteries! Thus, then, let no one despise or slightingly reject the strange things that are occasionally unfolded to us. We may not always know the why or the wherefore, but he who observantly traverses the broad earth—afar off or near—will often see many things far beyond his present comprehension, and seeing them, he cannot help exclaiming with one of old—" Marvellous are thy works, O Lord, and that my soul knoweth right well."

I am, sir, your obedient servant,
W. Parker Snow.
Home Cottage, St. John's Hill,
near Wandsworth, Oct. 17.

XLI.

Sir,—As Mr. Howitt, in his letter on "Spiritualism" in your impression of to-day, has thought fit to go out of his way to speak ill of the Jews, perhaps you will allow me, as one of them, to say a few words in return through the same "medium."

He says, "There is nothing more notorious than that the Jews, ever given to idolatry and necromancy, were forbidden this intercourse."

Now, infinite wisdom having made so great a mistake as to choose for a "nation of priests" such a wicked lot, I hope I may not be thought presumptuous in suggesting that Mr. Howitt himself may have made a slight error.

If he will be so good as to turn to Deuteronomy, xviii., 9—14, he will find, that instead of the Jews being specially perverse in this direction, they were cautioned against following in the wake of the other nations, who were addicted to this, perhaps worst of all abominations, and were told that in consequence of their doing so they were driven out from before us, and dispossessed of their land.

Mr. Howitt argues as if it were wrong for Jews, and Jews only, to communicate with familiar spirits, but if so, why did God punish the other nations for doing so?

As regards such absurdities as that spirits that pinch your legs under the table are not familiar spirits, and that those are "angels," who they admit tell lies, all I can say is, such is not the Jewish idea of what angels are, and if I am not very much mistaken, it is not the Christian one either.

He then says the founder of your faith abrogated this law against spiritualism; now, although this is no business of mine, it is such a "flimsy sophism" that I am tempted to tear it to shreds; for if Mr. Howitt believes him to be, as he says, the prince of spirits, surely the fact of his conversing with spirits would constitute no argument in favour of his doing the same.

In conclusion, allow me to express my surprise and regret that he considers being face to face with Satan a substantial gain; that he entertains the idea of converting the fountain of evil into the fountain of faith; and allow me to tell him, that notwithstanding we are so prone to abominations, our comfort is not in the Devil, neither do we require a proof of his existence to convince us of the existence of God. —I am, sir, one who is proud to subscribe himself,

Oct. 20.   An Israelite.

XLII.

Sir,—I find by Mr. Howitt's letter, in your number of October 20, that he possesses "a little table" of extraordinary virtue, in which spirits reside, or which serves as a terminus to some Jacob's ladder, passing through Mr. Howitt's roof or walls, by a "discontinuous" opening, analogous to the wounds inflicted on heathen gods by Homeric heroes, or Satan when the "griding sword with discontinuous wound passed through him."

With this "little table"—*modus operandi* not mentioned—a physician obtained a "spiritual telegram" concerning the death of a child one hundred miles off.

I in no way impugn Mr. Howitt's fact, but take it for granted—in argument.

But as to the *cui bono*. If spirituality be a miracle, why use a miracle to demonstrate by "spiritual telegraph" what could have been ascertained by material telegraph with little more expenditure of time? Surely if this thing be holy, it is applying holy things to the mere uses of a post-office.

But there is a purpose to which this "little table" might be most usefully and lawfully applied. A child died at Road under a murderer's hands. No earthly means have been found availing to discover this murderer, and the thoughts of a whole nation are turned to the discovery.

Here, then, is an employment for Mr. Howitt's "little table," of a most legitimate kind, doing two important things—first, delivering up to justice a cruel murderer; and, secondly, establishing beyond doubt, to the satisfaction of all men, the truth and utility of the modern society of spiritualists.

I have no prejudice either as to belief or disbelief. But belief must come in one of two ways, either by instructive perception or by logical evidence. If my mind be obtuse, and there be no link between it and the spirits of Mr. Howitt's table, it is clear that I must remain in a state of darkness. If the "little table" discovers the Road murderer, it ought henceforth to be regarded as an ark of the spirits, and not remain the private property of Mr. Howitt. Like Miss Rosa Dartle, I merely ask for information, and remain, sir, yours faithfully,

W. BRIDGES ADAMS.

Hampstead, Oct. 22.

[We have received such a flood of correspondence on this subject, that, in sheer self-defence, we are compelled to close the discussion. This letter is inserted because it gives expression to a suggestion which has been made to us by a score at least of our correspondents.—ED. *Star and Dial.*]

LETTER OF CHARLES BRAY, ESQ.

FROM THE "BRITISH CONTROVERSIALIST," AUG. 1861.

Considering the testimony now in favour of what has been called spiritualism, I think the subject deserves serious consideration. To treat it philosophically, it will be desirable to examine briefly the grounds of our knowledge, and our means of knowing. It will be necessary also to know, what is the natural condition of the mind, as distinguished from the preter-natural and super-natural. Unless we know this we cannot correctly draw the line between the subjective and the objective—between what has its source entirely within ourselves, and what we think has an external reality.

First, then, it is certain that we have no faculties that give us any knowledge of things in themselves, that is, of their nature or essence; we can know nothing but phenomena, their co-existences and successions. As Lord Bacon said, it is with "the order of nature" only that we have to do. The world is governed by "forces," but forces of which we really know nothing; we only hide our ignorance under the high-sounding names of attraction, repulsion, chemical, electrical, vital, &c. Thus, when we say a thing takes place by the force of attraction, we think we have explained it, but we have merely named a certain group of phenomena occurring in a certain order. We know nothing of attraction in itself, it is only known to us in its effects: no scrutiny enables us to lift the veil and look beyond. This is very generally admitted as applied to what are called physical forces, but less so as applied to mind; but mind is only known to us by what it does—that is, by its manifestations,—and we define it by the appearances it puts forth. Mind is only known to us in the cerebral causes of mental states, and in the effect as shown in bodily conditions; *disembodied* spirit, or mind unconnected with, organization, is without the range of our experience: we have no means of knowing, then, whether such a thing exists or not.

An ordinary observer believes in an external world because he says he feels it, he sees it; but what does he see? A minute, inverted image, lies, unknown to consciousness, on the back of the eye; this, through the nerves, produces an action on the brain, giving ideas, vivid in proportion as certain parts of the brain are large and perfect. Thus a seen *reality* turns out to be a mere conception of the mind. The objects of knowledge, therefore, are ideas; not things as is commonly supposed. Ideas are not purely subjective or formed within ourselves. Something without ourselves, which we call matter, or the object, but of the nature or essence of which we know nothing, acts upon the sense, and the sense upon the intellectual faculty, through the medium of the brain. Ideas are thus compounded equally of the object, the sense, and the intellect; and we cannot resolve an idea so compounded into its elements, for it has been well observed, "It is God's synthesis, and man cannot undo it." All arguments, therefore, based upon the essential difference between mind and matter, must fall to the ground; and when we speak of one as temporary and perishable, and the other as necessarily imperishable and immortal, we speak of that of which we know nothing.

The distinctions that we make between organic and inorganic, between that which feels and that which does not feel, between matter and mind, are very necessary and convenient for using the knowledge we really possess, provided we go no further. Then of matter I would remind the reader that Sir John Herschel tells us, that among all the *possible combinations* of the fifty or sixty elements which chemistry points to as existing on this earth, it is likely, nay, almost certain, that *some* have never been formed; that some elements, in some proportions, and under some circumstances, have never yet been placed in relation with each other: also, there is nothing, however solid, which is not capable of taking the invisible, imponderable, gaseous, or aëriform shape. It becomes us, therefore, to be very modest in defining the exact provinces of what we call matter, and we are certainly not in a position to dogmatize about "spiritual" manifestations. With respect to mind, the science may also be said to be in its infancy. We scarcely know what belongs to its normal state, and we have glimpses only of its abnormal conditions. It is with the consideration of the abnormal states of mind, however, that we have principally to do, to enable us to form a probable estimate of how much is merely subjective in the phenomena of spirit-rapping. Mesmerism certainly must be reckoned among the preternatural states of mind. After long discussion on the subject, most physiologists are now prepared to admit as much as Dr. Carpenter, viz., 1st. A state of complete insensibility, during which severe surgical operations may be performed without the consciousness of the patient. 2nd. Artificial somnambulism, with manifestation of the ordinary power of mind, but with no recollection, in the waking state, of what has passed. 3rd. Exaltation of the senses during such somnambulism, so that the somnambule perceives what in his natural condition he could not. 4th. Action during such somnambulism on the muscular apparatus, so as to produce, for example, artificial catalepsy: and 5th. Curative effects. Dr. Carpenter, however, has not yet seen sufficient evidence for belief in the higher phenomena of clairvoyance.

The power of reading the thoughts of others seems to be amongst the best attested of these phenomena. The nervous system is, however, believed by many to be, as the Germans express it, an identity and a totality, by which we become all-knowing and intelligent as far as regards all that has yet been known by mankind. The well-attested case of Davis, the American Ploughkeepsie Seer, is supposed to illustrate this. (See his Works.)

The automatic powers of the mind, as described by Hartley, and as illustrated by Faraday in table-turning, are normal powers, although unobserved by the majority.

Under the influence of somnambulism, of sleep-waking or sleep-walking, people are said to read and write with their eyes shut, and in the dark, and to do other wonderful things. This is accounted for on the supposition that one sense, under particular circumstances, may be so excited, and become so exalted, as to supply the place of another. Thus Dr. Carpenter, speaking of what Mr. Braid calls hypnotism, says:—"The exaltation of the muscular sense, by which various actions, that ordinarily require the guidance of vision, are directed independently of it, is a phenomenon common to the mesmeric, with various other forms of artificial as well as natural somnambulism."

He has repeatedly seen, he says, Mr. Braid's hypnotized subjects write with the most perfect regularity, when an opaque screen was interposed between their eyes and the paper, the lines being equidistant and parallel; and it is not uncommon for the writer to carry back his pencil or pen to dot an *i*, or to cross a *t*, or make some other correction in a letter or word. Mr. B. had one patient, who would thus go back and correct with accuracy the writing on the whole sheet of note paper; but if the paper was moved from the position it had previously occupied on the table, all the corrections were on the *wrong* points of the paper as regards the *actual* place of the writing, though on the *right* points as regarded its previous place. Sometimes, however, he would take a fresh departure, by feeling for the upper left-hand corner of the paper; and all his corrections were then made in their proper positions, notwithstanding the displacement of the paper.

The phenomena classed under the head of electro-biology, by which the will of one person appears to become completely under the control of another, are very wonderful.

The powers of sympathy are also much greater than are usually supposed. "True sympathy," says Mr. Combe, "arises from the natural language of any active feeling exciting the same feeling in another, *antecedently to any knowledge of what excited it in the person principally concerned;* and this is sufficient to account for the origin of panics in battles and in mobs, and for the electric rapidity with which passions of every kind pervade and agitate the minds of assembled multitudes."

Again, the mind is connected with the brain as intimately as each sense with its organ; and if the sense when exalted displays abnormal phenomena, not less so do the organs of the brain when either very large or unduly excited. Thus I have known an idiotic boy calculate the number of pounds in a million farthings much quicker than another on a slate, and we are most of us familiar with the extraordinary power of some other people in this respect. What the powers of the other organs are under excitement, or when of similarly unusual size, is not yet correctly known, but no doubt they are equally wonderful; the organ of locality, for instance, in dogs and cats, who find their way home over hundreds of miles of strange country! There is nothing more wonderful among the supposed powers of clairvoyants than those exercised by the carrier pigeon. No doubt these are the result of organization—of a peculiar modification of the organ of locality, it is said; and it is possible, at least, if not probable, that some men may possess rudimentary organs, sufficiently large, when exalted by mesmerism or otherwise, to give all the powers that are said—we must admit, on good authority—to pertain to clairvoyants. But of course this at present is mere hypothesis. Now, it becomes us to be very modest in speaking of what such men as Robert Chambers are said to have investigated and to believe; but in taking into consideration the question before us, as to the genuineness of the so-called spiritual manifestations, the abnormal conditions of mind I have mentioned must not be lost sight of. In fact, the subject can only be fully and properly investigated by those who are familiar with it, and the principal object of my communication is to point this out. I have little light to throw upon the extraordinary "spiritual" phenomena said to have been observed by others; what I have seen myself is certainly principally on the negative side.

The prevalence of the belief is undoubtedly evidence of *something* to believe in; but what? The faith has about kept pace with that in Joe Smith and Mormonism.

The believers *affirm* the existence of a "spirit world:" now there is no *natural* evidence for the existence of mind unconnected with organization.

The Hindoos and Greeks—the Pythagoreans at least, believed in the transmigration of souls; that is, that, according to our deserts, our souls are consigned to the bodies of animals, more or less high in the order of creation; but no such low place was assigned to any poor soul as that to which modern spiritualists put their progenitors. We are very naturally, therefore, opposed to the belief that the spirits of our ancestors, and of the great and good of the earth, can have been so lamentably degraded. But even supposing all to have taken place as related by spiritualists, it is far from proving the assumptions based upon it, and a belief in the phenomena is a very different thing to believing in the supposititious cause. For instance, as the spirits more often tell lies than the truth, what evidence is there that they are spirits at all, much less the respected spirits of our ancestors? In this case, we must at least bring in a verdict of "Not Proven." Knowing what *we* may suppose to be known only by our ancestors, is not sufficient proof, considering that it is impossible for us to ascertain how they came by their knowledge. Again, as to the reality of the phenomena, the question *will* force itself upon us, why do such things only take place before certain people, and under circumstances favourable to deception? If the spirits can carry Mr. Home about, and show their hands, and play accordions, and their object is to convert the scoffer and the sceptic, why do they not do it in open daylight, before all the world?

Few are sufficiently aware of the power of sympathy, to make us feel as others do, and believe we see what they do. Although I am, from cultivation, "hard of belief," this feeling of sympathy has, on one or two occasions, been almost overpowering in my own case. There is a natural dread of spirits, and their supposed presence in a dimly-lighted room puts us into a state to be easily imposed on; and this feeling is very much increased by the position in which people ordinarily place themselves, which is favourable for the transmission of sympathy, as described by Combe. My experience with Mrs. Marshall and niece seems very much to accord with that related by Mr. Novra in your last number,* and was then given at the time in the *Coventry Herald*. When I arrived at Mrs. Marshall's, there were about a dozen people in the room, in some confusion, the spirits being contumacious and refusing to act, ex-

* British Controversialist, July, 1861.

cept in requesting two sceptical gentlemen to leave the room, who, when I arrived, were standing outside the door. It was now determined to divide the parties, there being too many for scientific observation, and the six to whom I belonged, stayed; the others were to come another night. We were then three ladies, three gentlemen, and the two mediums, who also were ladies—Mrs. M. and niece. The party all sat round a small, very light, round table, the mediums together. I wished to remain out of the circle for better observation, but was not allowed. I therefore pushed in next, and very close to the aunt medium. I placed only one leg under the table, the other partly across the front of her chair, so that I could feel what she was doing with her legs. The spirits were almost immediately asked what we were to do with our legs—were we to put them out under the table? The reply was, Yes. One tap meaning no, three yes. I refused, however, to comply, and my leg received a tremendous wrench; by whom or how given I cannot say. I still kept it where it was, however, and there were several gentle twitches at my trousers, as if by two feet trying to pull it out. When we sat down, the table always turned— as it seemed to me, by the pushing of the elder medium's hands—till one of its three legs got opposite the leg of the younger medium, when it tipped and performed other tricks. The table also raised itself under our hands, and was supported, or supported itself, for at least half a minute. It was suggested then that we should all stand up, which we did, and the table floated away at least half a yard from the mediums, and went down easily, and not as if any support had been suddenly withdrawn from it. I have not the least idea how this was done. The table also danced to tunes played by the elder medium's son! but this appeared to me to be done by the niece's foot. In both cases, when I put my hands upon the table, and bore downward, it came to an immediate stand, and refused to rise or dance any more.

We then went to prophesying, and my Christian name was asked, the spirit replying by aid of the alphabet. Alfred was rapped out; but this, like every other answer through the same means, was wrong. I then asked who it was pulling at my leg under the table. The answer was, "Me," meaning the spirit; I then asked if the spirit would shake hands with me under the table. The answer was three taps, that is, yes. I put my hand under with some fear and trembling, thinking that, as the spirit had made so free with my leg, it might also take my hand, and mentally resolved to hold him fast, and learn, if possible, the difference between matter and spirit. But the hand of the spirit refused to clasp mine. Another gentleman made the same request, with the same result. By the aid of an apparatus and the younger medium's hand, the spirit also wrote some sentences: I forget what they were, but they were the merest truisms, having no possible relation to anybody or anything present. The spirit refused to write with any but the medium's hand.

Nothing satisfactory in any way was elicited. The elder medium tried to soften the spirits into better behaviour,—" Will the de-ar spirits tell this or do that?" &c.; but they remained decidedly contumacious. There was no lack, however, of marvellous tales of what they had done on previous occasions, at one of which, one of the ladies of our party had been present. For instance, she affirmed that she had written on a bit of paper asking the spirit to raise the table and put out the light, standing on another table with it, and it had done so.

By this time the respect and awe which we all naturally feel in the presence of spirits, had somewhat abated, at least, with the men, and we ventured upon one or two irreverent jokes. I observed the eye of the younger medium upon us, all the evening, watching the extent of our faith or credulity; and "good night" was now rapped out, and we heard the spirit depart, the rapping gradually becoming fainter and fainter, after which no response was vouchsafed to us, and we were told the *séance* was at an end, and it was hoped we might be more fortunate another time.

I must say that, notwithstanding the respectable people with whom the spirits, or rappings, or tables may be said to have held communion, what I saw appeared to me to be a barefaced and ignorant imposture. But I never was fortunate in seeing marvels.

The rising of the table was the only thing that seemed to me unaccountable, for it floated away from the mediums, and I thought I could see distinctly under it. But what are we to believe? that is the question. Spirits are said to have appeared before, almost from the beginning of time, in the shape of ghosts; but these took a personal form. It is true that, for decency's sake, the ghosts of their clothes always appeared along with them. But the cause of these apparitions is no longer a mystery to the cerebral physiologist, and arises from the involuntary excitement of the intellectual organs, of which numberless illustrations are to be found in the *Phrenological Journal.* The kind of appearance varies according to the number of organs brought into activity: diseased action, for instance, of Form and Size, producing, as described by a patient, ' whitish ' or grey, and transparent, cobwebby objects. A ghost club, however, formed in Cambridge, in 1851, believed in the objective reality of ghosts. I must confess that my difficulty lies in the testimony,—in the long list of respectable believers; not in the three million, or in Judge Edmonds, of America, whose whole list of deductions are the purest assumptions: but one such name as Robert Chambers has more weight than all these put together. If it were not for a few such names as his, I should find no difficulty in knowing what to believe, and I should say sympathy and humbug accounted for it all. But what have Messrs. Chambers, Hall, Howitt, Bell, &c. seen, that we have not? Surely they must have seen something more than the very questionable exhibition described by " spiritualists" generally. May not the abnormal states of mind we have described have been more or less mixed with their experiences, and they have mistaken the preternatural for the supernatural? Have mesmerism, clairvoyance, thought-reading, and other *possible* conditions of mind been mixed with their evidences, and enabled them to swallow the immense amount of unrealities that other investigators have felt and observed? I have seen nothing and heard nothing as yet to induce me to believe the "manifestations" either "spiritual" or altogether "genuine;" or that will enable me to suppose for a moment that we have been put in communication with the inhabitants of any other "spiritual world" than our own. Will T. P. B., or any one else, kindly take me in hand? I will go a great way to see credible evidence, and although I admit I am a little prejudiced in favour of the result of twenty-five years' investigations, I think I have a mind clearly open to the truth, which I put in importance above all earthly things. CHARLES BRAY.

ELUCIDATION OF CLAIRVOYANCE.

As a fitting commentary upon this series, and to show the extent to which clairvoyance may be assumed to account for the alleged communion with the spirits of the departed, I append the following: —"A *true clairvoyant* may be defined to be one who, by the opening of the *internal consciousness*, or spiritual sight, whether induced by any operation, or occurring spontaneously, has, while in that state of inner consciousness, and according to the degree of its development, a *sensational perception* of the objects of the inner, or spirit-world. Where this development does not exist, the state is simply that of natural clairvoyance, or cerebral lucidity. Some subjects appear to possess the faculty of spiritual clairvoyance; others, that of lucidity; while some few individuals have exhibited both faculties. If the attention of a true clairvoyant is directed to any distant individual, and the *rapport*, or connection between them, made stronger by using the hair or writing of the individual sought, or something else dentified in some measure with his mind or body, *as the connecting medium*, there are two ways in which the parties may become mentally present with each other. Firstly, the clairvoyant comes by the *rapport* with the man, into connection with the associated spirit; and then, from the reflection of memory, and from what may be called the *living phantasmagoria* of the spirit-world, the man and his affairs, and perceptions, and recollections, are laid open to the clairvoyant's inner vision. And as, from the proximity of the spirit-world to the mind, the associated spirit will be equally near, whether the man be in the next street, or in another hemisphere, the distance of the object sought will make no difference to clairvoyant inquiry. Secondly, as man, even in this mortal life, is internally a true spiritual organism, and *as such*, is, as we have observed, a subject of the laws of the spirit-world, the spirits of all men, as denizens of the spirit-world, may be equally near to each other, *according to their respective states*, no matter how far apart their natural bodies may be; and the clairvoyant in whom the proper state is induced, may come into *sensational* correspondence with the spirit of the man, and thence with his natural organism and memory, wherever he may bodily be present; yet, still, it is probable that the direct connection is *mediately* effected by the associated spirits. Which of these two modes of connection is the more common one, appears to the writer, after much experience, difficult to determine. So complete a counterpart of the man, and the scenery by which he is surrounded, appears to be afforded by the associated spirits, and the surrounding objective appearances, that the clairvoyant, having no means of comparison, owing to the closure of the external sensorium, may mistake the associated spirit for, and take it to be, the real man. But the general vividness of the perception, and the constant and frequently unexpected description of *natural objects*, rather inclines the writer to conclude, that the connection *is direct*, and that the *whole man*, both as to spirit and body, is thus brought before the inner vision. But the admission of these psychological causes does not preclude the possibility of there being some subtile, material, elementary connection, between the nervous system of the clairvoyants and that of the distant individual; something *analogous*, probably, to the odylic force of Reichenbach: and this connection may be induced by the action of the mind of the clairvoyant on the mind of the distant party, by which, as from an electric battery, a current may be set in motion, analogous to the currents passing along the telegraphic wires; but having this essential difference, that there is only a sensational perception at one end of the communication. This, then, appears to be the simple, rational, yet deeply interesting solution of the psychological cause of the certain facts of distant clairvoyance. There remains to be considered the psychology of what is called CEREBRAL LUCIDITY; that is, the power of distinguishing natural objects by an interior perception, independent of the usual visual organs, and even where opaque substances intervene. *How* the impression of outward objects is conveyed to the sensorium, is one of the most difficult problems connected with our inquiry: the fact that such is the

o

case, cannot be doubted by any one who has had sufficient opportunity carefully to examine the subject. The difficulty arises from the clairvoyant being unable to analyse the mode of vision, and point out its mode of operation, and the impossibility of an individual in the normal state, *sensationally* realizing the feelings or perceptions of a clairvoyant.

"One of the revealments of the higher stages of clairvoyance, or independent internal sight, is the knowledge, that an effluvium or atmosphere surrounds the mental organism, or spiritual body of every individual. Following the general law of nature, this sphere possesses the peculiar qualities of the organism from which it emanates. And hence arises the *repugnance* which is felt to the society of some persons, and the pleasure which is experienced in the company of others, and to it are referable all the remarkable instances of SYMPATHY and ANTIPATHY, so frequently observed. In these ordinary cases, the active cause is latent or hidden; but in the higher mesmeric, or rather psychic state, it often becomes sufficiently obvious, even to our physical senses: for we may here see, that similar to terrestrial magnetism, there is an actual blending of spheres. The magnet induces its quality or state on the iron, so that it becomes magnetical; and the operator induces his sphere on his patient or subject, so that the subject becomes, as it were, *one body* with himself,—the *egoism* or self-consciousness of the one, being blended with the *egoism* or self-consciousness of the other.

"Here then is the *psychological* cause for the *physiological* condition of the subject. The change of state induced on the animus of the subject, whether by the manifestations of an operator, or spontaneously, is the *primary cause* of the change in the condition of the cerebrum; the collapse of the cerebrum closes the external consciousness, while the union of the spheres emanating from the animus of both operator and subject, causes the latter to perceive, as in himself, what really is felt in the active cerebrum of the former. And this change of state affords, I believe, the true psychological solution of the whole apparent mystery of Phantasy, and many other curious mesmeric, otherwise spiritual phenomena. As regards phreno-mesmerism, the arousing into activity one particular organ of the brain, without the guidance, control, or balancing powers of the other organs or faculties, is a sufficient reason for the incongruous effects we see displayed."*

Although this article favours spiritualism, I give it for what it is worth; believing, at the same time, that it goes to show how large a portion of the foregoing phenomena, termed spiritual manifestations, are due to clairvoyance in connection with animal magnetism or mesmerism.

* "Somnolism and Psycheism," by J.W. Haddock, M.D.

LETTERS ON SPIRITUALISM.

SECOND SERIES.

SECOND SERIES.

MODERN SPIRITUALISM.

"The Spiritual Magazine." No. 20. August.

THE periodical which is now before us is the organ of a decidedly unpopular cause. "Spiritual Manifestations," as they are termed, are regarded by the majority with incredulity; by some they are denounced as the fruits of deliberate imposture. On the other hand, a very large body of believers, not only allege that they constantly occur under given conditions, but also hold that they are to be ascribed to the operation of a purely spiritual agency. In the investigation of the subject, these two points may be conveniently kept apart. The genuineness of the phenomena must be established before any necessity can arise for endeavouring to assign to them a cause. We are quite aware that there are many who will treat with contempt the suggestion that the matter is worthy of serious inquiry. The human mind has an unhappy tendency to ridicule all that it cannot comprehend. The egotism which sets up its own finite comprehension as the test of possibility, rejects with scorn everything alien to its experience or antagonistic to its pre-conceived ideas. It can scarcely be necessary to urge that such a mode of dealing with alleged facts is not only grossly unphilosophical, but would, if generally adopted, prove a positive barrier to the elucidation of important truths. As the world has grown in age, new wonders have been constantly crowding into view—so marvellous as to excite incredulity on their first discovery, but now become so familiar through habit as to awaken no surprise. Candid and impartial research can alone distinguish realities from illusions, and discriminate between genuine phenomena and the effects of fraud. Of course, a marvel apparently irreconcileable with known natural laws, and vouched for only by a single individual, is not to be held entitled to such serious treatment. But when a very large number of independent and respectable witnesses testify that they have repeatedly seen phenomena wonderful in their character, identical in their nature, and occurring always under certain fixed conditions, it is obviously our duty to sift their evidence, in order that we may either crush an imposture, dispel a delusion, or establish a new and possibly most important truth.

This is the position which the controversy with

regard to spiritualism has unquestionably assumed. In England and in America, thousands of men and women, esteemed for their piety, their intellectual ability, and their social worth, aver that they have been eye-witnesses, not once but repeatedly, of very strange manifestations, which can scarcely be accounted for by the operation of any known natural agency. They tell us that they have seen heavy tables lifted up a foot or more from the ground and held for some moments suspended in the air; men raised from their chairs and floated across the ceiling of the apartment; accordions and guitars, held in the hand, played upon by unseen fingers; bells carried about a room and rung at intervals by an invisible power, and passed from hand to hand of the quiescent circle; intelligible sentences written upon slates and slips of paper placed beyond the reach of any present; luminous hands appearing in the air, lifting articles from the floor and placing them upon the table; and a host of other marvels, to all appearance equally beyond the grasp of ordinary credulity. These things are said to have been witnessed, not by one individual at a time, but by a dozen or more, all of whom aver that they saw the same things at the same moment. They are alleged to have taken place, rarely in the dark, occasionally in semi-obscurity, but in the greater number of instances in fully lighted rooms. Other phases of the manifestations are reported of a different but equally striking character. The present number of the *Spiritual Magazine* contains the second of a very interesting series of papers on "Spiritualism in America," by Mr. Benjamin Coleman, which embodies some eminently curious details. In the United States the belief in spiritualism has taken root very deeply—its adherents are numbered by hundreds of thousands, and a large number of periodicals exist devoted specially to its advocacy. If the statements of Mr. Coleman are to be believed —and he is a gentleman whose word would be unhesitatingly taken on any ordinary matter—the phenomena are there developed even more remarkably than elsewhere. He tells us, for example, of a drawing medium, who has the power of sketching perfect portraits of deceased persons whom he never saw, and with regard to whose personal appearance he had no means of forming any idea. He relates his visit to another medium, to whom he was personally unknown, who, in answer to his mental question, wrote a communication to him from his step-son, sometime deceased, signing it with the young man's full name, and adding his own residence in London; and he states that he listened to some speaking mediums, persons in their ordinary state wholly illiterate, who, under what was asserted to be spiritual influence, spoke in public, for more than an hour at a time, with very remarkable eloquence and intellectual power. He recounts an instance, which he declares was certified to him on excellent authority, in which a communication was received through a medium, leading to the discovery of a lost document essential to the success of an important lawsuit; and he recites an example of an opinion obtained by the same means, which brought to light a new point, and put a stop to a harassing litigation. But setting aside all that he gives on the authority of others, his narrative of his own personal experience is strange enough to satiate the most ravenous appetite for the marvellous. At one *séance*, for example, at Boston, he states that a guitar was carried rapidly about the room above the heads of those present, a melody being accurately played upon it as it moved through the air—that bells were similarly floated about, ringing all the while—that the medium, in her arm-chair, was lifted on to the centre of the table, from which position he himself removed her—that his own name was pronounced in a loud voice through a horn—and that, when he complained of the heat of the room, a fan was taken from a drawer and waved before him, and a tumbler of water was raised and placed to his lips.

All this is no doubt passing strange, and those who have never with their own eyes seen anything of the sort may be well excused for shaking their heads in doubt. It is true that the striking singularity of some of the phenomena reported induces us sometimes to forget, that if we concede the possibility of one of them, we may without much difficulty admit that of all. Grant that a power exists which can raise a heavy table from the ground and hold it suspended in the air, it is clear that the same agency may just as easily lift a man from his chair, carry a bell, wave a fan, or play upon a guitar. The simple rapping upon the table, if not fraudulently produced, is intrinsically, though not apparently, quite as marvellous as any of the most elaborate manifestations. But these physical effects are by far the least interesting of those which the spiritualists allege to be of every-day occurrence in their circles. They complain, indeed, that the use of the phrases " Spirit-rapping" and " table-turning" has tended to give the general public a very low and inadequate idea of the scope and object of this class of phenomena. According to their doctrine, these strange freaks, which are played with material objects, are designed solely to arrest attention, and to convince the sceptical that unseen agencies are present, capable of holding communion with mortals; and this end having been attained, the real purpose of that which they regard as a beneficent dispensation acquires its needful scope and comes into full play. This purpose they hold to be the communication from departed beings to their surviving relatives of messages of solace, of warning, of encouragement, and of counsel,—conveyed occasionally by audible voices, but much more frequently in an alphabetic form. They appear to believe—and we are of course merely stating their theory, without expressing any opinion as to its claims to adoption —that the ultimate end of these " spiritual manifestations" is the advancement towards moral and religious perfection of the living through the loving ministrations of the dead—the proximate end being the counteraction of materialistic tendencies by the exhibition of cogent proofs of the reality of spiritual existence. Mr. Coleman's paper contains a few of the messages thus sent, and a host of examples of them are found cited in other publications. It is only fair to say that they are uniformly admirable in tone, and pervaded by genuine piety and sound morality. The literary merit of certain communications which have been dictated in the United States, purporting to come from eminent intellectual celebrities of past times, is certainly infinitesimal. But it is nevertheless true that credible witnesses assert that these were spelt out in their presence, as they stand, by raps given at the various letters as the alphabet was called over, and their evidence to this is the only point with which, in the present stage of the inquiry, we have to deal.

If the extraordinary narratives, of which we have thus summarised a few of the most salient points, were vouched for only by men utterly unknown, or of dubious credulity, they might scarcely be deemed worthy of serious attention. Even then we could scarcely avoid the reflection that the idea which constitutes the postulate of the spiritualists, so far from being novel, has had adherents in every age and every nation. The belief in the possibility of intercourse between spirits and mortals has found a place in almost every religious creed ever held by man, and pagan traditions and biblical records alike bear witness to supernatural communion. Nor can we entirely exclude the thought that these phenomena, if sufficiently attested to be accepted as real, would cast much light on many incidents in past secular history which stand greatly in need of some rational elucidation, in place of the wholesale rejection of a mass of evidence which has hitherto been our desperate expedient. But are they so attested? That is the first point to be settled. The principal witnesses are literary men of note, merchants, lawyers, physicians, and divines; ministers of divers sects, men and women of unblemished repute, artists, poets, and statesmen. Of minor witnesses the name is legion, but we have no personal knowledge of their claims to our belief. This much we know, that in America and in our own country there are many whose sanity no one doubts, whose general veracity no one would impeach, who aver that they have seen these strange things with their own eyes. It remains for us to say whether we will take their word.

If we stamp all those who declare that they have witnessed these so-called "Spiritual Manifestations" as liars, of course the inquiry will be at an end. If, on the other hand, we are willing to believe that, in the narratives which they have given us, they have honestly recorded the impressions produced upon their eyes and ears, we shall next have to consider to what causes these phenomena may fairly be ascribed. Four hypotheses have been put forward: fraud, self-delusion, the operation of some hitherto undiscovered natural law, and spiritual agency. The idea of fraud, as a general explanation of the manifestations, may, we think, be fairly discarded. Imposture there may

have been in cases where money was to be gained;
but seeing that many of the most striking manifestations testified to, took place in private houses, where
no paid medium was present—this being especially
true of the intellectual communications purporting
to come from departed relatives—it is difficult to
believe that those who formed the circle could have
been fools enough to practise a deliberate cheat upon
themselves for no object whatever, to say nothing of
the blasphemy against the holiest affections which
was involved in simulating a message from a deceased
parent, wife, or child. It is not easy to understand
what invisible mechanism would take a man out of
his chair, float him round the ceiling, and then replace him in his seat; and that must be a very
knowing apparatus for the production of raps which
would spell out to an unknown foreigner the name
of his step-son, who had been some years in the grave.
But in purely private circles—the vast majority of
those which are held—fraud is clearly out of the
question. If self-delusion be the chosen explanation,
then we ought to have it explained how it happens
that the same delusion operates upon a dozen or
more persons at the same time; or, to take a stronger
case, how Mr. Coleman and his companions all fancied that they saw the medium in her arm-chair
placed upon the table, and he imagined he lifted her
off, while they only thought they saw him do it. If
the operation of an unknown natural law be the
solution adopted, it must be one law capable of producing all the phenomena recorded, for they appear

to present themselves in very indiscriminate order at various *séances*. It is a current, but very grave error, to suppose that the most startling of these physical manifestations are opposed to known natural laws. It is generally said, for example, that the lifting of a table from the ground—one of the commonest of the alleged phenomena—is opposed to the laws of gravitation. Clearly it is not, if an unseen force be applied to it, powerful enough to counteract its attraction. An unseen force is no novelty in nature. Life is unseen—electricity is unseen—heat is unseen, until, by igniting matter, it gives birth to flame. But this force must be one capable of accounting for all the effects. It will not do to say that this phenomena results from hysteria, that from magnetism, the other from thought-reading, a fourth from the od-force, whatever that may be. If the spiritual theory be resorted to, a vital point arises. Is it a good or an evil agency? The advocates of the Satanic theory have this great stumbling-block to get over, that the advice given in the messages communicated is said to be universally good, the sentiments moral, and the doctrine piously Christian; and it can scarcely be supposed that the Author of Evil would labour for his own discomfiture. There may be a mixture of good and evil agencies; then we ought to discover how we are to discriminate between the two. For ourselves, we express no opinion on the subject; all we wish is to see the matter fairly investigated, with a total absence of that spirit of ridicule which is always offensive and proves nothing, and which is in the present case especially out of place. With the consideration of "*Cui bono*" we have nothing whatever to do. The first question to be solved is, "Is it true or is it not?" The second, "Whence is it?" If the first be answered in the affirmative, then, even should the second remain without reply, we may tranquilly leave the rest to the good providence of God.—*Star and Dial.*

I.

Sir,—The entire absence of that levity which so many affect when they touch on spiritual themes, must commend your review of this subject to all thoughtful readers. Like all earnest inquirers, the reviewer has evidently satisfied himself that the phenomena alleged by spiritualists are real; he sets aside "fraud and self-delusion" as inadmissible explanations of these facts, and very properly draws our attention to two other solutions which really do deserve serious consideration. These two are,—1st, "Some undiscovered natural law," and 2nd, "Spiritual agency;" 3rd, and lastly, the reviewer touches the most important point of all—viz., the moral and religious bearing of the whole question.

On each of these points I beg your permission to offer a few remarks, and I hope, from the candour which marks the whole tenor of the review, that the writer of it will afford me a fair consideration—especially as I have no theory of my own to offer—but shall adduce only authenticated facts.

1st. As to the supposed "undiscovered natural law," I would say that it has in all times (even in the most remote ages) been known to the more enlightened few (though ignored by the many) that there is "a spirit in man," as saith also the Scripture, and that by this spirit man could and did communicate both with God, who "is spirit," and with other (created) spirits—dwelling either within or beyond the bounds of this visible world. If this "natural law" then be resolved into a faculty, or element of man's nature, and if, as I believe, this be its more correct designation, it will be seen at once that this supposition, so far from superseding the other, namely, "spiritual agency," or from being opposed to it, necessarily implies its existence.

This view I do not offer as my opinion, for as such it would be worth nothing; but I state it as a fact that in all ages, in all nations, such a faculty has been recognised, and in this assertion I think the learned will justify me. Moreover, the Old Testament, no less than the New, amply confirms it.

This truth appears, indeed, like one hitherto "undiscovered" and now newly brought to light, because it had been, during the last two or three centuries, displaced by modern scepticism (falsely called philosophy), driven into dark corners out of popular view, and scarcely existing among the learned and judicious few; now, again, in our own day, it is beginning to challenge the belief of both orders, and to compel, by undeniable facts, the attention of the people, no less than that of their guides and teachers.

If spiritual agency be admitted, we come to the solemn question—How is the good to be distinguished from the bad? How is our safety to be ensured? I will suppose this question put to professed Christians, and then we are at once reminded that Scripture speaks much of "evil spirits" as well as of good—speaks of "trying the spirits whether they be of God;" and, lastly, recognises, as a special gift of God's Holy Spirit, the gift of "discerning" spirits. What is the obvious inference, if not that man's wisdom does not suffice for this trial, and that our only safety lies in having God's ordinance for our help? Let it be remembered also that God's gifts to His Church have a mutual connection and dependence, and, like the organs and functions of the human body, cannot act separately, and then we must feel that, to enable us to eschew the evil and retain the good, we require the endowments with which God has enriched His Church in their entirety and completeness. Now all this, I am aware, may seem to many not only mere opinion, but worse than doubtful. It is, however, a fact that all means of discernment short of that I have just described, have been found unavailing. Those who have relied on their own individual powers of discrimination have been too often deceived to their hurt. If any doubt this, I would refer them to certain facts recorded by Mr. T. L. Harris in his various works, especially that entitled "Modern Spiritualism." Without agreeing with Mr. Harris in all his theological views, I appeal to his testimony on matters of fact, and I am sure all who are acquainted with the subject will bear me out in the assertion that no man has had greater personal experience, or more extensive means of observation relating to this matter, than Mr. Harris.

And now, as to the last and chief point. Your reviewer states that "the advice given in the messages communicated" (by the spiritual media) "is said to be universally good—the sentiments moral, and the doctrine piously Christian." Now this is a question of fact, and I venture to hope that your reviewer will see that he has mistaken the facts of the case on this point. Certainly, Mr. Harris—and very many other enlightened and pious men—have said the exact contrary.

In proof, I will adduce only one or two quotations out of many which might be cited. Mr. Harris says that some of the "received spiritual teachings" are as follows :—" That sin is an impossible chimera" —that Christ, "our Redeemer, is not in any sense a Saviour of the soul from sin, death, and hell"— "that He never ascended glorified to Heaven"— "that He never made atonement for sin"—"that He never communicated the Holy Ghost"—that "there can be no regeneration because there is no degeneration." "This," says Mr. Harris, "I quote from the writings of the most conspicuous of spiritual media." So much for doctrine; and now as to morals. "Spirits declare," says Mr. Harris, "that where two are legally conjoined, and the wandering inclinations of either rove to another object, the new attraction becomes the lawful husband, or the lawful wife. Now, as a man of honour," says Mr. Harris, "I pledge myself that through mediumistic channels, all these things are taught as emanating from the spirits; and worse is taught, if possible, to those who penetrate the inner circles," &c.

I have before me a critique "On the Spiritualism" (a work of 500 pages) "of Judge Edmonds, Dr. Dexter, and the ex-Governor Tallmadge." The pamphlet which analyses their writings is anonymous; but the writer is known to me as a correspondent. I believe him to be a learned and conscientious man, and his verdict is nearly similar to that of Mr. Harris —above stated. But let your Christian readers judge for themselves whether the sentiments above quoted are "good," "moral," and "piously Christian." As a matter of fact it is "said" that they are quite the reverse. At least, we may conclude that in this affair of spiritualism we have no child's play, but a serious struggle between the powers of darkness and light, and that we are no further safe than as we put on the "armour," and submit ourselves to the ordinances which God has provided. Nor is this a question between sect and sect of Christians, but between Christ and Anti-Christ.—I am, sir, your obedient servant,

W. T. COLEMAN.

33, Blomfield Road W., August 8.

P.S.—It was not my object to say anything of the purely physical phenomena—such as the moving of heavy bodies, the action on musical instruments, &c., but I beg leave to observe that, in all ages, sound philosophy has taught us to refer the origin of all motion to spirit. We prove, every time by an act of the will we move a limb, that spirit moves matter. It has also been known, from ancient times, that the spirit in a living man, or other spirits acting through him, can, under certain conditions, exert this motive power without the palpable intervention of the body, *i. e.*, matter may be so moved without being touched. This is the foundation of ancient magic. The "powers of the world to come," with which the Christian may be even now endowed, are entirely distinguished from this "curious art" by their moral aspect, application, and, above all, by their origin, which is heavenly.

II.

Sir,—I am somewhat surprised that the liberal offer contained in your excellent review of the *Spiritual Magazine* has not been more generously responded to by the disciples of the spiritualistic faith. I have carefully examined the columns of the *Star and Dial*, since Monday morning, with the hope of seeing something from Mr. Howitt, Mr. Benjamin Coleman, Mr. Wilkinson, or some other able and well-known witness to the reality of the manifestations, but have thus far been disappointed.

It was my good fortune to be introduced, at a very early day, to that branch of the subject popularly known as the "rappings." I had the pleasure of knowing the Fox family, with whom the "rappings" in America originated. I had an opportunity of knowing to what trying ordeals they were subjected by an incredulous public, and also of knowing that every test applied to detect fraud or imposture resulted in a complete victory to the "mediums." During the past twelve years, I have witnessed nearly all the various phases of the manifestations, from table-turning and bell-ringing to trance-speaking and impressional mediumship, and am prepared to testify that much the larger proportion of that which has been communicated to me, or in my presence, has been not only of a highly moral character, but has been strictly in accordance with the truths of Christianity. If the proper tests were applied at the beginning of a *séance*, the revelations have invariably been of the most beautiful and exalted nature.

The "physical manifestations," such as lifting ponderous bodies, ringing bells, and playing upon musical instruments, are undoubtedly, as you state, "designed to arrest attention, and to convince the sceptical that unseen agencies are present, capable of holding communion with mortals." That they have a very important significance cannot but be acknowledged when it is known that many people who had spent nearly half a lifetime under the blight and darkness of atheism, have been brought by their instrumentality to a knowledge of the soul's immortal existence. The fact of an intelligent invisible agency once established, it does not take a long time to comprehend its nature.

No doubt many people in this metropolis fancy that the excitement has died out, that it was only a "nine days' wonder," got up to please the credulous, and must eventually be replaced by some other marvel. Such, however, is not the case. There has never been a more earnest desire to investigate this all-important subject than there is at the present time. *Séances,* private and public, are held weekly in various parts of London, and the manifestations are constantly increasing in interest. In company with some friends, I attended a circle on Wednesday evening, in Rahere Street, St. Luke's. There were several mediums present, but two ladies were selected by the spirits for the manifestations—Miss Dixon and Madame Besson.

After the circle had been opened by prayer (and among the true believers *séances* are seldom held without this devout beginning), Madame Besson sat down to a small round centre table alone. She placed her hand upon the top of it, when it immediately began to tip and glide about the floor. Pretty soon, her jacket was taken hold of by some unseen influence, and so firmly fastened to the bottom of the table, that a small piece was torn off in removing it. Shortly after, she was entranced, and began to make the motions which are gone through by a shoemaker in closing up a shoe or boot—pricking the hole with the awl, and afterwards drawing out the wax-end. She then turned to an elderly woman, who sat upon a couch near by, and told her that her husband's spirit was the influence; that he had been a shoemaker, and had made a pair of shoes for her (his wife) not long before he died. This was acknowledged to be entirely correct. Passing into a deeper trance, Madame Besson went through with the death scene of the shoemaker, being affected precisely (as was stated by the wife) as he had been in his last moments. She then arose, still entranced by the spirit, and addressed the widow, telling her of his (the husband's) bright home in the spirit world, and of the constant guardianship which he exercised over her, and would continue to exercise until they were again united. The language was such as might be used by the most pious and devoted teacher of religious truth. In this connection, it may be as well to add that Madame Besson had never before met the woman whom she addressed, she (the woman) having arrived in town from the country on the same afternoon. This influence leaving the medium, another spirit took possession, and delivered a short and effective address, when all the members of the circle (except Madame Besson) were ordered to join hands, and the gas to be turned off. Madame Besson was directed to keep her seat at the little table. Altogether, the circle was composed of seventeen, including the mediums. There was about an equal number of the two sexes. Soon after turning off the gas, spirit-forms began to make themselves visible to Miss Dixon, Madame Besson, and the other mediums, and every person present was repeatedly touched by spirit hands, in some instances five or six, and those who were sitting at the extreme sides of the room, some of them not less than twelve or fourteen feet apart, were touched at the same time. I had my face repeatedly patted, and my whiskers playfully pulled by a spirit hand, and although I sat as close to the wall as possible, my chair touching it, a hand grasped firmly hold of my shoulder from behind. Then there were loud clappings in the air, from the ceiling, and sounds in various parts of the room like the tinkling of Turkish bells. These sounds were heard almost simultaneously in every corner of the room, coming in the midst of what was otherwise perfect silence. Some present saw the operations of the spirits, as well as heard and felt them, but all were thoroughly convinced of their existence through the medium of two organs.

If it be asserted that the medium sitting at the table made use of her hands in touching the others, it may well be answered that it would be impossible for her to be present at both sides of the room at the same moment. Again, the stillness was such during the greater portion of the evening, that a person could not move without being at once detected; and besides, several times, while being taken hold of, I had my foot so far outstretched as to prevent any physical being from approaching near enough to touch my face without encountering my feet.

This was not done because I doubted the sincerity of any one present, but that my testimony might be of more value. Again, my shoulder was grasped from behind, and there was not a quarter of an inch of space between my chair and the wall. And, still further, the raps on the table, and the bells in the air, were heard in a distant part of the room at precisely the same moment that several persons were being taken hold of by spirit hands. Much else occurred of an equally startling and interesting nature, all of which can be testified to by sixteen credible witnesses; but I will not intrude upon your columns farther than simply to say that I have had spirit hands take firm hold of me in broad light.

I have given the foregoing sketch of a single experience with the physical manifestations, because I believe that to the novice they are the most interesting.

Once more assuring your readers that much the greater proportion of these manifestations are of a purely moral and religious nature, I will close by signing myself, yours truly,

A. W. BOSTWICK.

Exeter Change, Strand, August 9.

III.

Sir,—Your two questions, "Is it true?" and "Whence is it?" strike at the root of the tree of spiritualistic phenomena, however varied the shape of the branches and the hues of the flowers. Six years' testing at several hundred sittings, during leisure hours in the quiet of home life, has placed me in a better position for arriving at an accurate opinion than the man who has never been at a sitting, or only at one or two; but I pass these questions for the present, and lay hold of Mr. W. T. Coleman's letter, as it may frighten away a class of persons who are afraid of testing the phenomena, for fear the "devil" is the producer of them. I therefore state, that at the sittings I have attended I have never heard a sound, nor seen a sight, antagonistic to purity; but, on the contrary, I have been advised to prayer, to Bible reading, to repose in Christ—duties I had grossly neglected. To the Christian who believes the truth that an unseen devil tempted the pure Christ forty days, and that the devil still tempts men, it cannot be a matter of surprise that devils may come and attempt to deceive in a church or at a sitting; but, if so, they must also believe that an angel came and strengthened Jesus in the Garden during his agony, and that as "angels minister," they can and do minister at a church, social gathering, or a sitting formed expressly for the purpose of proving by signs and wonders that devils and angels are still in and round human beings. I have found the most energetic inquirers into the subject of spirit-power to be those persons who had no faith in either a "devil" or an "angel;" but by means of the proofs given, rugged and uncouth though some think them, they have "changed their minds," and several I know are now "Church members,"—a species of "devilism" much to be desired. I would frankly state, that I was rapidly imbibing Materialism, and that belief was acting in my actions. When I heard of the spirit-power manifestations I felt that if true they would hew in pieces the Upas tree of Materialism. I sought and found; and not that only, but the Bible was ordered to be put on the table, and a medium, with closed eyes and averted head, was acted upon by an unseen power—as the Quakers were said to be in olden times—and with agitated hand was made to turn over the leaves; his finger then stiffened, and pointed to the open page and verse, "Heard a voice saying, this is my beloved Son." Again the agitation, turning of leaves, and the finger pointed to "I am come that ye might have life," and so on, to a number of passages. In every instance, the finger rested on a verse which contained the principle that Christ was the Son of God.

I advise every one who is going to a circle, to go with a cheerful, thankful heart, avoid fun and frolic, otherwise your grieved angel friends may stand afar off, while you are fooled to the top of your bent by a class of unseen beings, whose absence is more to be desired than their presence. With your permission I will send an answer of "facts" to your question, "Is it true?"

JOHN JONES.

15, Basinghall Street, E. C., August 9.

IV.

Sir,—I should be glad if these remarks, suggested by Mr. Coleman's letter in your impression of Friday, might find a place in your paper.

In Mr. Coleman's letter, two points are alluded to which are said to be connected, if not to be the motive causes of many of the results we have lately heard of under the name of Spiritualism.

The third point alluded to is not a cause, but rather a caution.

And so to turn our attention to the two first points noticed—the solution, as they are said to be, of the sundry spiritual phenomena that have come before our notice.

1. "Some undiscovered natural law." Mr. Coleman says he is going to offer no theory of his own, but is about to deal solely with fact, which it is to be regretted is a determination he permits himself to depart from.

Assuredly his first statement is a fact. There is a spirit in man. No Christian would deny this fact, for he has sure proof of it when he reads that God said, "I will breathe into him (man) of my spirit." It is also a fact that now and then strange insights into that other life, and a conversation with beings not of this world, were granted by God's special grace to peculiar men—as in the well-known case of Saul, which is a sufficient instance. And it is quite true, again, that God made himself sensibly heard by certain men, speaking so that their ears received impressions of sound; and in such a manner that these men could again return answer. Solomon and Samuel are sufficient to mention, out of several instances related in the long course of history embraced by Bible narrative.

But it by no means follows, nor is it a fact, that this power, once or twice granted to men, is a "faculty" or "law of human nature." It is rather, taking the word "faculty" in its strict sense, not a faculty, but an accident of human nature. The expression "law," or "faculty of man's nature," indicates a power in every one, if they so choose to act in their direction of that power, to use the faculty. Hearing and seeing are faculties! All men not accidentally maimed can hear and see at will.

And if faculty be the right expression to give to the supposed power, I, and all other men, not hindered by accidental (or perhaps immoral) check— but this last is not clear—could thus at will communicate with other spirits, and possibly with the very Spirit of God, in such a manner as to call the sense of hearing into play.

We all know (I make a small digression to avoid any risk of being mis-rendered) that there is a spirit in us, which God has given, which works rightly or wrongly in us, as we, using or rejecting His help, act—by which spirit we communicate with Him, in prayer and in other such ways, the sense of hearing in no way being essential. We do not hear God's spirit talking to us, but we feel its impulse; nor do we know, save by experience, if our prayers are received or answered.

And I imagine it is begging the question when Mr. Coleman says that this spirit in man, mentioned in the Scriptures, and the spiritual agencies which gave rise to his letter, are the same.

Then to resume: As I cannot communicate with other spirits, nor can one or another person of my acquaintance do so, how can this power be a faculty of man's nature? My will is strong on the subject. I have often tried whether, by any means, I could hear the words or know the thoughts of absent or dead friends. My endeavours have always been unsuccessful; so also have been those of others of whom I have inquired.

Surely there is no faculty of man's nature in the case.

In the quotation, "Try the spirits," which Mr. Coleman mentions, he again appears to me to take for granted that which has to be proved. St. John says, "Try the spirits whether they be of God, because many false prophets have gone into the world." It was not the spirits—it was the prophets moved by the Spirit in them, that communicated to men; and by what the prophets said, "by their fruits" were their spirits to be known and tried. In neither case mentioned by Mr. Coleman does the Bible bear out his argument; nor does it bear testimony to spiritual agency of the kind alluded to in his letter.

As to the second point, "Spiritual agency." Here we have no proof offered us by Mr. Coleman. He only says, "If spiritual agency be admitted." Why should I admit it? It is not proved. I must repeat, that, by spiritual agency, I mean that which has lately come before the world, when we hear of answers audibly made to questions put, and what appears to me to come under another head, and to belong to another class of inquiry—tables moving, instruments sounding, &c.

To notice another point in Mr. Coleman's letter.

We, of course, prove an exertion of will whenever we move a muscle; but has it been known as a truth, from ancient times, that the exercise of the will can effect the inertia of matter without an instrumental agent? Has it again been satisfactorily proved in ancient times that matter can be moved by the power of will without the influence of touch?

And if it has, why may it not also be proved in modern times, and why is it not so proved? For I may say I am one of modern time; modern proofs suit modern times. I am not content with ancient proofs. (While at the same time let me ask, where are the ancient proofs?)

If these ancient proofs exist, and were worth anything, they would to some extent be proofs now. Why should we not have them to begin with?

It is said, at the end of Mr. Coleman's letter, that this "curious art" is not heavenly. How, then, can the spirit concerned in it have been put into human nature by God? As Mr. Coleman says in the commencement of his letter—"That spirit God breathes into man is of Heaven, till we suffer the Devil to work upon it and expel it."

I have thus, in ill-arranged, words endeavoured to show that this spiritual agency is not a faculty, and that the Bible does not bear out Mr. Coleman's argument in those points whence he appeals to it. I would, at another time, be glad to add more, if the kindness of the editor permits the insertion of these words.

W. P. K.

V.

Sir,—In common with your several correspondents, I much admire the candid and impartial notice of the *Spiritual Magazine* which appeared in your impression of the 5th instant, and while taking exception to one statement therein made, am happy to be able to bear testimony, as a constant reader, to such impartiality being one of the characteristics of your journal. In the course of your remarks on the so-termed "spiritual manifestations," you observe, "It will not do to say that this phenomena results from hysteria, that from magnetism, the other from thought-reading, a fourth from the odic force, whatever that may be." Now, with deference to the reviewer's opinion, I beg to submit that it is precisely by looking at the phenomena as the result of these or similar influences, and testing them by such views, that a satisfactory solution of the question can be arrived at. How otherwise explain the case of the shoemaker's wife, as detailed in the letter of Mr. A. W. Bostwick, than as a clear case of thought-reading? The party assemble under the impression that they are going to hold communion with the spirits of the departed, the proceedings are commenced with prayer, by which means they are brought into a subdued state of mind, and prepared for the reception of the marvellous. Now to whom, under the circumstances, were the widow's thoughts likely to revert but to her deceased husband? Madame Besson, being entranced, went through with the death scene of the shoemaker, being affected precisely (as was stated by the wife) as he was in his last moments. Just so, and as every clever thought-reader would do. Sir, the conditions observed are not very unlike those required at ordinary mesmeric *séances*, and the result is quite in keeping with the experience of those who have witnessed what are usually termed clairvoyant *séances*. I am prone to believe that people biologise themselves in all these cases. I do not dispute their being under the impression that they hear, see, and feel all that they detail, but, in like manner, do all who have been biologised. Should this opinion or belief of mine be incorrect, I would respectfully submit, that it is at least more dignified than to imagine that the spirits of the departed should occupy themselves in the frivolous amusements of " patting poor mortals' faces, and playfully pulling their whiskers." Again, as to hysteria, how comes it that most of the mediums are females, who are naturally subject to this affection? The magnetic force, and odic light, doubtless, will account for much of the phenomena which no spirit hands will explain.—I am, &c.

SCEPTIC.

VI.

SIR,—" Is it true?" is a natural question. My answer is—Yes; because my ears have heard, my eyes have seen, and my hands have felt, at my own home, and at the homes of my personal friends. I have enjoyed my few leisure hours during the last six years, in sitting several hundred times in "circle" in different parts of London, to witness manifestations of spirit power on substances animate and in animate. Except about ten sittings with paid mediums, all have been in the privacy of domestic life. Take this incident, out of many. I asked that an ordinary parlour table be lifted off two of its feet; at once it rose to an angle of forty-five degrees, and undulated in that position. I asked that it be motionless—the movements ceased. Every movement I suggested was made; it moved like a thing of life—no one's hands or feet were near that table. The room was carpeted. None but witnesses can realise the uniqueness of spirit manifestations as a whole; for, unfortunately, in giving some idea of what was witnessed, the incidental prefixes and affixes are omitted, and merely some leading fact given; and thus an impression of the apparent foolishness of the manifestation of spirit wisdom is created in the mind of the reader. I now turn to some of those leading incidents, with this observation, that if I place a bell, a pencil, an accordion, or other article on a table, and earnestly ask that the proof of the existence of unseen intelligent agency be given to me, by moving those substances in a way I suggest, or in any way prefer,—it would be absurd for me to turn round and sneer at, or deny the existence of the power that produced the phenomena; and on my head be the alleged foolishness of the phenomena, if the beneficent power who moved them so stooped to my lack of sense, to overcome my want of faith in a future life.

Movings.—I have seen heavy loo tables tilt about like light ones. I have frequently seen them rise one, two, three, and in one instance four feet off the ground, being one foot above my outstretched hands, no human being touching it, then gently descending like a feather. I have seen a chair move along a large drawing-room floor, pass in front of one of the sitters, and take a vacant space in front of the table; afterwards, I saw the chair lifted up till the seat was level with the table. I have seen a couch within six inches of me start off to about two feet from me, having on it a friend of mine who was lying his whole length on it. I have three times seen that person, while a few inches from me, rise up in the air. In one instance I held his hands, and when I loosed my grip he floated upwards, and over to the other side of the room. I and several of my friends having seen these facts, with us the question does not arise, Is it true?

SOUNDS.—I have an accordion, so have friends of mine; we know where we bought the instruments, and they are of the usual kind. Often and often have I seen those instruments, held by one hand only, at the opposite end to the keys, pulled by an unseen power at the other; and the keys moved, and sweet strains of music played. I have mentally asked that a certain air should be played, and my mental wish has been granted. I have heard music so sweet, so ethereal, so supernatural, breathing out of the instruments, that I have wept. On the 12th of June last, an accordion played in my hand, and the force at the other end was so great that I had to press the side of the instrument against the edge of the table, as my hand was too weak to contend with the force in action at the key end. I have heard sounds, as if in the table, on the table, and round the chairs on which we were sitting. I have heard sounds as of the moaning of the wind, the seething of the sea. I have heard sweet sounds of various tones. Having with my friends heard these things in our own houses, we have not to inquire, Is it true?

Touch.—I and my companions have been dozens of times touched and grasped by unseen power; the sensations were at times as if a firm hand laid hold of me, at others as if a gentle pressure touched and glided away. The last time was in June, 1861. While six of my friends were seated with me round a large loo table, and the hands of all were lightly placed upon it, I felt a pressure on my thigh. I at once put my hand down, and it was kindly patted as if by warm fingers. Mentally wishing that the spirit would shake hands with me, I placed one end of my pocket-handkerchief over my hand, but, instead of shaking hands, I felt the power gently pulling or playing with the handkerchief; and on feeling a small lump of something placed in the palm of my hand, I looked and found that a knot had been tied on the handkerchief; the loose part did not exceed four inches. As I have the handkerchief with the knot on it, I have no need of asking myself, Is it true?

Ghosts.—While sitting, several of the sitters have seen the apparitional or soul-form of the producers of the phenomena. I have not, but at the instant they have witnessed the entrance of those to me invisible beings, I have felt a sensible change in the air of the room—sometimes like a cold current floating past me—sometimes a warm aura seemed to press on me. I have twice seen an ethereal hand rise between the dress and the lace fall of a lady whose hands were on the table. It was a female hand, long and taper. It was about twelve inches from me. The lady never had been at a sitting before, but tears of joy were trickling down her cheeks when she saw it; why, her soul knows. I and those who have seen these sights have not to ask, respecting angels appearing to our Saviour, the prophets, and the apostles, Is it true?

Voices.—I and others have heard voices, no one near. On one occasion I heard a prediction, that a certain event would happen on a particular date on the following month—on that day, the event took place. When, therefore, I read biographic, classic, and scriptural histories of prophecies, said to be heard by voice, I am disposed to believe, and not trouble myself with the question, Is it true?

I could go on and tell of visions—trances—cures —warnings of evil—directions for good—given at these sittings while I was present, and these facts, which joking at us cannot eradicate from our memories, enable us, with a right good heart and will, to say, that we are ready to attest with our signatures, and if need require, by our oaths, before any legal tribunal, that it is true!

It is right to say that the pressure of business

engagements in this beautiful world of God's wisdom has for the last two years prevented me attending many circles, but the past evidences I have had of spirit-life after death are to me, who have suffered the loss of wife and five children, a very joy.

JOHN JONES.

15 Basinghall Street, E.C.

P.S.—If space be allowed, I will, in a day or two, answer the second question you put—Whence is it?

VII.

SIR,—A letter appears in your impression of Friday, to which I beg you will allow me to reply. It is on "Modern Spiritualism," by Mr. W. T. Coleman, who, it may be well to state, avows himself a firm believer in "spiritual manifestations," and in the remarks he ventures upon the question, exposes his consummate credulity when he disparages our "scepticism," and pities us, no doubt, because we are not so imbecile as to sit in darkened rooms, got up for the occasion, until the weak-nerved owner of the palpitating heart is almost ready to mistake its throbbings for the "knocking" of a polite spiritual visitor "at the door."

Well, Mr. W. T. Coleman believes that, by this agency, tables have been moved and knocked, and dulcet harmonies evolved from harp and lute, until the ambitious minstrel, caring not vainly to compete with talent invisible to the naked eye, feverishly resigns his cunning fingers to repose, and vows attentive ear! Such things are done; yea, more! We are told what really is beyond the power of man to know, and so cannot dispute; and what we could not "know," because we know it is false. Well, the phenomenon, he says, is to be explained in this way. "Even in the most remote ages it was known to the enlightened few that there is a spirit in man, as also saith the Scripture, which can communicate with God and created spirits." This "natural law," as he calls it, "must, if resolved into a faculty or element of man's nature, imply the existence of spiritual agency. In all ages, such a faculty has been recognized—moreover, the Old Testament no less than the New confirms it." I may say that the New Testament does not mention it at all, so it is safe to say that the Old cannot do less. "There is a spirit in man, saith the Scriptures," saith Mr. W. T. Coleman. He might better have said an "immortal soul," which, while a close prisoner in this house of clay, he knows can never see the spirits he suspects to exist, because the material eye is between them and his spirit, so that he can neither regard the shadowless figure, nor hear the noiseless march, neither can we "communicate" with them, but only with the Great Spirit, and that not by knocks or raps, but in sincerity and in truth. It savours not of a truth-seeking spirit, to debase Holy Writ by decking an untenable argument with "Thus saith the Scriptures;" nay, rather but the Scriptures teach that God at sundry times and in divers places spake by the mouth of holy men, but in these latter days has consummated all by the gift of the presence of his Son. We need no other communication from the invisible world than we have here, and more no man can know. But would you review the past? —it is indelibly seared on the page of history. The future?—seek not the counsel of spirits; the holy angels, even, do not know their Father's omniscient will. The present?—"To-day, if ye will hear His voice, harden not your hearts."

Let us seek to become wiser and better men. By heeding the unprofitable loquacity of those who profess to raise spirits (but would be more terrified than the Witch of Endor if they saw one), we derange our nervous system till we cannot accumulate riches on earth, and by carking anxiety divest our thoughts from laying up lasting treasure where thieves break not through and steal.

In fine, I ask for proof of the existence in man's nature of the element of which he speaks. I deny *in toto* that he can show it in any living man.

And, as to spirit acting on matter, I ask him if he ever saw matter move, unless by natural or mechanical agency? Did he ever see a door unlocked and opened without mechanical agency, or by anything that he could fairly attribute to spiritual agency? Or have we heard as much as we ever shall of the doings of these spirits, and are they about to retire in disgust? Let them: they should have come boldly from under the table—they could then have eluded our grasp; but, methinks, if seated at a table, and I felt my foot embraced by a so-called spirit, a lightning-like motion would give voice to these dumb knockers, and by it we could make a shrewd calculation as to their age at time of death, their country, and their sex.—Yours truly,

W. A. ADAMS.
17, Cheapside.

VIII.

SIR,—Eight years of close and careful investigation into the phenomena of modern spiritualism has, in my case, resulted in the conviction, that the vast majority of the manifestations are genuine, and done without trick, contrivance, or collusion, and that many of the wonderful phenomena developed at spiritual *séances* are produced by invisible spiritual intelligences, and are not the result of any hidden and merely natural law. The question opened up for consideration in the pages of the *Star* is not so much "Do the phenomena occur?" That seems to be admitted. Indeed, unless it be admitted, we are forced to the conclusion that the testimonies, to matters of fact, and things seen, heard, and felt, of tens of thousands of disinterested, intelligent, and hitherto unimpeachable witnesses, are utterly valueless, and that the witnesses have either become impostors, are self-deceived, or have been made the dupes of designing persons. There are many reasons for believing none of these inferences to be true;— 1. For persons who have been witnesses are, many of them, well skilled in a knowledge of all the natural sciences, while those who are the mediums are often illiterate and unlearned. 2. Although tens of thousands of persons, in England and America, have had the phenomena produced in their presence, no single instance, with which I am acquainted, of the discovery of any trick, has yet been established. 3. The testimonies are to matters of fact seen under every variety of circumstances, appealing to all the senses, and testified to by all who have been present at the *séances* where they took place. 4. Although the occurrences transpire at places widely apart, sometimes originating quite suddenly,' and in the presence of persons who have never seen similar phenomena, yet the descriptions of the transactions which take place are substantially the same in all instances. 5. It is not conceivable that tens of thousands of mediums could produce these things by arts of deception, and yet never in one case confess, make known, and expose the jugglery. So hopeless is the case of the adherents of the theory, that the modern spiritual phenomena are the results of trick, that this view of the subject has been given.

over to those, and to those only, who never have examined the question, and who write from prejudice rather than from knowledge and investigation. If, then, the phenomena occur, how are they produced? There are seven theories:—

1. That they are produced by spirits or disembodied human beings, some bad and some good.

2. Ditto ditto, together with automatic cerebral action of the mediums.

3. That they are produced by spirits, by automatic cerebral action, and by the influence of powerful magnetisers.

4. That they are produced by powerful embodied human beings acting mesmerically; by the voluntary and involuntary action of the cerebral, spinal, and sympathetic nerve centres of mediums, acting through the medium of and using an imponderable and all-pervading fluid, designated by Reichenbach "Odyle."

5. That they are partly automatic, partly voluntary, partly mesmeric, partly the result of known and unknown natural laws, but mostly produced by invisible intelligent agents, inhabitants of the supermundane or spiritual world or worlds.

6. That they are produced by known and unknown natural laws, without the interposition of disembodied spirits.

7. (And, lastly, by those who know little or nothing about the matter), that the phenomena are the result of trick or mechanical contrivance.

To theory No 5, after serious investigation and

in spite of the influence and opposition of friends and well-wishers, I have been compelled to give my adhesion. As to the character of the teachings, the conclusion at which I have arrived is this: that no teachings received from either embodied or disembodied spirits are infallible and worthy of unquestioning assent; and that we ought to try the teachings of disembodied as well as embodied beings, and only receive such as are supported by corroborative evidence, and agree with our moral sense and our highest conceptions of natural and spiritual truth. Many of the teachings derived through modern spiritual mediums are questionable—some are positively bad—but the larger proportion inculcate excellent moral and spiritual truths. An epitome of the arguments adduced in opposition to the views held by those who believe in the spirituality of modern mysterious phenomena will be found in the August number of the "British Controversalist," and a reply to those arguments will appear in the September number of the same periodical.

I would rather be in a minority of one with truth, than in a majority of all the world with error. Allow me to thank you for your fair and manly criticism of a despised, unpopular, but nevertheless earnest, intelligent, and truthful belief.—I am, yours truly, T. P. BARKAS.

Newcastle-on-Tyne, August 12.

IX.

Sir,—Your correspondent, Mr. Bostwick, has expressed his surprise that neither Mr. Howitt, Mr. Wilkinson, nor myself, have taken advantage of the reopening of your columns to a discussion of the very important subject of modern spiritualism. I write, therefore, to say that my friends are away from town on their summer tour, and I am saying all I have to say at present in the pages of the *Spiritual Magazine*.

The tone of your review of my notes on American Spiritualism is so extremely fair and temperate, that I have nothing to complain of or to combat. Your correspondent, Dr. J. W. Coleman, who is entitled to every respect for the conscientious scruples he has on the religious bearing of this subject, will no doubt be answered by others more competent than myself. I would only take this opportunity of saying that Dr. Coleman is not related to me, and only agrees with me on this subject so far as to acknowledge his belief in the reality of the phenomena which so many unthinking persons are disposed to vituperate. As the doctor is called by some of your correspondents "Mr." Coleman, he may wish, as I do, that no mistake may occur as to the identity of our sentiments. Permit me to say, that I will show the evidence in my possession, of some of the extraordinary facts witnessed by me during my recent visit to America, to any serious investigator.—I am, sir, your obedient servant,   Benjamin Coleman.

48, Pembridge Villas, Bayswater, Aug. 13.

X.

Sir,—Allow me a word or two on this matter of Spiritualism. We know there can be no effect without a commensurate cause, for it is certain and plain that nothing can do nothing. Well, I have, with other friends, seen a table raised from the floor without any human, or what is called physical, power underneath to raise it. I have seen an accordion, when held bottom upwards, playing as it were of itself, and heard it give forth sweet strains of music. Now, the force, or power, or agent, was clearly there, though unseen; nor does it seem to me of consequence whether that force be called electric, magnetic, or od, for that force, or power, or agent, was as plainly directed by an intelligence possessing thought and feeling, which thought and feeling, with a motive and a purpose, was indicated in the music; therefore the question is still reiterated, and still arrests us—What and whence is this intelligence? Does electricity feel and think? Is there any such thing as feeling, thinking, loving, or hating, apart from individual, intelligent existence?

The only conclusion I can possibly come to (and that, with many, many others) is that it was (to us) an unseen being acting by (to our physical eyes) an unseen agency. It seems to me, if we cannot thus believe our eyes and our ears—our rational faculties and physical senses—we must be blanks, and believe in nothing. But besides these physical phenomena, I have several friends who say they can see these spiritual visitors, as separate individual existences, when they operate in these manifestations. This cannot be all fancy, because they cannot imagine it at their wills, and still stranger would it be to imagine facts not previously known. And it cannot be all disease, because they give every evidence of mental, moral, and physical health.

I test it thus—"You, the seer, say you see a spirit form with us, trying to make its presence known to us—to prove you see it, describe its appearance, tell its name or age, and how long since departed," &c. This has been done, as I know. Facts of personal history have been told before, unknown to the seer or medium.

Again, other friends pass into a trance or sleep; unseen power entrances them, and they speak as from unseen individuals, from those whom we usually talk of as dead and gone—the burden of their message usually is that they come to claim our love and reunite with us in friendship; that they are still interested in us, and watch over us—part of the "great crowd of witnesses," "God's ministering spirits," as 'twere his eyes and ears—brought more manifestly to us. You can ask questions of them, and they will give you their credentials.

Some of your correspondents say, "It is contrary to nature's laws:" I say facts cannot be contrary to natural laws—and these are facts. But another says, "Oh, it's clairvoyance—thought reading." Very well, if it is, it is admitting that a spirit in a material body may see a spirit in another material body—*i. e.* that mind can read mind.

Another says—"Oh, they were biologised." Very well; who biologised or magnetised them? Who did the facts? They could not imagine them, and by their fancy make the physical manifestations. No, sir; many have tried all these explanations, but cannot rest on them. This may account for one fact, that for another; but nothing (it seems to me) can cover the whole facts, but spirit, individual intervention, by God's permission, and according to a law.

But then comes a most important point. Are there nothing but bad, evil, and devilish spirits that walk the earth both when we sleep and when we wake? Some honest clergymen are afraid of this, and have preached accordingly—that they are not human spirits at all, but demons. But, methinks, it is bordering on blasphemy to say that God has given all power to evil, and none to good spirits. We know, in all seriousness, there is enough of evil—spiritual, moral, and physical—but is there no good left? The olden Jews believed in nothing but evil, for they said Christ "cast out devils by Beelzebub, the prince of devils," but we know better. Good is good all the world over; and if the foolishness of preaching manifestations lead me to nobler and higher thoughts of God, to deeper prayer to him, to a fuller dependence on his providential government, and to a clearer understanding of the Bible testimony; if it has made my prospects brighter, and explained the

great enigma; if it has made me and many others happier, and I believe wiser and better—then if it be of the devil, all I can say is, God speed the devil, for he must have become a reformed character.—
Yours, &c., T. WILKS.
Worcester.

XI.

Sir,—Allow me to thank you very sincerely for your renewal of the discussion on Spiritual Manifestations in the current numbers of the *Star and Dial*. I was greatly disappointed by its abrupt termination in the autumn of last year, and am of course gratified to a corresponding degree by its resumption in your pages now. Last winter it operated on me, and many others, like a charm. I shall not soon forget the eager looks and wrapt attention of the fireside circle to which I read the paper on each succeeding evening, and the animated conversation that followed upon subjects the most sublime and mysterious. The carking cares and dull projects relating to earthly matters were then put on one side, and the higher topics of mind and spirit took their place, surely not without benefit to the conversers. I anticipate during the coming season a renewal of these high pleasures, and I think in this way much good may be done, for many who have a distaste for direct religious conversation may be by this means, and doubtless have been, allured through this singular and inresting subject to reflect upon the nature of spirits in general, and their own souls and destinies in particular.

And here, sir, allow me to put the question—May not these novel manifestations (granting them genuine) be now singularly opportune, as furnishing a check to the material tendencies of this dull, plodding, mechanical age? May they not be just what are required to draw the mind away from those earthly subjects which are at the present day so all-engrossing? Utilitarianism is the characteristic feature of this middle of the nineteenth century, and it requires something unique and startling in order to arouse the minds of people in general; to call off the attention of the tradesman from his ledger; of the working man from his avocation; of the aristocrat from his fashionable pursuits; of the lady from her crinoline; of the gay youth from his betting-book; and even of the religious from that dull, apathetic, mechanical way in which their customary devotions are too commonly performed. We had, sir, well nigh lost sight of the realities of another state of being, in consequence of being absorbed in this; and, in my opinion, the mysterious phenomena now so general are meant as a counteracting force, in order that we may better realise the powers of the world to come. This, I think, furnishes a reply to the " Cui bono?" so often put. The mind of man instinctively yearns for some token of a spirit world, some signal to beckon him

"Into the land of the great departed,
Into the silent land."

The highest intellects that have ever appeared among us seem to have lived in the past and the future, the distant and the ideal, and to have cherished those Divine musings, those "thoughts that wander through eternity," which speculate upon and anticipate a future state; and can any one say that it is not the will of the Most High that in the latter ages of the world this state should not be revealed more fully? Indeed, as time rolls on, something of this sort seems to be required. Every day we are growing more remote from the era of miracles, and although this fact does not retract from the value of their evidence viewed philosophically, yet it does from its recognition and effect. I submit, then, that the phenomena may be of use in removing the doubts of the honest sceptic, of furnishing growing testimony to the truths of religion, of humbling the pride of the scoffing rationalist, and of teaching us all the great truth, that there are more things in heaven and earth than are dreamt of in the philosophy of the worldly wise.

I cannot, sir, close these few rambling observations without expressing my surprise at what has been so dogmatically and positively asserted by some of your correspondents, namely, that matter cannot be operated upon but by mechanical agency, when scarcely a minute passes without my lifting my hand to my head by an effort of the will. The muscles, tendons, &c., of my limbs act at once in obedience to this mental impulse, in some mysterious manner, and therefore it cannot be physically impossible for the will to act upon matter generally, as shown by Spiritual Manifestations.—I am, sir, yours very truly,   J. A. L.

Kettering, August 14.

XII.

Sir,—I thank you for publishing my letter of the 12th, particularly for having adopted the incognito, which, with your kind permission, I will continue, as it is a literal designation, being a thorough-going sceptic in the matter of these "Spiritual Manifestations." Sir, the thanks not only of your correspondents, but the public generally, are due to you for the liberal manner with which you have re-opened your columns to the discussion of this subject. A question of more vital importance cannot possibly occupy them if true—and if not, the sooner it be exploded the better, through the agency of open controversy in your enlightened journal. Having avowed myself a thorough sceptic, I am prepared to do battle with the spiritualists, and may probably incur some derision when I state the fact that I have never been present at a spiritual séance. But I am emboldened to say that, had I witnessed all that has been written concerning these manifestations, and all that has been witnessed even by your ingenuous correspondent, John Jones, I should still disbelieve my senses when in opposition to my reason. Setting aside the awe which attaches to these mysterious proceedings, from their supposed connection with the spirit world, I would ask, is there anything more extraordinary in the phenomena detailed by Mr. John Jones than the thousand and one marvels performed by M. Frikel and his contemporaries, in the art of legerdemain, that we should forego our reason and be cajoled by our deluded senses? Not that I would be misunderstood to pronounce the whole phenomena as caused by sleight of hand. I would rather ascribe them to ecstacy and magnetism, which, although apparently bordering on the spiritual, are entirely physical in their nature. Dr. Ashburner, in his translation of "Reichenbach's Researches," in a note on light, says, "To apply the term spiritual to the class of phenomena under discussion is to remove them from the domain of physics into the region of the absence of ideas. The instant the human mind loses the idea of matter, it wanders in a haze in which clear consciousness is no longer present—it approaches, in a degree, the state to which narcotics reduce the perceptive faculties, and which, carried to its extreme limits, proceeds to fatuity and unconsciousness." Again, "There are organs of the brain, which, when over-stimulated, leave the individual a victim of ecstacy. The imagination, said to be a mental faculty, but, in reality, the result of a combination of the actions of several organs, if indulged in without regulation and very strict control by the intellectual powers, may lead to an ecstacy as incompatible with rational conviction as the open-mouthed fatuous wonderment of the idiot is with the higher, calm, reasoning power of the philosopher. Could man be brought to the conclusion that the numerous fallacies, the reiterated falsehoods, which have resulted from his imagination having conquered his reasoning faculties, are the causes of all the evils surrounding him, how ready would he be to abandon his errors? Alas! When is man to be enlightened to this extent?"

It is not my intention to discuss the quality of the spirits, whether good or bad, nor the merits of their teachings. I am content to leave that matter to the spiritualists to settle amongst themselves; neither do I wish to invade that territory which I should have thought men calling themselves Christians would not have dared to approach with levity—viz., Holy Writ. But as spiritualists propose to reclaim materialists by these means, and thereby attempt to justify their unhallowed orgies, I cannot forbear referring them to the parable of the Rich Man and Lazarus, and, quoting their Lord and Master's words, "If they hear not Moses and the prophets, neither will they be persuaded, though one rose from the dead." This must be the dawning of a new dispensation, if these spirit communications are to be permitted and inaugurated A.D. 1861. I am induced to forward the enclosed extracts from "Grimes's Etherology, and Phreno-philosophy of Mesmerism," in support of my position :—

"The belief of many excellent persons in the communion of mesmerised subjects with the spirits of the departed dead, is undoubtedly a delusion into which they have been led by their own credulity, and the peculiar condition and superstition of the subject. When a subject is under Etheropathic (mesmeric) influence, to a certain extent he can be easily made to believe that he sees or hears the supernatural inhabitants of Heaven or Hell. He can be inspired, and generally is, with the notions of the operator, especially if he is clairvoyant enough to perceive the state of the operator's mind. Under these circumstances, if the subject is questioned, he will sometimes surprise, delight, or horrify the operator by merely echoing back to him his own superstitions. I am acquainted with a most respectable gentleman who was a universalist, who became converted to a belief in the existence of perdition by a subject who described to him the exact appearance of his mother and several other dear relatives who were dead, and who had never in life been seen by the subject. It did not occur to the credulous gentleman that his own mind was like a mirror to the mind of the subject, and that his own thoughts reflected the images of departed friends, but he really supposed that by clairvoyance the subject actually looked into the eternal world, and from its countless myriads selected his relatives, and described them with perfect accuracy. He therefore proceeded to question the subject as to what his mother said, and whether she had any communications to make to him. He was informed by the subject in reply, that his mother was in heaven, and was desirous to warn her son of his errors, and to assure him of his imminent danger of falling into eternal perdition. Overwhelmed with awe, and terrified with these solemn revelations, he sunk on his knees, and in an agony of conviction surrendered his former faith, and from that day to this has acted consistently with the resolves of reformation which he then made. There is at this moment a large number of very respectable persons in this state, who sincerely believe in the reality of communion with spirits by means of Etheropathy (mesmerism). To ridicule it will only make their belief stronger by exciting the principle of stubborn opposition; but I think they will become convinced of their error when they find that subjects can be made to believe or to see anything which whim or caprice may suggest, provided they have not been previously committed for or against it. Many persons have become convinced of the existence of supernatural spirits, from the (supposed) evidence afforded by Mesmerism, from the supposition that it proved the existence of spirits, and was therefore favourable to religious belief. The truth, however, is, that neither Mesmerism nor Etheropathy (nor table-turning) sheds any light whatever on this subject, it leaves it where it finds it."

I beg especially to recommend the above to the notice of Mr. John Jones and others of like experience, and remain yours, &c., SCEPTIC.
August 15.

XIII.

SIR,—None of your correspondents on Spiritual Manifestations appear to have seen, heard, or felt any of them, unless it be in a room or dwelling-house. Can any of them produce any witnesses to them in the centre of a field? If not, they ought to say why not.

They refer to the Old Testament in support of their theory, but they forget that the garden, the road, the field, and the doorway were more frequent localities of such manifestations than the interior of any building. Of course, a table, &c., could be raised from the middle of a field (if raised at all by spirits) to an indefinite height, and it would add thereby to the present number of believers.

Your obedient servant,
JAS. M. BUCKLAND.
South Place, Reading, Aug. 14.

XIV.

Sir,—The question " Whence is it?" is speedily answered if the querist is a Christian. I have only to point him to two great events in Christ's life— His temptation by the Devil, and His support in agony by an angel—and we have the acknowledgment of two invisible persons of opposite morals acting upon the one individual. I say persons, because, though invisible to the majority of mortals, because of the opaqueness of most human eyes, yet by many whose eyes and bodily structure are sensitive, those apparitional forms are seen. We have no announcement from Matthew to Revelation, of any physical convulsion in the human organisation, or of a change in God's mode of acting on, with, or for man ; and the declaration that signs and wonders have ceased is the ignorant assertion of ignorant men, and diametrically opposed to the last words of Christ—" These signs shall follow them that believe ; in my name shall they cast out devils, heal the sick," &c.—and diametrically opposed to biographical history, classic and theological, from the days of the Apostles down to August, 1861.

From those who are not Christians, the question of " Whence is it?" is natural and fair. And my answer is, that the phenomena of inanimate substances moving without visible touch arises from the invisible power of invisible intelligent beings in the air around us, and that these beings have form and substance as surely as the unseen air has, which sometimes is so strong, so powerful, as to tear up an oak tree by the roots, and lift a farmer's waggon off the ground and toss it over the wall into the next field. And I see no reason why the unseen gases which make air and water, and produce the vegetables which make the seen body of man, may not produce substances unseen by us to feed unseen beings. Let us reduce this idea to demonstration. First, by remembering that all fragrances from fruits, petals, &c., ascend upwards—they must have form and substance, or there could be no fragrance. Secondly, the facts called spiritual phenomena are acknowledged; the question is therefore narrowed to —Are they produced by an unknown natural law, or by unseen intellects possessing physical power? My answer is, that six years' experience of no ordinary kind has settled the answer as "Yes," to the second question. Because when seated in a room with others round a table we cannot produce any phenomena; but when we ask that a named solid substance be moved, it is done. When we ask for music—say some of our favourite Irish or Scotch melodies—it is given with a pathos exceeding what we have listened to when produced by musicians. We are at once compelled to yield to the conviction that angels still minister; and when that conviction is buttressed by communications respecting dates, ages, names, and reference to incidents unknown to those present, but afterwards found to be true, we have no leverage for the assertion that " Spirit Manifestations are produced by an unknown natural law."

These phenomena take place only in the company of persons called seers, prophets, or mediums—but those persons have of themselves no more power than the barometer. The machine is there, but the storm wind comes and goes as it wills, without the power of the barometer or of man to prevent; so the spirit comes and goes when it will, without the power of the medium or of the sitters. Whence it is may also be inferred from the following fact, given to me by one of the leading officials belonging to the corporation of London:—" Having heard that 'fire' had descended on several of the great Irish assemblies during the revivals, I, when in Ireland, made inquiry, and conversed with those who had witnessed it: that during the open air meetings, when some 600 to 1000 persons were present, a kind of cloud of fire approached in the air, hovered and dipped over the people, rose and floated on some distance, again hovered and dipped over that which afterwards was found to be another revival meeting, and so it continued. The light was bright—very bright—and was seen by all, producing in all awe." Whence was it? Ask those who had the guidance of the chariots of fire which were used for Elijah, or the producer of those tongues of fire which were seen resting on the Christians in Jerusalem some 1,800 years ago. Therefore I judge that unseen intelligent beings, good and bad, are the producers of spiritualistic phenomena; and that assertion, verified by hundreds of persons well known in divinity, law, physic, and commerce, is the answer to the question, " Whence is it?"

JOHN JONES.

15, Basinghall Street, E.C., August 12.

P.S. In answer to " Sceptic," I state that to produce spiritualistic phenomena I went through a series of experiments. I have tried electricity, odic force, magnetic force, arrangement of mediums, and will, without success; but when I gave up and mentally acknowledged myself foiled, the manifestations commenced, and accordions have played, and tables have been raised off the carpeted floor, &c.—rather tough work for even imagination to place to the credit of " thought-reading."

J. J.

It requires no stretch of the imagination to admit a modification of magnetic force which affects the brain and its organs, producing consciousness and clairvoyance in a subject who is, by the process of magnetic induction, brought into communication with it.

We may well question, supposing, for the purpose of argument, the possibility of the existence of disembodied spirits, why they should exhibit powers superior to those of the embodied state; thus rendering the wondrous mechanism of the body a useless appendage. Surely it were an injustice to involve spiritual beings in a tabernacle of clay for the mere purpose of foiling their aspirations and clogging their faculties with organs of perception, without which they could the better perceive.

XV.

Sir,—Thousands of readers will thank you for re-opening this question, and it is to be hoped that through your means a great fact or a great fallacy will be established, for no question can possibly be of greater importance.

Allow me to suggest that it will probably help the solution if "Sceptic" will allow his senses to try the test, for it is very unlikely that Dr. Ashburner's paragraph will apply to him, and if he can be induced to be an eye-witness, and his reason and his senses act in accord, the result will be looked for with great interest.

Seeing the high respectability and standing of many of the numerous supporters of the cause, surely it is time to drop the Frikell or Houdin argument, and we have certainly as many instances of the obstinacy of reason as of the delusions of sense. —I am, sir, yours respectfully,

Another Sceptic.

Brixton Hill, August 16.

XVI.

Sir,—I am willing to believe that all your writers on spiritualism may be sincerely aiming at the elucidation of truth, but so long as the controversy is between two diametrically opposing parties, proselytes and sceptics, truth is in imminent danger of being swamped during the struggle for victory. If the question be not discussed in the dispassionate spirit of true philosophy, the hope of enlightenment is at once defeated. So was it during late discussions, the first of which I presumed to open with Mr. Carpenter, at St. James's Hall. My objections were received by him with becoming courtesy; but directly he permitted himself to be addressed by those who substituted ridicule for argument, without an atom of reasoning, there was an end to all hope of elucidation.

The proselytes of spiritualism are too often content to blazon their unexplained facts, and I for one have never presumed to deny them; the bigoted sceptic is content with hooting down these facts, and laughing to scorn the affirmations of honourable men, whose extreme credulity has exposed them to his shafts, and has done more harm to their cause than even the rancour of their enemy.

As I must censure the diffuseness of your correspondents, I will study to be brief. The belief that the spirits of those we love are ever around us, is the deepest consolation for the devout Christian in bereavement. This spiritualism may yet be proved, even shorn of the imputation of illusion. It may be that the demon of Socrates, and the friendly spirit of Tasso were real entities, but I believe that the popular manifestations of the day, psychical and physical, that unhappily savour more of caprice than holiness, may be referred to Nature's known laws, and that it is only the intensity, that shrouds in mystery ideas and actions and forces at once clear and simple.

It is no more profanation to analyse these phenomena of mind and matter than to discuss the theory of the rainbow, or the lightning, or the comet, for it would lead us at once through Nature up to Nature's God. The laws which we cite in elucidation are those the great Creator himself has made. The mysteries of the mind, and the wonders of science are equally bewildering; the projectility of ideas, and the transit of the electric telegraph equally astounding. Receiving, therefore, every assertion as a fact, I will not presume to assert, but content myself with the form of proposition, for the question is yet merely in abeyance. It may be granted that mind is projectile, for what is thought, dream, or vision, but the visit of an intellectual element to another sphere? The *intensity* of these phenomena, under hyperexcited action of the brain and the concentration of nervous power, with the superadded influence of memory and association, and especially of electro-biology and mesmerism, or the odyle force of Reichenbach, constitutes those displays that have been somewhat irreverently termed preternatural. It is this concentration of nervous force that explains at once the mystery of clairvoyance, deuteroscopia, glamourie, and prophetic eestacy. It is only a question of degree, and not of kind.

As thought and memory are thus unconsciously centred in one idea, the faculties also may be exalted by this concentration. By the deprivation of other organs of the body, one organ or faculty may be so intensified, that fluency of speech—perfection of melody-mental vision—may be raised to such a lofty pitch as to astonish even those who can explain them.

The projectile power of volition or the will is displayed even in the lifting of a finger; the concentration of this volition may explain the whole phenomena of table-moving, nay, even the body-lifting of Mr. Home.

Reflect on the wondrous shocks of the silurus and the torpedo; the accumulation of their natural electricity is equally perilous and fatal as the high-charged electric jar. Even pathology may adduce facts in illustration. A fragile girl of fifteen is the subject of hysterical convulsion, and during this unconscious spasm she will require perhaps six strong men to hold her. When her nervous electricity is expended or again diffused, she may be almost knocked down by a feather. These natural conditions, like the electric charge, require a lapse of time for concentration; just as the table-movers must sit for a time in solemn conclave ere the spiritual gyrations are effected. When we compare these electric actions, and, I might add, the dance of the middle ages, &c. &c., with the power of a magnet in lifting a bar of iron, may not the animal electricity, a centrifugal force, become so intense as even to lift Mr.

Home to the ceiling? It is only a question of degree.

I may thus seem to be straining a point, but I do not advance a theory in these propositions. As the ultra spiritualist is seeking for fresh causes, I would thus remind him, without presumption, of those established laws of the Creator displayed, in less degree, every hour before us. You see that, in these brief comments, I waive the subjects of collusion and delusion. I do not challenge the truthfulness of *séances* or affirmations, but I do challenge the *rationale* of those who blindly jump at a conclusion, and vaunt their dogmas without reasoning on the facts before them, and form a *supernatural* theory in the face of established laws. But the clear solution can only be arrived at by dispassionate discussion. The devout spiritualist should meet in open arena the physiologist, the divine, and the chemist; thus only shall we elucidate the beautiful and wondrous phenomena of the Creator's world, and thus only may we transfer this sublime subject to the arena of scientific discussion.

WALTER COOPER DENDY.

London, August.

XVII.

SIR,—Those who believe that the periodical press is one of the most powerful instruments for teaching either truth or error, must rejoice to find a journal which admits a view of more than one side of a question; where, without being obliged dogmatically to answer the question which has been propounded, we may have our say without fear of being sentenced to the rack for not answering "Yes," or of being ordered off to everlasting fire and brimstone for daring to say "No;" or, as a merciful alternative, passed over to penitential purgatory, for objecting to the nature of the question or the mode of putting it; and giving, instead of a point blank answer, some reason for the truth that is in us.

The discussion on "Modern Spiritualism" which has been revived in your pages by a review of a periodical said to be "the organ of a decidedly unpopular cause," is, up to the present time, of a somewhat one-sided character, although two great canons of this creed are on their travels, and a third tells us he is occupied in his appropriate place. It is true that "Sceptic" has brought his great gun to bear on "Mr. John Jones," but most of the talk has fallen to Mr. Jones and his fellow believers.

Do quiet, rational men, think it Quixotism to enter the lists against the champions of this system? Or do they fear to use the only weapon which can secure a victory?

When the advocates of a system assume a position as the basis of action which is common to themselves and others, he who dares to attack that basis must expect to meet the opposition, not only of those whose system he would overthrow, but of all those whose root springs from the same postulate. Hence the disadvantages of an attack that is for ever to demolish the system and scatter all its parts to chaos. And yet it must be admitted that the assumption of a position as the basis of a system or a belief is often the origin of all the error or all the truth which is subsequently raised to form the superstructure—a superstructure which we are permitted to admire or condemn, swallow at a gulp, or criticise in detail, but the base of which we must not touch.

And yet, to criticise properly "modern spiritualism" we must get beneath the dancing tables, the musical accordions, and all the other sights and sounds which go to make up the group of phenomena called "spiritual manifestations."

The basis of "modern spiritualism," like the basis of that spurious "ancient spiritualism" which tells us of the Witch of Endor and her tricks—its very foundation, its very life, springs out of, and is created by, the assumption that individual human spirits exist separate and apart from the nerves and arteries, bones and muscles, which form the material portion of a human being.

The postulate of "modern spiritualism" is not the basis of the true ancient spiritualism—that which runs through the main pages of Holy Writ—viz., that the body is resolved into its original elements, and that the spirit returns to God who gave it.

And yet, he who dared to attack the basis of "modern spiritualism," would have to defy more than "the thunders of the Vatican." All the spiritual churches, of whatever sect, would combine to cry him down to the best of their ability; and all they lacked in the power of speech would be lent them by the poets of that ponderous school who see no poetry in every-day life, and who are too weighty to imagine for the future of our race the infinite goodness and glory which matter and mind, combined, will produce for the happiness of man.

And where is the reason—where is the utility—where is the truth in lumping together a lot of phenomena, and presenting them to the rational being to examine, as a proof of the truth of an assumption —a postulate of reason?

Every phenomenon which every spiritualist ever saw may be, to the seer, a fact; but every rational being will, and must, account for that phenomenon compounded of cause and effect—in his or her own way. Moreover, is it not a fact that no phenomenon, nor any number of phenomena, can prove the existence of spirit?

The proof of the existence of matter in all its forms—phenomena—is of its kind. The proof of the existence of spirit in all its forms—noumena—is of its kind. The two are totally distinct, and must be so, so long as reasonable men assume the existence of these two entities as the sum and substance of the Universe.

Should you honour these remarks with a place in your pages, I hope that no readers of them will imagine that they are reading dogmas; for I freely grant that which I as firmly demand—the rational examination of all that is written: and as you were so good as to publish some former thoughts of mine on this subject, to which both my name and address were added, I hope you will kindly permit these to appear as from yours obediently, A Critic.

I regard the Pneumatology of the Bible as affording no evidence whatever favorable to the supposition that we are capable of holding communication with the spirits of the departed. In Genesis, I read, that "The Lord God formed man of the dust of the ground, and breathed into his nostrils the breath of life; and man became a living soul." Also, that He brought "a flood of waters upon the earth to destroy all flesh," both man and beast, "all in whose nostrils was the breath of life." The spirit (Pneuma) here spoken of, is evidently the animal life or soul, *i. e.*, breath—wind—derived from the surrounding atmosphere,* which common-sense meaning has been grossly perverted by the spiritualists in all ages; against whose teaching I would warn my readers in the language of Isaiah; "Cease ye from man, whose breath is in his nostrils; for wherein is he to be accounted of?" c. ii., v. 22.

XVIII.

Sir,—To introduce new truths that are to supersede old errors has always been a somewhat prolonged and tedious operation. I have no hope that the introduction of spiritualism, in the place of the Sadduceeism and materialism of the present age, will prove any exception to the almost universal rule.

It will be admitted that the majority of educated people deny the probability, or even the possibility, of direct and palpable interference on the part of disembodied agents, in the affairs of this mundane sphere. Such interference is not acknowledged, and even the extraordinary events and spiritual inter-

* Vide Ezekiel, xxxvii., 1—14.

positions described in the Old and New Testament receive but a partial and timid recognition.

Your correspondent who signs himself "Sceptic" acknowledges the importance of the investigation, and does not desire to be charged with ascribing the whole of the phenomena to sleight of hand, but would rather ascribe them to ecstacy and magnetism. I have investigated magnetic and mesmeric phenomena for upwards of twenty years, and spiritualism for upwards of eight years, and have arrived, after rigid opposition, as the only satisfactory solution of the question, to the conclusion that mesmerism, biology, mechanical contrivance, and optical, auditory, and tactile illusion will not account for one-tenth part of the phenomena I have seen produced, nor one-twentieth part of what I have seen or heard described as having been witnessed by others. "Sceptic" will admit that I give mesmerism a wide latitude when I say that magnetisers have the power of producing, with more or less certainty, the following effects. They can render rigid any of the muscles of their patients, whether voluntary or involuntary. For example, they can catalypse the muscles of the arm, or retard or accelerate the action of the heart. They can render inoperative, or entirely change, the normal characteristics of the five senses of their subjects. In other words, they can render their patients blind, deaf, dumb, incapable of smell, taste, or feeling; or, they can produce spectres, which are entirely subjective, making those under their influence believe that a table is a race-horse; that they are hearing beautiful music when no music is being played; that they are partaking of the most delightful viands when they are not eating anything whatever; that they are enjoying the most delightful scents when surrounded by the most obnoxious odours; that articles which are in reality cold are intensely hot; and those that are really hot are very cold. Mesmeric subjects are subject to every conceivable delusion. Mesmerisers have also the power to control susceptible subjects, without their being conscious of any influence being exerted, and that, too, at great distances. Mesmerisers have the power of placing their subjects *en rapport* with themselves, so that whatever is done to the operator shall be felt by the patient, and whatever is thought by the operator shall be read by the patient.

Another remarkable phase of mesmeric phenomena is, that the mesmeric subject when perfectly awake, is entirely under the will of the operator, and does whatever the operator wills him to do, without a word being spoken, a sign made, or the mesmeriser and subject seeing each other. Mesmerisers have also the power of rendering their subjects clairvoyant. In the first stage the subjects have the power of reading the mind of the operator; next, of reading the minds of those with whom they are placed *en rapport* by the magnetiser; and, finally, the power of describing what is being done in distant places, when neither the operator, nor any one in his locality, has any knowledge of the place to which the attention of the clairvoyant is directed. With the exception of the last, or independent clairvoyance, I have personal knowledge of facts which illustrate the whole of the above statements, and the testimony of well-accredited persons makes clairvoyance a fact as certain as the electric telegraph. It will be seen that from this stand-point I was not likely to give ready credence to the interference of super-mundane agents, when I knew so many things apparently supernatural could be accomplished by merely mundane agencies. And such was the case; I witnessed phenomena, received the testimonies of friends, read almost every work that was written on the subject, and could not bring myself thoroughly to believe in the super-mundane nature of the manifestations until I had personal evidence of the highest phenomena, and could not resist the conclusion, unless I took this position, that no amount of evidence can possibly prove direct and manifest intercourse between the inhabitants of the natural and spiritual worlds.

"Sceptic" will acknowledge that all persons are not equally susceptible to mesmeric influence; that some persons are very difficult to impress; and that the proportion of very susceptible people is not more than ten per cent. of the whole population. If this be conceded, the difficulty of accounting for all persons who go to spiritual *séances*, coming under the spell of a magnetiser., and that, too, immediately on their entering the room, is almost insuperable. Speaking of myself, I have submitted to the manipulations of the following eminent and powerful mesmerists—Mr. S. T. Hall, Dr. Darling, Captain Hudson, Mr. Oliver, Mr. N. Morgan, Mr. Chadwick, &c., &c.,—and although I yielded myself up to their influence, I have never felt the slightest mesmeric effect produced upon me, and am therefore not at all a likely person to be mesmerically affected during a spiritual *séance*. Mesmerism covers a mere fraction of the ground, and "Sceptic" and others will have to seek for some other cause or causes to support an unsupportable hypothesis, or do what would be much more philosophical and to their credit—investigate the question fully before giving another opinion.—I am, yours respectfully,

T. P. BARKAS.

49, Granger Street, Newcastle-on-Tyne.

Thanks are due to Mr. T. P. Barkas for the corroborative evidence he furnishes that mesmerism and clairvoyance are sufficient to produce much of the phenomena termed spiritual. It would, however, have been more satisfactory had he as candidly informed us of the nature of the "personal evidence, of the highest phenomena," which he could not withstand, in spite of his large experience of the powers of mesmerism. Admitting the full force of the argument as to the difficulty of accounting for the fact that the majority* of persons attending the *séances* appear to be similarly, if not equally, affected, still it is no less a fact that the revelations come through an ecstatic medium, and as the visitors or sitters, composing the circles, are content to receive those revelations as communications from the spirit world, I think that circumstance is alone sufficient to account for all those complying with the required conditions, coming under the influence not only of the medium, but also that of their own organs of credenciveness, commonly called wonder or marvellousness. I believe no amount of evidence can possibly exist which can prove direct and manifest intercourse between the inhabitants of the natural and spiritual worlds, inasmuch

---

* That all do not, at all times, I believe is not maintained.

as I do not believe in the existence of disembodied intelligent spirits; when a man or other animal is dead, he is dead. The union of the body and the life constitute the living being or soul. The life being a constituent of the body can no more have an individual existence apart from it, than the body can continue to exist without the life; no more than the magnetic power of the magnet can have a separate and distinct individuality. Magnetised iron becomes a magnet; when it loses its magnetism, it is dead or inert. The force is dispersed, and its whereabouts, if existent, is not cognisable to mortal ken—being resolved in the universal medium.

XIX.

Sir,—The correspondence upon this important and interesting subject has now assumed formidable proportions, and did I not think that it is incumbent upon those who have paid attention to the question to report the results they may have arrived at, I should probably be disinclined to add to the series of letters provoked by your impartial review of the 5th of August. However, as nearly eight years have elapsed since my own enquiries into the subject began, and as it has constantly occupied my mind since, while my opportunities for investigation have been very favourable, it may be profitable for me to say a few words upon the entire subject, and to state what I consider to be the position in which it is desirable that "spiritualism" should be placed, in order that an impartial decision shall be attained as to its verity or unverity.

I will, if you will permit me, first state the manner

in which I became acquainted with "spiritualism;" then offer my results for consideration, and lastly touch upon the views which I have been personally led to entertain in respect of the reality of the phenomena.

In the autumn of 1858 I purchased and read the work of Judge Edmonds and Dr. Dexter, containing presumed communications from the disembodied intelligences of Swedenborg (always spelt Sweedenborg in that volume) and Bacon. At the time I read the book my knowledge of Swedenborg and his writings was homœopathic, being limited to Emerson's essay on him in "Representative Men;" consequently I had no power of judging the probability of the communications really emanating from the Swedish philosopher. A close study of his writings, together with numerous facts which have come under my notice since, has led me to the conviction that the "spirit" Swedenborg and the theologian of the last century are not identical. One reason for this conviction is to be found in the doctrine of progress proclaimed by the "spirit" Swedenborg, who must, from the nature of his present teachings, have been far beneath the seer of Sweden in mental calibre while on the earth. Another reason may be drawn from the doctrine of the philosopher, that man on earth, by his deeds, thoughts, and tendency, creates for himself a heaven or hell analogous to those deeds and thoughts. We are, I think, forced to admit this, or to admit that it is possible for spirits—viz., disembodied intelligences—to go mad after leaving this world. Now all our innate convictions tend to the conclusion that derangement is mortal and temporary, leaving the mental constitution untouched after decease. Hence " Swedenborg" and " Swedenborg" do not seem likely to be the same.

With Bacon the case is almost identical, but as the topics discussed by the spirit Bacon are dissimilar to those treated in the writings we possess of the mortal Bacon, it is more difficult to decide. Yet I think we may safely assume that the Lord Chancellor —whose memory Mr. Hepworth Dixon has so nobly rescued from contumely—is not identical with the spirit Bacon.

However, when I had read the book, the matter assumed to me this position. The judge and the doctor—men of integrity and honesty—have fearlessly published this volume, and the marvels contained in the introduction (similar to those we have heard so much about since), rest upon their testimony. They may have happened, but, I argued, is it not too soon to ascribe these things to supernatural or extramaterial agencies! I am not going to appeal to the history of hallucination, but I will rather ask, whether some unnoticed faculty of man has not now first come into play? I ended my perusal of the book, not with a denial of the circumstances narrated, but with an opinion that they were not assigned to their right origin, and that until mental philosophers had considered in all its bearings this new series of phenomena, we need not necessarily, or more than temporarily, attribute the effects to ultra-mundane intelligences.

My experiments in 1854 and 1855 were so barren of result, although conducted with perseverance, and with integrity on the part of my fellow-students and myself, that I was almost disposed to abandon the question as, perhaps, unworthy of study, but at any rate not advanced enough for consideration.

I have elsewhere ("Spiritual Magazine," vol. i, p. 283-4) narrated the particulars of three singular apparitions to myself—apparitions unexpected and important in their results to me. I have also endeavoured, from the early part of 1856 to this present time, August, 1861, to reproduce, by the faculty of imagination, the apparition in question, but without effect. Never have I been able to reproduce, in the remotest degree, either in dreams involuntarily, or while awake by an effort of will, the form of the deceased friend, who spontaneously fulfilled his promise of appearing to me. I am, therefore, compelled to acknowledge that these apparitions were not produced by myself mediately or immediately, and in this conviction I am strengthened by the testimony of thousands in all ages of the world's known history. That spirits, therefore, can appear under certain circumstances, was the result which I came to in the early part of 1856.

To proceed. In that year I became greatly more interested, in consequence of the apparitions, in the question of spiritual manifestations, then making slow headway against public opinion—I had almost written public vindictiveness. I became acquainted with a gentleman who, to my astonishment, had been pursuing the study regularly, and with few interruptions, for a quarter of a century. He liberally placed his results before me—he explained his method of procedure—he invited me to witness the manifestations at his house—to ask my own questions, previously and carefully prepared, and freely to criticise the results obtained.

Of this permission I availed myself, and your readers will probably be interested in knowing what passed.

The medium in the case was a young lady of average education—more given to the art of cookery and preserving, than skilful in metaphysics, religious discussion, or scientific inquiry. The gentleman who conducted the investigation was careful in the extreme to register every circumstance which took place, and the mode of communication was this :—

At page 466 of the translation of Baron Reichenbach's "Odic Experiments," edited by Dr. Ashburner, in a note, you will find that in some persons, in the proportion of about one in a thousand, a curious faculty is found, viz., that on their inspecting a glass or round vessel of water, or a round or oblong piece of rock crystal or glass, such object becomes to them clouded, and the images of little figures and places present themselves to the eye. These sometimes are the likenesses of individuals who can be recognised; sometimes scenes well known to the seer; sometimes, and most frequently, scenes distinct indeed, but unknown and not to be identified by the seer, and lastly, scenes of an unearthly and spiritual character.

Now this faculty of vision, whether spiritual in reality or not, was possessed by the young lady, some seventeen years of age at the time, whom I mentioned above. Instead of a glass of water, or a crystal, however, a large silvered looking-glass was used, and as this hung against the wall, the young lady, looking into it, described visions and read off sentences without hesitation or tautology, of intellectual superiority to the tone of her conversation when away from the mirror. There was nothing apparently mesmeric in this, inasmuch as she was in her normal condition, and able to turn from the mirror and speak upon any other subject during the sitting, which, on an average, lasted an hour and a half. The light being too much for her eyes, as it streamed towards her from the mirror (though invisible to all others present), she wore a pair of smoked spectacles during her inspection. In this manner answers were delivered, distant places seen, and even books dictated through the young lady's eyes. The words appeared on a species of cloud; or, in the case of a book, the page of the book lay open like any other volume before her, and she read it off. In this manner upwards of twenty closely-written quarto volumes have been produced within a few years, and the experiment only came to an end in consequence of the young lady's death, in 1858.*

* This is most unmistakable clairvoyance, abnormal cerebration, and quite another thing to supernaturalism, or what is understood as " Spiritualism."—Vide Appendix.

In the same manner I have once, and once only, been able to see in a crystal written words and sentences which were recorded immediately; and that it cannot be imagination is proved from the fact that I have never, although having the liveliest wish to see, been able again to have any vision, except something so vague as to be quite indistinct and useless.

By the use of this mode of communication with what I cannot but call "spirits," I have received some seven or eight quarto volumes since 1856 until now. The contents of the volumes are chiefly metaphysical and religious, and in all cases support the purest and most liberal Christianity.

I am afraid of trespassing too much upon your space, or I would proceed to narrate other things which I have seen; but, I would rather leave that until another time, merely now concluding by a few observations of a general nature.

As to this mirror-seeing—many persons would deny the fact *ab origine*, others set it down as an optical delusion, and a very few would consider it worthy of scientific investigation. If the appearances are themselves true, I would beg scientific men not to pass them by; but to study their nature, that the reason for them may be made plain. If the faculty exist at all, it must exist in consequence of some scientific law; if it be a hallucination, it is equally worthy of study, as furnishing, perchance, some key to the hidden mysteries of cerebral disorder and incipient insanity.

Of these spiritual manifestations altogether, it

may be said, that, whatever their nature, they should be investigated, in order that the public generally may be instructed, and the reason elicited why they appear amongst us accepted alike by the educated and scientifically inductive mind and the intuitive perception of the less well-instructed classes of our population.

In another letter, I would bring forward other methods of presumed intercommunication; but in this I have specially drawn attention to the faculty of vision, inasmuch as it seems nearer the domain of optical science than other modes of spirit manifestations.

I care not whether the ultimate end of the discussion prove the "Spiritualists" right or wrong, so long as we can ascertain truth. I cannot but, for lack of evidence to the contrary—from the want of any adequate scientific solution—declare my sincere conviction that the phenomena are spiritual. If any other explanation be possible, I am ready to receive it. My common sense, without the aid of spiritualism, assures me that the immortality of the soul is a necessity; but it also tells me that until some better destroyers are found for spiritualism than ridicule and contempt, I must remain, sir, yours obediently,*

A SPIRITUALIST.

---

* Until the soul is proved to be an entity, that is, having an independent existence, I cannot admit the *necessity* of its immortality, by which I understand an intelligent sense,

or consciousness, of individual, personal existence. If the soul is material, it doubtless will continue to exist in some form or other, but not necessarily have intelligence, or a sense of individuality. If it is *immaterial*, there is evidently an end of the matter. Not matter and nothing are synonymous terms.

XX.

Sir,—Your correspondent "Sceptic" has certainly given us some strange contradictions in his letter of the 15th. First he says,—" I would ask, is there anything more extraordinary in the phenomena detailed by Mr. John Jones than the thousand and one marvels performed by M. Frikell and his contemporaries in the art of legerdemain;" and further on he writes,—" Not that I would be misunderstood to pronounce the whole phenomena as caused by sleight of hand." So that first it is no more than M. Frikell can do by sleight of hand, and then it is something different. Again he tells us: "But I am emboldened to say that, had I witnessed all that has been written concerning these manifestations, and all that has been witnessed even by your ingenuous correspondent John Jones, I should still disbelieve my senses when in opposition to my reason." So that we must first ascertain what "Sceptic's" "reason" would lead him to believe, and that will be the limit to which we must go. I think I need not remark on the absurdity of such reasoning as this:—If we see a table go up to the ceiling, we are not to believe it is there, because reason has not yet been able to tell us how it got there.

I have a strong conviction in my own mind from whence comes this power, and I think the Word of God warns us that because men " received not the love of the truth that they might be saved," "strong delusion" should be given them "that they should believe a lie."—2nd Thess. ii. 9, 10, 11. It may not be palatable; nevertheless, it is God's word; and that which I think will alone put an end to it is when "the Lord Jesus shall be revealed from heaven with his mighty angels in flaming fire, taking vengeance on them that know not God and that obey not the Gospel of our Lord Jesus Christ."—Yours truly,

WATCHFUL.

Exception has been taken to the remark that had I witnessed all that has been written concerning the manifestations, that " I should still disbelieve my senses when in opposition to my reason." I would explain, that as my reason tells me there can be no individual spiritual existence, independent and apart from the material form, (which together constitute the living being) that on perceiving the phenomena I should nevertheless disbelieve that they were the effects of supernatural agency or disembodied spirits. In other words, although my senses might perceive whatever should be presented to them, still my reason would not succumb to the impressions made on them. So that being of those who have not accepted the " strong delusions," I am not of those who have " believed a lie."

"Watchful" charges me with strange contradictions in my letter of the 15th. I certainly ask "is there anything *more extraordinary* in these phenomena than the thousand and one marvels performed by M. Frikell?" but 'I nowhere say, "that it is no more than M. Frikell can do," therefore there is no inconsistency in my subsequently saying "that I have no desire to be misunderstood as pronouncing the whole to be sleight of hand." I should not have noticed so pitiful a charge, but that it is a glaring instance of "Watchful's" own want of veracity, and total inability to form *correct inferences*, fully bearing out the arguments of the writer in Blackwood. The inference intended was, that there is nothing wonderful or extraordinary in people being deceived with their eyes wide open, even though the deception should consist in their own false inferences.

XXI.

Sir,—After much beating about the bush, we have at length stumbled upon a trail which it may be well to follow. Your corespondent, Mr. T. Wilks, truly says, " We know there can be no effect without a cause, for it is certain and plain that nothing can do nothing." Here we are in perfect accord. Will he and his co-spiritualists be content to make this their stand-point?, The phenomena of spiritual manifestations not having been witnessed by myself, have been questioned, not denied. I think, as the discussion proceeds, the distance between spiritualists and materialists, so called, will be considerably lessened if not entirely bridged over. I do not assert that it is impossible for a table to rise and be suspended in mid air; but I deny that the cause can be other than physical, let it be what it may. I do not say mechanical force. From what we know of forces, whether electric, odic, or magnetic, or any other, let the Spiritualist define them as he may, they are still physical. Thought, the most subtle phenomenon known to man, is purely physical. Admitted that the force which raises the table is there and unseen, it does not necessarily follow that the mind or intelligence directing it should be that of a disembodied being. Why not that of some one present, even though it be the medium, possessing both thought and feeling, a motive and a purpose?

Thought is as subtile, if not powerful, as electricity; the effects are witnessed, the cause is unseen. We do not see people think, but we may and can divine their thoughts. It is curious that a spiritualist should ask the question,—"Is there any such thing as feeling, thinking, loving, or hating, apart from individual intelligent existence?" That is a question, I boldly reiterate, and as boldly meet with the rejoinder, Show me the monstrosity and I will forego the accumulated experience of ages, my reason and my belief in truth—and become a worshipper at the shrine of spiritualism. As suggested in my last letter, it is no unusual thing for our eyes to be deceived by the facile manipulations of the professors of sleight of hand. We know and admit the deception with perfect equanimity on such occasions.

How often have our ears been sported with by the ventriloquist. But knowing the cause, we do not ascribe the effect to supernatural agency, whatever our forefathers may have done in ignorance of the natural laws which produce these phenomena. The whole senses may be entranced by the mesmerists, those of touch, taste, and smell, in addition to those of hearing and seeing; but we may still reason on these things without becoming perfect blanks and believing in nothing, which belief, by the bye, if such be possible, attaches rather to the spiritualist than the materialist. Will any of your correspondents explain their notions of spirit? I know full well when they attempt to define they must come over to us, and make substance of it, or take refuge in an incorporeal intelligent being, sans parts, sans organs, sans everything, which is a nonentity—naught but the "baseless fabric of a vision."

The magnetic or odic force, as shown by Reichenbach, is visible to certain sensitives; therefore, we have an explanation of the apparitions said to have been seen, the mediums, or certain of the sitters, doubtless being the subjects. A luminous emanation or aura proceeding from an entranced or ecstatic person under the enjoined conditions and surroundings, a previous belief in the possibility of communicating with the spirits of the departed, the anxious and almost breathless watchings, the passive state of abstraction thereby induced, the mind being reduced to an almost infinitesimal point, may well suffice to overcome the reason, and lead to a belief in the presence of supernatural visitors. I maintain clairvoyance or thought-reading, and prevision, all well-known phenomena, will do the rest, and withstand the tests applied by Mr. T. Wilks, and explain the facts of personal history said to have been related, which may or may not have been previously known to any one present. I do not dispute the facts, but I deny the premises. I am not one to limit nature's laws. Mind, in a material body, and we have no evidence of its existence in any other, neither can we have, may and does act on mind in another body—in other words, mind can react on mind. But mind is the result of a natural law; we only perceive mind in nature, and being in, of, and a part of nature, we cannot go beyond it. When we go beyond ourselves we are beside ourselves. Where have we any real experience of intelligence without a brain? I know the answer, but it resolves itself into nothing more real than a myth or conceit of the imagination. When I say people biologise themselves, I mean that by preconceived opinions they can induce a state of susceptibility, whereby the most extravagant impressions cannot be resisted, as is well known to the mesmerist and biologist. There is no more powerful mesmerist than the imagination; and because your correspondents cannot satisfactorily account for the phenomena witnessed, they jump the difficulty, and ascribe them to unseen supernatural beings, as superstitious—*i. e.*, ignorant man has done in all ages; for what is superstition but the measure of our ignorance? Sir, I have felt it incumbent upon me, after the space you have allowed me to occupy in your journal, to prove the possibility of the so-called spiritual manifestations being produced by natural laws; and I think, so far as I have shown parallel phenomena can be induced by man acting upon the credulity of his fellow man, I have succeeded. With regard to the lifting of tables and chairs, and men floating about in mid-air, and all such appearances as seem to require mechanical contrivance, I can only say that I have had no experience of the kind beyond dreaming that I have been gliding through the air, sometimes in an apartment, at other times over trees and hedges, and plantations of shrubs, and knowing what the uncontrolled imagination does picture to itself in dreams, and what men, women, and youth of both sexes have been made to fancy they behold when thought to be in their natural state and wide awake, I am inclined still to think the spirit circles are the subjects of their own credulity—*vulgo*, monomaniacs —at least, for the time being. Doubtless the whole effects are subject to the control of universal law, but I see no occasion for explaining phenomena so varied by any one law. Mr. J. Jones admits that he cannot produce the manifestations. He is only a seer, and somewhat of a prophet, I suppose. Again, it is admitted that mediums are necessary, and that they are entranced—that is, in a state of ecstacy. Therefore, it is necessary, perhaps, in order to answer the question, " Whence is it?" that their peculiar temperaments and idiosyncracies should be ascertained. However, let not Mr. J. Jones lay the flattering unction to his soul that because he cannot explain it by natural laws it cannot be explained. I think we have made some progress towards an elucidation of the mystery. If otherwise, it does not make his extra-mundane theory correct. With respect to the religious aspirations of " J. A. L.," I have nothing to say, though I believe he may find his answer in this letter. Conjointly with him, I much regretted the abrupt termination to the controversy last autumn, and sincerely hope the present may lead to more satisfactory results. Sir, I have no desire to shock the feelings of your readers, but I cannot help incidentally alluding to Mr. J. Jones's garbled quotation which he is pleased to give of the last words of Christ. I can understand his suppression of a portion of the passage, and with permission, will supply the omission, and I challenge Mr. Jones to abide by that test as a proof of his own sincerity and truthfulness of belief: " And these signs shall follow them that believe; in my name shall they cast out devils; they shall speak with new tongues; they shall take up serpents; and if they drink any deadly thing it shall not hurt them; they shall lay hands on the sick and they shall recover." Now, if Mr. J. Jones (signs and wonders not having ceased) will drink any deadly potion that I may mix, without providing himself with a better antidote than spiritual dependence, I will at once become his disciple and a believer in modern spiritualism.

As regards inanimate substances moving without

visible touch, does the iron attracted by the magnet require an intelligent being to direct it? Yet it is influenced by an invisible power. The current of electricity towards the pole is the sole directing power which points the needle of the compass to the north. I am at least justified in assuming this, as it is an admitted truism in philosophy, as already remarked by your correspondent, that it is not desirable to multiply causes.

When Columbus astonished his delighted auditory by making an egg stand on end by flattening its base with a rap on the table, he was considered a perfect Solon; but in these reflective times, with a better insight into the law of equilibrium, it is a parlour pastime with the youth of our land to set an egg on end by simply shaking it to mix the albumen and yolk, and gently balance with a steady hand. Behold, then, the wide-world wonderful phenomenon! Yet it is the same egg, and the same law in action: the conditions alone are altered. It were impossible to balance the egg in its natural state. Does this point a moral?

We need not to be reminded of the influence of the elements nor of their power, which is patent to all mankind. We have no knowledge, nor can we form any rational idea, of life other than as we behold it in the living object; neither can there be life without circulation, nor circulation without a system, nor functions without organs. These are not postulates, but self-evident facts which cannot be disproved;

therefore the materialist will not surrender his faith in nature at the bidding of the spiritualist. The will can alone act through living organisms. We require a nervous system for the exercise of will. The dog wills ere it moves a muscle or exerts a limb; and this will, though of the nature of spirit so far as it is a subtle force, is the physical result of impressions from without. The spiritualists are strong with their modern facts; let them combat these facts, which are plain, demonstrable, and as old as the hills.—Truly yours,

Sceptic.

XXII.

Sir,—Mr. Barkas tells us of the extraordinary effects which have been produced by mesmerism and the will of one man on another. How can these statements be true? Reason is against them, because if they did not touch one another how could a man's arm be made rigid without splinters or other solid substance? How could one man will another man to think water brandy, and ice red-hot coal? It is preposterous, and contrary to reason. Besides, the council of physicians have exercised their powers of mind, and their reason has been made manifest by the public official declaration that mesmeric action and biology are fictions—" a delusion and a snare;"

and so thought I, till I, some fifteen years ago, put myself in a position to judge for myself, by turning to be an amateur mesmeriser and biologist, and producing all the phenomena related by Mr. Barkas, so that the principle is solved that the will of one man can, without sight or voice, act upon another person. And to me it appears that the discussion on spiritualism will open men's eyes to the existence of natural phenomena connected with man's own natural powers, and of true science or knowledge of the powers of the being called Man.

I have endeavoured to show these powers, in my book on the "Natural and Supernatural," published last January by Baillière, of Regent Street. I need not therefore now consume space, but point out the unseen reason for the phenomena—namely, the existence and emission of chemical heat from any human being; that issues and radiates like heat from a coal fire, and is felt more or less intensely by all persons when ill or weakly. This may be proved by any father, sister, or brother, by asking them to extend the open hand, then pass the points of your fingers slowly at the distance of an inch from the wrist to the point of the long finger. Do this for four or five times, and the person whose hand is open will feel a hot or cold current passing along the hand, and the test will be that you, the operator, will feel a strange sensation in your fingers when over the portion of the hand where the person feels the current most powerfully. That something between the two hands is the unseen power, which, directed by an active mind or will, produces the extraordinary phenomena detailed; that power issues from man under the same law that the unseen magnetism issues from a horse-shoe magnet, grasps the needle, and carries it up to the shoe.

As I said last week, in a private letter to you, that I considered that I had occupied enough of the space in the *Star*, and meant to withdraw, except to give a summing up, I avoid the question of spiritualism, except to state that science has no greater advocate for spiritualism than Dr. Ashburner, quoted by one of your correspondents as an antagonist.

JOHN JONES.

August 18.

Mr. J. Jones's recantation of his faith in invisible intelligent beings, as the cause of the phenomena, strongly reminds one of the adage "give a man rope enough and he will hang himself." At all events, in the above letter he suspends both the argument and the spirits. It is consoling, after such an exhibition of spiritual faith, to find him eschewing invisible intelligences, and endeavouring to account for the manifestations in a manner at once both natural and rational. He admits that it, at length, "*appears to him that this discussion will open men's eyes to the existence of natural phenomena connected with man's own natural powers, and of true science or knowledge of the powers of the being called man.*" Voilà tout cela!!

It seems to me, that there cannot be a doubt in the mind of a philosopher who examines this subject carefully, that there is a peculiar form of vital force, which Mr. Jones is pleased to term chemical heat, and which has, with some propriety, been denominated *Animal Magnetism*, and which is concerned in producing all the phenomena of

U

animal life, and all the wonders of Spiritualism and Mesmerism. We come to this conclusion as the only one which will account for facts which we are not able to controvert.

"If we take a magnet and bring it near to a piece of iron, and make a number of passes across the iron, the peculiar motions of the magnet are communicated to the iron, so that it becomes a magnet itself. This is *Induction*. A piece of iron cannot be placed near a magnet for any considerable time without becoming in some degree inducted, losing its own independent action, and submitting to the influence of the neighbouring magnet. Precisely so it is with the inducted subject; the cases are nearly as parallel as the different natures of the two bodies will admit."

This will go far to explain why nearly all persons attending the spiritual *séances* are similarly influenced, being *en rapport*, or in contact, with mesmerised—that is magnetised—persons, they become subjected to the general influence.

Dr. Ashburner has no greater faith in the existence of *immaterial* beings than he has in free-will. Here is a line: "To our limited ken, all Nature's truths are material." Surely this is comprehensive enough! Again—"*A force which is a material agent, attended by, or constituting a coloured light, emanates from the brain of man, when he thinks—that his will can direct its impingement—and that it is a motive power.*" Moreover, he takes the Baron Reichenbach to task, for applying the term *immaterial essence* to light. So much for the Doctor's Spiritualism! On the subject of the cataleptic patients having no free-will, nor, in fact, any will at all, he says, "This is the subject which is the key-stone of all the objections to the application of magnetism, or of mesmerism to the human system. To show that man is not a free agent is bad enough, but to prove it by physical facts should be atrocious. The instinct of those who have large organs of cunning, acquisitiveness, and self-esteem, is instantly on the alert, and forgetting that they do not wholly belong to the baser animals, they give way to the lower feelings of their nature."

[We have received a vast number of letters on this subject, which are for various reasons unsuited for publication. Some are unconscionably lengthy; one is not only written on both sides of the paper, but is actually crossed, presenting insuperable difficulties to the printer; very many convey only an expression of individual disbelief; others embody offers to stake sums of money on the result of experiments—a mode of proceeding which seems to us scarcely appropriate in such an investigation; and not a few indulge in very insulting personalities with regard to those who have written thus in support of the doctrines of spiritualists. Our correspondents should bear in mind that all letters must be as brief as is compatible with any exposition of their views; that they must embody either the results of personal observation or sober argument, based upon facts already made public; and that they must be free from injurious remarks upon adversaries. Prolixity, vagueness, attempted facetiousness, or personality will always suffice to ensure the exclusion of their communications.—Ed. *Star and Dial.*]

XXIII.

Sir,—I suppose we may go on defending and denying the phenomena of spiritualism until the termination of the American war, or perhaps Doomsday, unless some new mode of settling the vexed question be introduced. Allow me to suggest to the leading spiritualists in London the propriety of forming a responsible committee for the examination of the subject, to consist of three intelligent believers and nine intelligent, candid, and unbigotted unbelievers, selected from various professions, and having among their number a few gentlemen well versed in physical and psychological laws.

The details as to the *modus operandi* may safely be left in the hands of the twelve gentlemen forming the committee of inquiry.

I would also suggest that the names of the twelve investigators be published, and that each member of the committee of inquiry pledge himself to a public avowal of the conclusion to which the investigation has led him. Without such open expression of opinion, the examination, for all practical purposes as regards the general public, would be useless.—I am, sir, yours respectfully,

T. P. Barkas.

49, Grainger Street, Newcastle-on-Tyne.

XXIV.

Sir,—I beg respectfully to propose to those who are desirous of ascertaining the truth or fallacy of the alleged spiritual manifestations which are at present attracting so much attention, a very simple test, to the application of which no really philosophic mind can, I think, offer any objection.

Let a public *séance* of spiritualists be held in the open air, and by daylight, and there let them, surrounded by competent witnesses, openly demonstrate to the world the existence of those phenomena in which they profess to believe.

This may, perhaps, by some be considered as too vulgar a test, to which objection I reply, that no unprejudiced seeker after truth will shrink from the employment of any means, however common or literal, that will finally confirm or disprove the accuracy of the subject he is endeavouring to investigate. —Yours respectfully,

S.

Hampstead, Aug. 22.

XXV.

Sir,—You have had compliments enough from both sides for your liberality in re-opening your columns to the discussion of the modern phenomena above-named. I cordially join in what has been said in this regard, but desire now rather to economise space and time, and so, by your leave, will at once direct attention to the branch of the subject to which I feel myself more particularly related, from my experience having principally lain therein, viz., that which occupies the main part of the communication of Mr. Walter Cooper Dendy.

The admirable spirit in which Mr. Dendy writes renders it a pleasure to enter upon the discussion with him, because one feels sure that whatsoever is advanced bearing upon the points in dispute will receive fair consideration from him.

Mr. Dendy has the candour to admit the facts, and to discard the suppositions of deception on the one hand and delusion on the other. Nevertheless, even he is not short of attributing "extreme credulity" to the "honourable men" who give their testimony to the actuality of the facts. The adherents of spiritualism who have been made so by thorough and severe investigation—and they really are the main body of its literary defenders—can afford to smile at this imputation, well knowing how hard they were to convince; many of them having to confess that it was only after years of observation and critical inquiry, after having exhausted all inferior hypotheses suggested by themselves or others, that they were literally forced to the conclusion (not the assumption, as is generally or recklessly imputed to them), that nothing else was adequate to explain the facts. But let this pass. Mr. Dendy imagines they have not considered his hypothesis, and so, with excellent temper, albeit in somewhat obscure phraseology and consequent lack of perspicuity, he propounds it as a complete solution of the " mystery." What, then, is his hypothesis? This:—" Mind is projectile, for what are thought, dream, or vision, but the visit of an intellectual element to another sphere? The intensity of these phenomena, under hyperexcited action of the brain and the concentration of nervous power, with the superadded influence of memory and association, and especially of electrobiology and mesmerism, or the odyle force of Reichenbach, constitute those displays that have been somewhat irreverently termed preternatural." Add to this " the projectile power of volition or the will," and " the concentration of this volition may explain the whole phenomena of table-moving, nay, even the body-lifting of Mr. Home."*

---

* I am indebted to Mr. H. G. Atkinson for the following explanation of table-turning, which is the best and most explicit I have met with, though written more than seven years since. He says, " it is a force, projected and directed by the unconscious sphere of the mind or soul;" and admonishingly adds, "but we must try and maintain a wise and sober course, and not be led away by appearances."

Now, it is at once "granted" that "mind is projectile." The fact has been demonstrated many a time, as any one may learn who consults the annals of mesmerism. I have myself impressed my thought upon a friend, and induced mesmeric sleep and trance at distances varying from a few feet to above 200 miles. But how does the principle herein involved explain the facts in spiritualism assumed to be related thereto? Instead of obtaining through the medium an echo of your own thought, you are quite as often startled with thoughts not only different from, but in direct opposition to your own. The same results arise in relation to feeling and volition. Often the utmost anxiety has been felt and expressed for certain things to be granted; they have been resolutely denied. Feelings claiming indulgence have been rebuked; opinions at variance with those of both the medium and the person or persons present have been uttered and maintained. And as for table-moving by concentrated volition, instances are on authentic record of tables being lifted in spite of not only the concentrated volition, but likewise the muscular energy of those present—*vide* a remarkable instance of this kind detailed in the appendix to a volume by Judge Edmonds and Dr. Dexter, of New York, in which a very solid table of cherry-tree timber was raised, with Governor Tall-

---

Again, in another letter, Mr. A. writes, "I have a capital medium, and am making experiments in table-talking. Here is a matter that will revolutionize the world of thought."

madge, of Wisconsin, on the top of it, against the utmost efforts of the rest of the company to keep it down.*

When Mr. Dendy has applied his hypothesis to the facts, he will discover, as I have done years and years ago, how far short it falls of explaining the "mystery." He will haply also discover that it is not the spiritualists who "blindly jump at a conclusion, and vaunt their dogmas without reasoning on the facts before them," but much more pretentious men. In the meantime I would beg him to understand that they do not "form a supernatural theory in the face of established laws," or imagine that "nature's laws" are in the slightest degree violated by the influx and interaction of spiritual forces. Rather do they maintain that in virtue of "established laws" disembodied spirits can and do act upon embodied ones and upon unorganized bodies, and thereby cause the manifestations under discussion. This is their induction from the facts, and they respectfully maintain its validity, and deny the adequacy of any hypothesis which excludes the operation of spirits.

One word in reply to your other correspondent, "Critic," who also writes in a commendable style of fair inquiry.

He says—"The proof of the existence of matter

* If the table rose to the ceiling in this case, it must have been a rather ludicrous and somewhat unenviable position for the Governor!

in all its forms—phenomena—is of its kind. The proof of the existence of spirit in all its form—noumena—is of its kind."

Agreed. But at least some " phenomena," as voice and speech, expression of countenance, writing, playing on an instrument—in fine, performing any intelligent operation cognizable by any of the senses —even rapping or moving a table by design—involve " noumena." Therefore it is not " a fact that no phenomenon, nor any number of phenomena, can prove the existence of spirit."

The argument could be carried much further, and the reverse of his position made clear; but so able and candid a thinker will do this for himself. He, too, will see that in accordance with the strictest logic, as well as in agreement with indomitable fact, the position of the Spiritualist in this discussion is not successfully assailable.

I am, &c. L.

Liverpool, Aug. 20.

Had " Critic " stated that no phenomenon, nor any number of phenomena, can prove the existence of *disembodied* spirits, his position would have been more unassailable than the Spiritualists. In the absence, however, of a strict definition, his opponent has apparently an advantage, of which he has not been slow to avail himself. But the phenomena adduced as involving *noumena*, are those of intelligent, *organised* beings! and it remains to be shown that there can be such a thing as disembodied, unorganised sentience, before like effects can be attributed to the spirits of the deceased. Materialists do not deny the existence of spirit, but they dispute its identity apart from and in-

XXVI.

Sir,—I am happy to be able to confirm the views of your correspondent "A Spiritualist," as regards the facility of proving the existence of the spiritual dependent of matter. To the question, "What is Life, Light, Mind, Electricity, Magnetism, &c. ?" we reply, they are phenomena, *i. e.*, conditions of matter. No one disputes the existence or reality of whatever *is*. All the foregoing phenomena cease with the dissolution of the materials which are their cause. Nothing exists in Nature but cause and effect. Neither do we despise the inspired language of Scripture: but we claim the right to put our own interpretation upon it, according to the light that is in us. Thus, when it is written, "God said, Let there be light, and there was light," it must be borne in mind, the spirit of God *first* moved upon the face of the waters. If the phenomenon of light was the first act of creation, it will be admitted we have authority for saying the waters, at least, existed prior to the fiat, "Let there be light." We believe in the eternity of matter as the primeval source of all spirit. Matter *is*—*i. e*, it is real, tangible, visible, demonstrative either of itself or in its effects, and however changeable, still exists in some one or other of its forms, even as "*noumena*," which is but phenomenon. But effects can have no existence apart from or independent of causation, which is material, the body, so to speak, of spirit. We may believe in Spiritual phenomena resulting from any of the beforementioned imponderable agents, which are the real powers of nature, without believing in spiritual entities, the objective character of ghosts, or disembodied intelligences, though, doubtless, we shall be accused of "*Gross Materialism.*"

world by means of crystals and such media. I have, for over thirty years, been in the habit of investigating the question by means of crystals. And since 1849 I have possessed the celebrated crystal, once belonging to Lady Blessington, in which very many persons, both children and adults, have seen visions of the spirits of the deceased, or of beings claiming to be such, and of numerous angels and other beings of the spiritual world. These have " in all cases supported the purest and most liberal Christianity." The faculty of seeing in the crystal I have found to exist in about one person in ten among adults, and in nearly nine in every ten among children; many of whom appear to lose the faculty as they grow to adult age, unless they practise it continually.

The most determined sceptics have been convinced of the reality of the visions, on many occasions, by discovering that they had themselves the faculty, much to their surprise. The nature of the visions seen has been of the most varied character. Among the most interesting have been visions of Scripture scenes and events, such as the ark floating on the waters, the Crucifixion, the New Testament miracles, feeding the multitude, walking on the water, the Last Supper, &c. I may add, that every possible means have been taken by persons of sceptical mind to ensure that there was no kind of delusion in the matter. And as a vast number of children, and others who have never known each other, have witnessed the same beings, or beings having the same appearance, and declaring themselves to be the same personages, it does not seem possible that, if these seers had predetermined to tell us untruths, they should all, or nearly all, being numbered by scores, tell us the same untruths. All that has been seen in the crystal during the last twelve years, while in my hands, has been perfectly consistent, although seen by very numerous persons. The spirits—which I feel certain they are—which appear, do not hesitate to inform us on all possible subjects which may tend to improve our morals and confirm our faith in the Christian doctrines; but they will say nothing that may only tend to gratify curiosity. As to a knowledge of the future, they confess that they have little more than we mortals possess. Yet in some cases, they have informed us of future events, on which the peace of mind of individuals depended, or by the knowledge of which some evident benefit might ensue. The character they give of the class of spirits who are in the habit of communicating with mortals by rapping and such proceedings, is such that it behoves all Christian people to be on their guard against error and delusion through their means.

I could add much interesting matter, but refrain from taking up your space. I may do so at a future time. In the face of the thousands of facts of which I am possessed, the writings of your correspondent "Sceptic" become vapid and valueless. A line or two on his numerous beggings of the question. He says we have no evidence of mind in any other than a material body, "neither can we have."* This I deny; for I have had abundant evidence of mind of the highest order in these spiritual beings showing themselves as visions in the crystal, to the eyes of children, whose faculties were very far below the intelligence and information they displayed. He says that there cannot be life without circulation, &c. True, if he mean animal life; but there may be, and is, spiritual existence.†

Yours, R. J. Morrison.

* The mind is built up, as it were, bit by bit, from the experience of the senses, as we raise a house or other building; and so long as the senses remain intact, the superstructure may be perfect in all its parts, and honourable to the builder; but no sooner does the material, that is, the senses, exhibit symptoms of decay, than the building becomes impaired, and either is restored, taken down piecemeal, or falls to the ground. If the senses continue unimpaired, the mind, like any other fabric, will withstand the shock of time; but it is, nevertheless, liable to be levelled with the ground, even in its pride of strength, by any convulsion of nature, or other sudden catastrophe. If, as Lord Brougham says, the mind does not *age* with the body, it most demonstrably deteriorates as the senses decay, and must ultimately perish with the body to which the senses belong.

† Is there no dogmatism, nor begging the question, here, in the assertion that "*there is spiritual existence?*" We have evidence of the fact, that neither animal nor vegetable life exist without circulation, the only life known to us. We have no experience of spiritual life, and, I repeat, "neither can we have;" for if there be such, as it belongs to another sphere, or state, we can have no experience of it in this.

[We have received such a deluge of letters on this subject that we are compelled to close the discussion. Many of the letters are well written, but they are almost all too long. Every writer seems to suppose that it is his duty to exhaust the subject. Nor is it possible to make a selection, for each communication is either a reply to some previous correspondent, or opens questions which would involve replies, unmanageable in number and in length. Besides, the discussion appears to be interminable, except by the abrupt process we are now adopting. There is abundant evidence that a large number of persons either have seen, or imagine they have seen, manifestations of spiritual presences. On the other hand, a large number, not to say the overwhelming majority, of persons obstinately disbelieve their testimony. We do not see how the latter are to be convinced by any reiteration of assertion. We ourselves have not witnessed any of the reported phenomena; nor, were we to do so, are we sure that we should trust the evidences of our senses. In pursuance of our vocation as journalists, we placed our readers in possession of facts respecting the progress of a new phase of belief, and we must now leave it to each individual to examine or not for himself, as he sees fit, into the truth or falsehood of the statements made, and into the nature of the phenomena which are said to exist.—*Editor of the Star and Dial.*]

APPENDIX.

As an appendix to this subject, and a rejoinder to Mr. R. I. Morrison's letter, I extract the following from a note of Dr. Ashburner's, in his translation of Baron Reichenbach's Researches, pp. 466—7.

"Lately I have had opportunities of making experiments relative to the influence of odic light emanating from water, from glass, or from crystals, upon the nervous systems of certain sensitive persons, which tend to illustrate clairvoyance. They are so easily repeated that time only is required for thousands of corroborations of the events I have noticed; and although we have in England many *stupidities*, who, like the Baron von Reichenbach's critics, will carp at facts, which their maladroit minds will turn to ridicule and calumny, the simplicity of the apparatus required for these phenomena will speedily ensure a sufficient number of verifications. The persons who form the subjects of these experiments should be of highly sensitive nervous systems, and, as far as I have observed, should have heads well developed about the organs of ideality, marvel, veneration, and hope; comparison, tune, time, and constructiveness, adhesiveness, philoprogenitiveness, and caution; and rather the contrary as respects amativeness, combativeness, self-esteem, cunning, and acquisitiveness. A phial of clear and colourless glass, capable of holding eight, ten, twelve, or more ounces of filtered water, or a clear globe containing a pint-and-a-half, or a quart of water, answers the purpose well. The vessel should be completely filled with water, clean and clear. It should be mesmerised by some healthy person with a large brain, by darting the odic sparks from the fingers upon the surface of the water, at several hundred strokes, and by breathing upon it for some minutes. The vessel should be then closed, so that no bubbles of air are admitted; and when properly secured should be placed in the hands of the sensitive person, who is to look continuously into it, uninterrupted by the proximity of too many persons, whose odic forces may tend to spoil the experiment. The mesmeriser of the water may be near; but it is better that not more than one or two persons besides, agreeable to the sensitive person, should be present. I have placed vessels of water so prepared in the hands of numerous sensitive persons, most of them quite unaware of the object of my requesting them to look steadily at the water. Some, in the course of a few minutes, have seen beautiful visions of persons and things that have given them delight. Others have seen objects which have terrified them: Some have described vividly, charming country scenes, with elegant companies of ladies and gentlemen gaily attired, at boat-races on a river. Others have seen hunting gentlemen, in scarlet uniforms, on fine horses. Some have seen funerals and churchyards; others sick rooms, with death's heads flitting about the surface of the bed of sickness. Some have truly predicted to me the approach to the house of friends, who were to knock at my door at stated hours. On one occasion, a visit from my friend Mr. Hoffmann, of Mayence, was predicted by a person, who described him accurately without ever having seen him, except by the agency of the crystalline bottle of water, which she had held in her hand for the first time in her life, and without knowing the object I had in view in requesting her to look into it.

"At the moment I had a conviction that Mr. Hoffmann was either at Macclesfield or Liverpool; but he made his appearance in my room in ten minutes—the time my sensitive subject had intimated. A number of people have now repeated such experiments, and I am told that several persons who had failed, at first, in perceiving anything in the vessels of mesmerised water, had, by dint of patience and perseverance, after many repetitions of trials for half-an-hour and an hour at a time, become highly clairvoyant. The curious facts that have excited so much attention in relation to a crystal ball, bought by Mr. Morrison at Lady Blessington's sale, and those relating to the numerous fits of clairvoyance induced in Mrs. Woodard, by her looking into an oval piece of glass, are analogous to those I have stated. After witnessing very numerous instances of clairvoyance, I can have no doubt but that the brain, apt for the purpose, is stimulated to the production of the phenomena by some relation which it bears to light, perhaps to this imponderable matter in combination with the odic force." How this supports Mr. Morrison's experience of the exhibition of mind of the highest order, in what he is pleased to term spiritual beings, I am at a loss to conceive. It appears to me that the prolonged fixed gaze has produced a state of exaltation of the brain, and the objects of memory have become so intensified as to appear, as it were, visible in the crystals. Thus the scenes perceived by children partake of the Scripture narratives with which their minds are imbued; while those of larger growth behold those scenes with which they are either more immediately familiar, or with which their memories have been more strongly impressed. That this is only one of the many phases of electro-biology, or mesmeric induction, there cannot be a doubt; as for instance, the fact of one in ten being sensitive among adults, and nine in ten among children, it being well known that youth is more susceptible and credulous than adult age.

What is here assumed to be the spirits is nothing more than intuitive, or clairvoyant perception of the mind of some one present. "In these, as in all other visions, when people fancy they see spirits or ghosts, impressions unconsciously evolve embodyings projected on the vision. Such is our tendency to associate everything with persons or objects, according to our familiar conception." Why should we conclude that there is any more reality in these visions than in the diversified scenes of landscape, and other objects, evolved in the mind in our dreams? Looking at the phenomena in this light, it is easily understood why "the spirits say nothing that may tend to gratify our curiosity as to a knowledge of the future, and confess that they have little more than we mortals possess." *Vide* Job xiv. 12; also Eccles. ix. 5. Seeing that these spirits are little more than the interreflection of our own minds, the matter is clear enough. "*Clairvoyance* or prophecy is no greater step from our ordinary condition than seeing would be to a blind person, who would say 'I could only take up nature bit by bit before, and put these bits together, and then form but a very imperfect conception; but now I recognise all at once; the distant, as well as that which is near.' You set free the inner faculties, and open 'the eye of the mind' to the outward influences of the grosser sense; and knowledge flows in unobstructed. You are as one who was blind, but can now see. The new sense and the old are equally intelligible, and both inexplicable. You cannot explain a process, where there is none. The imperfect sense, the blind have a process to explain: but in clear seeing there is no process, but the fact. That somnambules should read the whole influence from a person, and even his entire history, from a touch, or from a bit of hair, or even from such an object as a piece of leather touched by the person; or from the influence hanging about another individual, who has been in company with, or otherwise influenced by, the person in question,—is the same class of phenomena. Herewith we find the principle of memory, and how it is that in such cases as that of the Swiss historian, Zschokke, the history of a stranger is brought under review, just as if the memory of one person was transferred to another.— Here again we recognize a basis for palmistry and future seeing;—facts, of course, like all other facts,—medicine, for instance,—affording wide opportunity for imposition, assumption, and folly."*

"The path is difficult, secret, and beset with terror. The ancients called it ecstacy or absence, a getting out of the bodies to think. All religious history contains traces of the trance of saints: a beatitude, but without any sign of joy; earnest, solitary, even sad; 'the flight,' Plotinus calls it, 'of the alone to the alone.' Μυσις, the closing of the eyes, whence our word mystic. The trances of Socrates, Plotinus, Porphyry, Behmen, Bunyan, Fox, Pascal, Guion, Swedenborg, will readily come to mind. But what as readily comes to mind, is the accompaniment of disease."†

"Some modern fortune-tellers have been supposed to be in league with Satan, on account not only of their successful impostures, but from their actual performances and revelations. Some, again, have a faculty of talking to (or charming) sores, felons, and burns, in such a way as to take the soreness out; they actually perform this apparent miracle whenever the patient is in any degree susceptible to Etheropathic induction, but not otherwise. I suspect that some persons are clairvoyant when asleep and dreaming, who are not so when awake; and that, therefore, in their

* Man's Nature and Development. Atkinson and Martineau.
† Emerson on Swedenborg.

dreams they perceive things which seem like communications from spirits of another world, warning them of the death, or sickness, or treachery of friends, or of anything else that concerns them; that would account for the truthfulness of some remarkable dreams. The impressions which some persons have had that they were to die at a certain time, may also be derived from a species of clairvoyant or abnormal perception, producing what is called presentiment or prevision."*

Emmanuel Swedenborg, one of the greatest men that ever lived, possessed the extraordinary power of independent clairvoyance. He was literally a "Seer," and it is supposed that he obtained much of his wonderful scientific knowledge of nature by the exercise of this power; but his supposed communion with spirits and many of his peculiar ideas doubtless originated in his own credencive fancy. It was perfectly natural for one educated in the popular belief concerning supernatural beings, to imagine, when he discovered his wonderful clairvoyant perception, that he was indebted to these beings for his peculiar advantages over his fellow men. A good and virtuous man, such as Baron Swedenborg, would imagine that his inspirations proceeded from good and happy spirits, who kindly and benevolently sympathised with him. But, were he conscious of his own moral depravity, he would be likely to clothe this spirit—whom his creative fancy called "from the vasty deep" of superstition—with characters like his own, selfish, malignant, and revengeful."*

These manifestations only go to prove that which has already been known to the few:—viz: "the existence of faculties in man beyond sense, experience, and reason; which faculties are chiefly called forth under abnormal conditions, but are seldom exhibited in a wholly pure state. In this state, men listen to the voice of intuition,—

* Grimes' Etherology.

fancy themselves inspired,—are carried away by the delusion,—and delude the world with their wanderings."*

Mr. A. Bostwick concludes a letter in the September Number of the " Spiritual Magazine" thus—" At a late circle, when the conditions I have mentioned were observed, the medium was magnetically drawn to a gentleman seated in the corner of the room. Grasping his hand, she said he was a stranger to the circle, and addressed him reprovingly and exhortingly, upon some moral failing. To his inquiry as to who was addressing him, her answer was, " Be satisfied, I am a Spirit, friend, and brother." A gentleman present seemed to know the person thus addressed; and, on the breaking up of the circle, spoke apologetically to him, and said that mediums sometimes erred. His answer was, " It is singular: all mediums address me in the same manner and strain. There is a foundation of fact in what they all say to me. What she said as to my being a stranger here, is true. I was admitted on using a friend's name." I meet this with the following quotation from Mr. H. G. Atkinson, " Man's Nature and Development," p. 280. " The knowledge which mesmerism gives of the influence of body on body and, consequently, of mind on mind, will bring about a morality we have not dreamed of. And who shall disguise his nature and his acts when we cannot be sure, at any moment, that we are free from the *clairvoyant* eye of some one, who is observing our actions and most secret thoughts, and our whole character and history may be read off at any moment! Few have the faintest idea of the influence these great truths will have upon the morals of men, and upon our notions generally. Yes, there are, indeed, more truths in heaven and earth than are told ' of in our philosophy.'"

I cannot do better than close this exposition with the following extract from Grimes' Etherology and Phrenophilosophy of Mesmerism, pp. 171, 2.

" The mode in which the organs of the brain normally

* H. G. Atkinson.

produce consciousness, after they are impressed by emanations from external objects, must be understood in order to enable us to understand Clairvoyance.

"They produce consciousness precisely in the same way in Clairvoyance as they do in the ordinary normal perception. The difference between Clairvoyant perception and common normal perception is in the manner in which the Phreno-organs are excited by the emanation ; or rather it depends upon the different modes by which emanations reach the Phreno-organs to excite them to action. In common perception, the motion of Etherium is restricted to pass in certain prescribed avenues, which we denominate *the senses;* but in Clairvoyance, in consequence of the *insulation* being overcome, the emanation passes directly to the brain through the skull, or through the feet, or hands, or sides, or through any other part where the insulation is especially weakened. . .

"In common perception, the emanation is permitted to reach the brain only through certain limited, defined, and restricted avenues or senses; and even through these passages, the pure and unencumbered motions of Etherium do not seem to be allowed to pass. In the sense of taste, the motion of Etherium is conveyed to the external organ by a *liquid* which dissolves the substance tasted. In the sense of smell, the motions are conveyed by currents of *air*, which are adulterated or mingled with atoms of the odorous substance perceived. In the vibrations of air, in the sense of sight, the emanation is conveyed or moved by currents, pulsations, or rays of light.

" But in Clairvoyance, the brain seems to be excited by Etherium in a different state—by emanations which are ordinarily excluded by insulation—and which are introduced in opposition to the insulating guards. When this more pure emanation is fairly introduced, and a current of it caused to proceed from a distant object to the subject, it passes directly through the skull, or some other abnormal passage, and reaches the organs of form. colour, &c., and excites them so as to cause them to produce a state of consciousness, the same as if the subject had seen the distant object with his eyes. I wish the idea to be distinctly understood, that consciousness and perception of every kind is, *in all cases*, produced by the Phreno-organs of the brain; that in common perception, and in Clairvoyance, the brain operates in the same manner. In both cases the *Phreno-organs* must be excited, and must perform *their* functions before perception can take place. It is a great error to suppose that in Clairvoyance a person can perceive without his *brain*, because he perceives without his senses. It is absurd to suppose that a person perceives *color* without the *organ* of color, because he perceives without the *eyes*. In order, then, to explain Clairvoyance, it is only necessary to admit that the Phreno-organs of perception may be excited through other avenues than the external senses." But all this goes to establish the truth of the science of Phreno-Physiology, and I doubt not that many would rather that "table-turning," or the so-called "Spiritual Manifestations" were true, and that Phrenology was false.

"Some have the power, when looking into a particular stone or piece of semi-transparent glass, to perceive, in a Clairvoyant manner, which is well calculated to excite astonishment in a superstitious and ignorant mind." Thus we have an explanation of the most wonderful of phenomena, that of Clairvoyance, without resorting to the aid, interference, or suggestions of disembodied spirits, either celestial, terrestrial, or diabolical.

A state of ecstacy or trance, the being *en pneumati*, is a temporary suspension of the external senses; the mental faculties being still active. This suspension of the senses being the result of reduced vital power, if too much prolonged, would terminate in the total extinction of the spirit (pneuma)—in other words, death would ensue. The mind being the manifestation of the living organism, *i. e.* cerebral phenomena, must necessarily perish, it ceases to be manifested on the dissolution of the material. "Mind is a living essence, and all life is, from the very first conditions of its existence, subject to change, and therefore to *death.*"

No one can explain, or attempt a reasonable explanation, how defective or diseased physical organs can affect an *immortal, immaterial* spirit, supposed to have a separate and independent existence—on the other hand, admit the spirit or life to be the result of natural physical forces existing in matter (though inert, until called forth by suitable conditions), and the phenomena of life and mind, in all their phases, at once become intelligible.

An answer to Professor Owen's defence of Spiritualism, in his " Footfalls on the Boundaries of another World," is supplied in his own words, in the following passage:—
" The body is gone: what continuous links of identity remain? The mind, the feelings. Transform these, and *every* link is severed connecting FOR US, a Here with a Hereafter.

" It is not WE, in any practical sense, who survive, but others. A human being dies on earth; a seraph or a demon appears in heaven or in hell."

" I was never so willing to believe philosophy in any thing as this; it is a pure enthusiasm, wherewith sacre truth has inspired the spirit of philosophy; which makes, I confess, contrary to its own proposition, that the most calm, composed, and healthful state of the soul that philosophy can seat it in, is not its best condition; our waking is more a sleep than sleep itself; our wisdom less wise than folly; our dreams are worth more than our meditations, and the worst place we can take is in ourselves."—*Montaigne.*

THE END.

BILLING, PRINTER, 103, HATTON GARDEN.

www.ingramcontent.com/pod-product-compliance
Lightning Source LLC
Chambersburg PA
CBHW030734230426
43667CB00007B/710